Perfectly Japanese

TWENTIETH-CENTURY JAPAN:
THE EMERGENCE OF A WORLD POWER

Irwin Scheiner, Editor

Perfectly Japanese

Making Families in an Era of Upheaval

Merry Isaacs White

UNIVERSITY OF CALIFORNIA PRESS
Berkeley · Los Angeles · London

For Charlie and Doris

University of California Press
Berkeley and Los Angeles, California

University of California Press, Ltd.
London, England

© 2002 by the Regents of the University of California

Library of Congress Cataloging-in-Publication Data

White, Merry I., 1941–
    Perfectly Japanese : making families in an era of
upheaval / Merry Isaacs White.
        p.   cm.—(Twentieth-century Japan ; 14)
    Includes bibliographical references and index.
    ISBN 0-520-21754-3 (Cloth : alk. paper)—
ISBN 0-520-23505-3 (Paper : alk. paper)
    1. Family—Japan.   I. Title.   II. Series.
HQ682 .W484 2002
306.85'0952—dc21

                                    2002005535

Manufactured in the United States of America

10 09 08 07 06 05 04 03 02
10 9 8 7 6 5 4 3 2 1

Contents

Figures

Acknowledgments

My colleagues in Japan and America have borne with me as I tried out ideas and related stories with them. I want to thank particularly Kate Hartford, Leslie and Mei-mei Swartz, Jonathan Lipman, Ellen Widmer, Jean Jackson, Mitzi Goheen, Sheila Smith, Sachiko and Yoshimitsu Ide, Takie Lebra, Shoko Kashiyama, Ronald Dore, Nakamura Noriko, Catherine Lewis, Suzanne Vogel, Dr. Henry F. Smith, Joseph Tobin, Iwao Sumiko, Hironaka Wakako, Mariko Sugahara Bando, and Hirose Yoko.

Colleagues and staff in the Anthropology Department at Boston University have provided a working environment that allowed me to live several lives, to support my teaching and my students as I shuffled between class and the computer, and I am very grateful. The E. O. Reischauer Institute of Japanese Studies has offered me a quiet haven to work and commune with Japan specialists all these years: I thank my colleagues and friends there, particularly Helen Hardacre, Andrew Gordon, M. J. Scott, Margot Chamberlain, Ruiko Connor, and Galen Amstutz. The University of Hawai'i at Manoa also offered me a home where, in addition to the joy of teaching novel topics in a new environment, I have written much of this book at a window from which I could gaze on the beautiful Pacific. There I offer my aloha and mahalo to Sharon Minichiello, Victor and Cleo Kobayashi, Ricardo Trimillos, Mary Hammond, and Dru Gladney. Another ocean gave me the same daily solace as I wrote on the island of Islesford, off the northern coast of Maine, where Ashley Bryan, Joy Sprague, Susan Krasnow, Marian Baker, Warren Fernald, Cynthia and

Dan Lief, and others kept me going with coffee, white gingerbread, and conviviality. Thanks in abundance to my patient friend and editor, Sheila Levine, and to Dore Brown, Edith Gladstone, and Mia Lipman at the University of California Press.

I also want to acknowledge the support provided by the grants and fellowships from the American Council of Learned Societies, the Japan Foundation, and the Social Science Research Council, which helped me to conduct fieldwork and data gathering during the long research process. Japanese officials and experts in family policy, as well as academic scholars of family studies, have all been most generous and supportive and I am deeply grateful. Ashino Yuriko, Atoh Makoto, Kashiwagi Keiko, Miyanaga Kuniko, Hara Hiroko, Doi Takeo, and many others have been invaluable companions and guides. It goes without saying that my greatest debt is to Ezra Vogel, whose consistent encouragement to "listen to the people" and to see "what makes the data sing" still guides my work.

The largest share of thanks is to my own family. My daughter, Jennifer, shared the first round of my fieldwork in Japan: it was she and her Tokyo school friends and their families who showed me first the power of interestingly off-the-map family accommodations at a time of increasingly powerful imperatives to conform to educational and social norms. Jenny's talent, hard work, and her unfailingly intrepid sense of possibility continue to inspire my love and pride. My son Benjamin, who set Japanese reporters buzzing with fears for my newborn infant's safety when I brought him to a women's studies conference, survived this event and prospered after his total immersion in "radical feminist activity" and his wit, wisdom, and editorial skills have helped me through several drafts of this work. Henry Isaacs, my brother, demonstrates more than anyone I know that family is not an abstraction: it is a place for celebrating and guiding children and for giving all of us a touchstone of love. This book is dedicated to my uncle and aunt, Charles and Doris Isaacs, with thanks for their humor and love, and for providing me with models of irreverence needed even in perfect families.

Are Japanese Families in Crisis?

The power of official versions of family life in Japan—the patriarchal Confucian lineage family, the home as the source of respite, solace, and nurturance—startled me when I brought my young son, age two months, to Tokyo in 1978 for a conference on women's studies. My son's picture appeared for three days running in a national newspaper as evidence of his mother's dangerous feminist priorities. The articles argued that I had put him at risk by bringing him half a world away from the paternal roof and before the end of the traditional three months' "seclusion" period guaranteeing the safety of a newborn child. This rhetoric brought me face to face with the norms and attitudes I had been viewing as an outsider. And a few years later, when I reported a prevalent Japanese attitude that women with children in school should not work but stay home to provide a backstop for their studying children, the news media in Japan took my words as an American expert's warning that women who work away from home are putting their children's futures in peril. When I told my Japanese friends about my mother's admission to a nursing home with advanced Alzheimer's disease, they were concerned. They wondered aloud: had I considered living with her, hiring a live-in nurse—anything but admit her to an institution?

I thus experienced both the model and the living complexities of family life in Japan. Knowing as I did that many of my friends themselves were not sticking to the standard menus of approved family behavior and were constructing their own very personal strategies and modes of coping, I realized that their reactions to my life reflected the standard model, rather than their improvisations, of family life. In my small world in America my own deviations (which included divorce) had become more or less acceptable; but exported to Japan, they turned into embarrassingly public revelations of private disorder. Where Americans tend to believe that the public representation of one's life should bear a reasonable resemblance to the private realities, Japanese feel that what doesn't meet the public eye need not conform to orthodoxy (the duality of *tatemae* and *honne*—"ideal form" and "reality"—excuses behavioral deviations from the norm as long as they remain private and as long as the individual or family punctiliously maintains the facade of *tatemae*).

A much younger Japanese friend told me that her husband was having an affair and, though he didn't know it, that she too had a lover. She said this "balance" made family life go on in a stable setting. I was at first dumbfounded at the ease with which she expressed these things. I had thought of their family as an example of happy accommodation between work and home life—and it was, though not as I had imagined. When another friend said that she and her siblings had decided to take turns moving, a year at a time, to their parents' home to care for their needs in old age, I saw this as a useful but difficult way of handling both Confucian ideology and practical needs. And I commiserated with fathers posted away from their wives and children, about the conflict between children's need for stable and consistent schooling experiences and employers' demands for total commitment to work.

Can such families be "perfectly Japanese," as the book's title suggests? Newspaper headlines present a story about families that appears to presage the end of Japan-as-we-know-it; they describe families riven by divorce, absenteeism, and abandonment and intimate strongly that these problems will bring Japanese society down. Official rhetoric and commentary impugn unfilial individuals who, by their irregular lifestyle choices, treat the family as a pit stop for its members. Images of the selfish mother, absent father, careless children, and neglected grandparent demonize members of families who appear to be ignoring their responsibilities. Official "scripts" for family, embedded in policy statements and rhetoric in media commentary, encourage the preservation of home as Japan's "social security." As in the past, these scripts reengage family as the symbol of what it means to be Japanese. And as evidence of their compliance with this script, families are above all encouraged to reproduce. Members of families who appear to deviate from the model of family life consonant with state needs—who choose not to have children, who put job or profession over the role of mothering, who live with parents well into their thirties ignoring the call to marry and grow up, or who place elderly relatives in nursing-care facilities—are subverting Japan's future by their noncompliance with scripted roles. Yet in spite of these images, and policies placing pressure on families to comply, ordinary families see themselves as organic *and* makeshift, serving their members *and* cobbled together—not centrifugal, deviant, or subversive. Somehow, they bridge the gap between official family norms for the "perfectly Japanese" family—in which the elderly are cared for at home—and the complicated lives of families in today's circumstances—in which, for example, a woman works two jobs to pay for extra home help for her senile father-in-law instead of performing those tasks herself.

Where do families get the resources to "make do" in attempts to fulfill the expectations of traditions and policies? Where do those who do not try to achieve that endorsed version get support (economic, social, and emotional) for their own makeshift families? This book attempts to show the play, or agonizing struggle, between versions of family life that strongly conflict: a national Family on the one hand, and on the other the ordinary and very plural and changing families where lives of individuals intersect, converge, and diverge over life courses and in the context of changing economic, social, and legal influences.

One arena in which families are engaged beyond the ideologies and policies of official Japan is that of consumer industries, in marketing and media. Families often get what they need to make up for the lacks of other agencies outside the walls of the home, from the goods and services provided to help fill the gap. These aids have proliferated, as we shall see, as a kind of ad hoc agglomeration of social services to reduce the strain on families even as they deviate from official notions of the good family and are unattended by social programs and public support. Such aids as prepared meals, private child-care centers, home improvements for families with a handicapped member, and home visitors for the elderly have been provided by a "family support" industry that flourishes in today's Japan. Those who can afford to buy the services and goods can, obviously, be more successful in their attempts to bridge the gap between the official uppercase version of Family and a makeshift disgrace. Those who cannot afford them demonstrate the increasing gulf between the haves and the have-lesses in Japanese society but still often look more like Family (where the household appears to be self-sufficient and women who must also work outside the home are "250-percenters") only because keeping up appearances leaves them with no energy to rebel.

In every household, versions of family against which to measure one's own home abound. Television is particularly powerful, and "home dramas" (Japanese soap operas) present several kinds of scenarios, from the emancipated single professional woman's trendy apartment, to a four-generation farm family managing to keep grandfather's agenda of continuity front and center. In one particularly evocative recent series, the morality tale of the present unfolds.

A career woman in her thirties finds her work life compelling yet barren, as she devotes herself to climbing the corporate ladder to success and becomes tough, hard-bitten, and "unfeminine." She speaks in rude, clipped language, is abrasive to others, and is demanding and thoroughly unpopular with her staff. A young wife, in her late twenties, is perky and energetic and displays her happiness in her stay-at-home role through her loving care of her five-year-old daughter and her career-track husband. He can devote himself to work because of her efforts to keep him undistracted by domestic concerns. This is the core cast of characters of *Poka Poka* (a homey word meaning "warm and comfortable"), a program offering a template for family values. This television series preaches to the converted housewives who watch at 10:20 A.M. every day, confirming the choices of women who stay at home and—satisfying the greatest concerns of domestic policymakers today—reproduce and care for the elderly. The happy home life extolled in this program may appear as a near caricature of women's devotion to domesticity but it aligns very closely to the image touted as solution to Japan's social and demographic problems.

In one episode, characters played out the question in viewers' minds as to whether or not people can find happiness in fulfilling their scripted roles. In a small restaurant where the husband and his workmates relax after work, a younger man claims he will never marry because a wife becomes unhappy and "no fun." The husband has a hard time convincing the young man that he, and his wife, are happy. He finally takes the young man home with him so that he can ask his wife directly if she is happy. They find the young woman (having put the daughter to bed in a happy giggly mood) smiling as she folds the laundry. She is confused but happy to see them. Her husband asks her to join him and his workmate in a beer. At first she shyly demurs but finally pours herself just a quarter of a glass. Her husband asks her, "Are you happy being married?—Be honest." She becomes pensive and slowly explains that she enjoyed college and work but—pause and beatific smile—her life is now complete, and she is . . . very happy. "Are you happy with *me?*" he asks. She looks at him directly and says, "Yes." The younger man leaves, convinced, and the husband hugs her and smiles as he helps fold the rest of the laundry.[1]

The audience of women at home, it is to be assumed, feel that this scenario justifies their own choice as both romantic and practical. That this choice requires such a blatantly sentimentalized defense underlines the fact that families, particularly women, appear to be entertaining quite different options and are seen to be in need of moral rearmament in order to be as happy as the young woman in the drama.

The television program described above is an example of the restylization of the Japanese Family in face of critical concerns about the future, a future whose security and continuity is in doubt because of the varying choices of families. Conservative politicians and policymakers see families as both victims and perpetrators of antisocial influences and keep family making on the state agenda. The media are not alone in extolling family values: recent policies enacted or proposed appear to be manipulating what families do if not what they value. We can use the sense of crisis generated through demographic data and portrayals of a nation at risk to explore the ideologies and the actualities of everyday life in families. A look at models for the Japanese Family during the Meiji and the postwar eras, as well as families, plural, in the present, reveals how the ideologically perfect family is interpreted—or ignored—in the strategies and goals of ordinary people. For example, the call to have babies now reveals the pushes and pulls families experience as they cope and muddle through, each in its own way.

MAKING BABIES FOR THE STATE, AND KEEPING GRANNY AT HOME

According to Iwao Sumiko, chair of the Commission on the Shrinking Birthrate, a body created to investigate the reasons behind the critically low birthrate (in 1989, 1.57 births per woman of reproductive age; in 1999, only 1.34), politicians often miss the boat. She says programs and media messages to encourage women to stay home do not increase the birthrate in any case, and the socially conservative Komeito Party's promotion of child-care allowances for those who stay home to rear children is not sufficient either. The commission delivered to the government in 2000 a list of 160 measures to increase the birthrate, treating a wide range of structural, cultural, and economic issues. These measures, Iwao says, recognize the diversity of reasons people have to delay or omit childbearing.

One issue is that young people are delaying marriage—some to their early thirties and beyond. Like the doubting workmate in the television drama, young people may need to be convinced that marriage and family building are fulfilling endeavors. There is, Iwao explains, no pressure on the young to marry now: single men have no energy left after work to seek their own spouses and women are running from the usual implication of marriage, child rearing. Behind the baby bust is an even more frightening story line of the abandoned elderly and a society with neither private nor public resources to support them. Keeping elder care in the province of family relies on having some family member—probably a woman—at home to care for Granny, a scenario most admit is unlikely in the next generation. Other systems of caregiving are insufficiently funded or bureaucratically stagnant. In April 2000, a nursing-care insurance program was to be launched to pay for professional, nonfamily care of the elderly. However, only six months before the start of the program, a delay in collection of premiums was instituted and payments to families who agreed to care for their own elderly at home were substituted. Iwao said that this revision is "totally out of line with the spirit of the new insurance scheme which aims to shift some of the senior-care burden from the family to society."[2] This revision produced a strong reaction among the public, particularly angering women who felt locked into the role of chief caregiver of their husbands' parents, and often their own parents too, as bilateral kinship responsibilities have become common.[3]

The family values that policymakers sustain overlook the economic necessity for women's work, as well as the richly diverse and changing ways people engage in making families: three-generational households or no-child households, families separated by work assignments or divorce, or those still legally married but living separate lives under the same roof. They work and live in the real world as they try to accommodate the ideal of "Family making," the attempts by agencies, institutions, and markets to create something manageable and predictable and economical to run, like a car with low service needs and high efficiency. How did this official version of Family develop?

THE *IE* FAMILY STRUCTURE

The traditional family represented by the *ie*, which John Pelzel describes as both the long-term "house" and the family who inhabits that house at one point in time, has been seen as the perpetuating social organization at the base of Japanese society, one that also provides a model for other forms of social organization. The *ie* is said to organize power, both within the household as a valorized hierarchy by age and gender and among households in the same lineage, whose duties and privileges are managed through the traditional relationships based on a succession in main (*honke*) and branch (*bunke*) families.

As Pelzel notes, Chinese and Japanese traditional family structures shared ideological roots in Confucian relationships, but in the Chinese case, joint inheritance by all sons, with management in the hands of the eldest, was the ideal, while in Japan, unigeniture (with a preference for primogeniture) gave eldest sons exclusive primacy in the households; younger sons left to make their own homes. This practical arrangement, according to Pelzel, minimized potential for dissension among brothers and their wives or at least removed it physically from the main household, making the ideal easier to engage in the Japanese than in the Chinese case.[4] However, several factors complicated the picture, namely resources, residential patterns, and reproduction.

Succession and inheritance are relevant in practical terms when there is something to succeed to and inherit. Families with no inheritable real estate, occupation, or other property and resources might find it harder to organize themselves around maintenance of a lineage family, or even an "ideal" *ie* household. Ideology can motivate solidarity and security, but only when ideals are in tandem with conditions conducive to continuity and productivity. Succession by one son does increase a family's chances of remaining intact for generations but does not guarantee it— nor does remaining intact depend on the presence of a capable eldest son. In fact, one of the sources of durability of the traditional Japanese model of family, according to some scholars, is its flexibility: where there is no son, or no competent son to act as the trustee manager of the *ie* for its ancestors and descendants, an adopted son-in-law or even an eldest daughter can perform this role. As Marion Levy describes such a family, it can take the form of a collection of roles to be filled by those who can well maintain the functions of those roles: a family as "civil service."[5]

At the beginning of the Meiji period (1868–1912), Japanese leaders witnessed major transformations resulting from domestic legal and social changes, rapid industrialization, and the influences of foreign contact. They responded by attempting to shore up what was to them the essence of Japanese culture and society, the Family. *Wakon yōsai*—Japanese Spirit, Western Technology—was the slogan guiding change. The Family was the bedrock location of this spirit. Faced with the threat of colonial and cultural takeover and the inevitability of dealing with powerful new foreign trading partners, Japanese leaders created an "ancient" tradition to preserve the "integrity" of Japanese culture. The form of family codified by law in 1898 was the patriarchal Confucian lineage family, the *dōzoku,* of which the *ie,* the extended family household, was the incumbent representative Family that managed the household in service to ancestors' spirits and acted as steward of resources to be passed on to descendants. This Family was also charged with the transmission of "Japanese spirit" to the nation's descendants in a smooth transition to a modern nation-state. In a similar way the postwar civil code created a family on whose back recovery and economic success would ride, homogenizing the model but not the experiences of people whose families were, in actuality, often far from the norm.

Descriptions of family making in Japan characterize the relationship between family and state as both natural and embattled. Those who see congruence between "naturally" evolving family forms and societal structure and development see even the extraordinary mobilization of families in wartime as evidence of preexisting consonance. The construction of a modern nation-state in the Meiji period was, in this view, a seamless evolution because of the availability of a patriarchal (Victorian) model to be codified as Japan's official Family. Industrialization and urbanization could be managed without alienation and anomie owing to the availability of younger sons for a modern labor force in a stem family system that "naturally" placed its non-inheriting sons outside the walls of the ancestral home. Reconstruction after the war could be managed through the Family, even through the "reduced" family of the emerging middle-class nuclear household. Its gender-based division of labor, in which a single male wage earner, dedicated to corporate goals, supported a stay-at-home mother, and she in turn their children, acted in service to national productivity.

The postwar family template with its separate spheres for men and women might appear to support individualism or, indeed, to support women's autonomy but—paralleling the case in American suburban families in the 1950s—this configuration actually constrained women and alienated families from community and other support systems. In fact, functions that had been managed in wider social units, inside and outside the household, were now left to a diminished unit with reduced resources of men, women, and children to manage them. Shrunken families had to take responsibility for their own "social welfare" in relative isolation, especially in neighborhoods where such nuclear households had limited and short-term ties with one another. Urban life, and most particularly life in large anonymous apartment complexes, did not tend to foster mutual cooperation among nuclear family units. This "privatized" social welfare system contained in a very small and private family unit put pressure on individuals, marriages, and parent-child relationships; especially around the issues of support for dependent kin and child care, it meant a great burden for working mothers. The division of labor said to be functional for reconstruction (husband at workplace unencumbered by domestic concerns; mother at home devoted 100 percent to husband and children) cannot hold when the nuclear household must add one or two dependent elderly needing care and when, to remain middle class, the family must depend on the second income brought in by a working mother. In a rapidly aging population, with longevity for women reaching eighty-three, for men seventy-nine, and with one in every four persons to be over sixty-five years old by 2020, it is more than ever likely that families will experience directly the decisions and responsibilities of elder care.

A continuous three-generation household would have managed these matters smoothly, conservative leaders think, but a reconstituted, pro tem extended family will have to do. Officials extol the 60 percent of rural families in which three or more generations reside, but the rural population is only 20 percent of the whole: most families live in cities. Most urban families are nuclear households for much of their life span, and this fact means that stress and dislocation characterize most people's experience, unsupported by the *ie*-based "family-welfare system," a fact that official, and even scholarly, Japan may have missed. Indeed, official priorities may exacerbate these issues.

MODELS OR MAKESHIFTS?

In Ariyoshi Sawako's bestselling novel *Kōkotsu no hito* (*Twilight Years*), a working woman must cope with the care of a senile father-in-law who is rejected by community adult day-care services. She must manage his complete physical care, giving up her job for the role of caregiver. This novel struck a chord with families burdened by such dependencies, but little has been done in the public sector to provide care that does not reinforce the guilt families feel in using it.

Even middle-class families, less concerned with the norms of the *seken* (watchful community) than with their own practical survival, must some-

times make conscious and somewhat dramatic moves to maintain themselves. One couple, whose eldest son is married and lives overseas, went
on their knees to beg their younger daughter, about to marry, to bring
her (somewhat reluctant) husband to live in a separate condominium in
their building to care for them as they age. Without official Confucian-
ism to support filiality, members still invoke family ties in the framing
of nurturance and responsibility. Families are indeed organic entities,
and members expect to be part of something larger than themselves,
larger than the neolocal nuclear units they may temporarily establish at
marriage.

"Coping families" may be at odds with "family values" but still attempt
to perform those functions posited by official rhetoric. Other families—
unlikely to be seen as families at all under official renderings—might be
called "families of choice" if that did not imply the very rare freedom to
select lifestyle. The ability of gay couples, for example, to cohabit and
legally maintain a residence together is restricted not only by public opinion but by the laws and bureaucratic systems (such as family registries)
that organize and control the public representation and support of households. Most of all, families-that-are-not-Family in the official version cannot fulfill the needs of productivity, reproductivity, and maintenance of
the growing population of elderly.

Matthews Hamabata discusses the distinction between families adher-
ing to traditional cultural preferences and those who routinely ignore
ideals, making adjustments to secure family continuity each in its own
way.[6] In the upper-middle-class "business families" he describes, women
managing kin relations in service to the prosperity of a family (their natal families' as well as their husbands') make linkages beyond the patrilineal to a wider *shinseki* or kin network well beyond the strict principles
of a Confucian *ie* where positions and roles demand rigid accountability
to patriarchal authority and hierarchy. Hamabata demonstrates that the
ie principle provides a suggestive frame, but the core realities lie in what
he calls the "rough and tumble" of the *uchi,* or ordinary private makeshifts
of family life. The families we will see here are even further from the *ie*
model than his.

The exaltation of the lineage-based household was supported by Japa-
nese sociologists and folklore scholars of the prewar years such as Ariga
Kizaemon (1897–1979), whose work emphasized the large household
and lineage as the essential, prototypical, distinctive Japanese family.
Meanwhile, however, ethnographic work noted that it was exceptional.
Empirical and historical studies in the postwar period showed local vari-

ation and change in Japanese families, and more recently, studies of family life cycle have been popular, but the *dōzoku,* or lineage-based large-family bias of the prewar school of family studies, still remains.[7]

Now, however, because the *ie* is so little part of most people's consciousness, the idea of the "corporate household" does not drive choices and planning, except in those families such as Hamabata describes, where property, political position, and social status seem to demand it. Ezra Vogel's study of postwar middle-class suburban families notes a remaining residue of *ie* thinking in the late 1950s and makes the important distinction that the *ie* concept is more relevant to the heirs in the main household, the *honke,* than it would be in *bunke,* branch households with less to preserve.[8] Vogel also says that economic interests in business, shopkeeper, craft, or agrarian families will bind descendants in *ie*-type relations to their progenitors. Vogel, like Levy and Pelzel, emphasizes the socioeconomic functions, rather than the ideological and cultural aspects of *ie* consciousness, and demonstrates that in families such as those of company workers and other middle-class urbanites, without a strong material motivation, the corporate household will not be sustained.

If we are to understand families and the motivations that inspire them to creative management against the forces separating members in time and space, taxing resources, and making demands on them to adhere to programs and ideals they cannot enact, we must engage ideas of family that incorporate and transcend *ie* models. Knowing as we do that family making has for well over a century been a national enterprise and that pre- and postwar ideals have never been part of the lives of the majority of people, we must treat families on the ground, as they are, and listen to their own meaning making in its diversity and fluidity.

As Hamabata does, we look here at contrasts between an ideal and the messy realities. Where he sees the archetypal *ie* still operative as a "design for living" for the wealthy business families he describes,[9] we will here look at the more generalized rescripted family ideal at the heart of official policy. This is not the traditional *ie,* but a compliant, productive, and reproductive middle-class family, able to manage the care of its own dependents across generations, but operating smoothly as a nuclear family with a clear division of labor between husband and wife, at least during some of its life course. This family was idealized as the bedrock of national prosperity in the postwar years but is no closer to representing the realities of twenty-first-century families than is the prewar model.

This book will attempt to show how "ordinary" families have managed to survive diversifying, even destabilizing, influences making them "deviant" from ideals constructed by state interests, and to remain viable in their very disorder. Current discussions of family mission focus on problems and where they will be fixed: are families to take on the responsibilities for social stability as "surrogates" for the state? Or will the state, still using official renderings of family functions, act as "surrogate" in the provision of care and support, given conditions in which families find it difficult to live up to those readings? (Naturally, laid-off corporate workers, double-time working housewives, and solitary elders do not see the lack of fit between official versions of family and real lives as evidence of deviance.) If the gap is to be bridged, and different strategies and models of family find acceptance and support, a stable society can survive the onslaught of demographic, social, and economic change in the new millennium. It is the attempt to deny these differences and the real sources of these changes that have created a sense of crisis in Japan; enforcement of singularity and glorification of even the recent past will not solve it.

MARKING TIME

In the past decade since I began the formal study of family lives in Japan, both public and private versions of family have had to confront the fallout of real social and economic changes. The majority of housewives now take part in wage labor, families are split by job relocation or informal "within-the-house" divorce, and workers are displaced by restructuring and forced into early retirement or unemployment with the collapse of the bubble economy. In apparent reaction, more stridently asserted versions of the normative images of Family have appeared, as policy and practices in the official sector find it hard to accommodate those demographic and social changes that make existing expectations and provisions at best outmoded, at worst tragically unfit to support families. Value-laden pronouncements abound in the press and in political oratory, such as "Are you abandoning Granny?" and "Why are women on a birth strike?" The latter is reminiscent (to those who can remember) of wartime exhortations to give birth to strengthen the nation. Contemporary exhortations serve to support policies that have been scrabbled together to deal with rising divorce rates, greater longevity, absent fathers, alienated teens, and other greater or lesser "pathologies" that seem to put the orthodox view of Family, and the nation, at risk.

The time has come to talk about families as viable entities in contrast to the organic, singular, homogeneously experienced Family that we might have attempted to describe in the earlier postwar years and that some Japanese scholars and Western observers continue to maintain as a model. My earlier work has addressed social life and families not as harmonious, organic, and complementary but as background for the individuals whose lives were controlled or marginalized by the social institutions in which they studied, worked, and consumed. Like most people, I took families for granted and saw them as residual, passive recipients of ideology and official policy rather than active producers of culture and social innovation. Putting real families first instead of the expectations for families made a considerable difference in my perspective. The reflections on families over almost four decades threw new light on my informants' history and my own history in Japan (and indeed in the United States, too), illuminating the differences between the Family (the institutionalized, conservative, somewhat nostalgic norm) and families (collections of relatives who support one another in various ways). Hamabata's description of family life on the "inside," as the "rough and tumble center of warmth and acceptance, emotional depth, the locus of the heart" is where we begin.[10] The decades of family life I have experienced in Japan since the early 1960s have been various and changing. The families I'd interviewed seemed to have experienced most of life's vicissitudes and joys without losing the grace and name of family. They seemed to hold on well, though few of them resembled ideologues' "beautiful family traditions" or looked as devastated, fractionated, ravaged, or decadent as media scaremongers depicted them. The younger families had less need to maintain the normative family and expressed their resistance to it more publicly. They often made counternormative, private choices without looking over their shoulders.

These are the stories of several postwar generations, written, I hope, from a perspective that avoids both relentless negativity and blind optimism. Using stories of both individual and family life courses, I try to give a broad base for thoughtful consideration of family life and social change over several generations that may raise even more questions about the relations between modern families and modern states. In the following chapters we trace the norms, the moods, the social and economic realities of families over the postwar era. We see families as economic units of production and consumption, families as sentimental or emotional evocations, whether as way stations, conduits, warehouses, or even as "state apparatus." Chapter 1 frames the discussion with the cries and alarms of contemporary commentators worried about the shrinking birthrate and looking for someone to blame. The population "crisis" begins our treatment of the felt need for a national family and bears some resemblance to the forces that created the Meiji and postwar-era "ideal" families. Chapter 2 takes two families, the bookends of a century, from a merchant family of the Meiji era to an end-of-the-twentieth-century family making do and getting by on its own, codeless but not clueless. Chapter 3 charts postwar families as constructions of a "democratic" model supporting reconstruction and growth. Looking at children, chapter 4 begins a set of portraits of elements of family that continues in chapters 5 and 6 with descriptions of women's and men's roles and the lives of the elderly. Chapter 7 brings the gap between the "national" Family and ordinary families into sharp focus through a treatment of the responses of consumer industries, goods, and services to the fractionated realities of family. In a brief conclusion, we consider how understandings of imminent disaster may themselves promote conditions in which families will have to struggle even more to maintain themselves.

Conditions of family life in Japan today reflect societal and demographic changes the nation has undergone. What we observe here will happen, in one form or another, in most of the developed world. Stripping away ideologies to display realities will be a necessary component of social policy as all our populations shrink and age in the future.

SOURCES FOR THE STUDY

I began fieldwork for this study in 1990, observing and interviewing families in several age cohorts, particularly including those in their late fifties and early sixties who had been raised at the end of the war and during reconstruction. These people were now facing retirement, empty nests (and / or "renesting" adult children, still at home or returned, for lack of an independent income or for other reasons), and freedom to pursue something new. In a kind of "renesting," some of these families included elderly who had become physically or financially dependent and now lived in a newly constructed extended family. Another group consisted of families of people in their late thirties, often with younger children. There were twelve families in the older group and ten in the younger group, but there were also extended interviews conducted with a range of families of other ages and other household compositions. Representations of a variety of lives are included: five of the core group are families of shopkeeper and working-class lifestyles, and another four in the core group are families who, because of recent disability or unemployment, have suffered a serious economic decline. The remaining thirteen would be called middle class in anyone's terms. Rural agrarian families reside in Gumma and Nagano prefectures and in Hokkaido and Okinawa. Families in the core group of twenty-two lived in Kansai, Kanto, Gumma, Nagano, and Sendai. My interviews with them continued from 1990 to the winter of 1999–2000.

In addition, I interviewed officials in the Ministries of Health and Welfare, Education, Labor, and Justice. Looking also at the agencies in which policies are interpreted and carried out, I met with workers in family planning clinics, therapists in family practices, volunteers working with the elderly, day-care workers, teachers, and people in other institutions directly involved with families and individuals. I learned how history, individual life courses, and social institutions have intersected within the complex subject of family life. Looking at policy as ideology, process, and bureaucratic detail engaged me in the struggles experienced by those who must interpret and enact it. As official Japan promotes larger families, Ashino Yuriko (of Japan's Family Planning Association) notes, it paradoxically diminishes support for and fractionates families. How this happens in the gaps between policy and practice became clearer to me as the study developed.

We will see here young married couples who experience fleeting togetherness until the first child is born; a *nyū famiri* (new family) working on a fifty-fifty division of home tasks; a family whose work is "home work" in an apartment over the shop; a family separated by job shifts; a family with grandmother as babysitter for the younger generation; a marriage without children still daring to call itself a family. I am deeply grateful to all of those who opened their homes and lives to me, and I hope I have not transgressed against that openness: I have disguised all cases in various ways to protect confidentiality. I hope too that I have captured the vivacity of their self-portrayals and their profound honesty.

PART ONE

Making Family

A Nation Begins at Home

CHAPTER I

Why Families Are a National Security Issue

An official at the Ministry of Health and Welfare listened as I asked about apparently "pronatalist" social policies, seeming to many to be strategies for increasing the birthrate. He leaned back in his chair, laughed, and said, "No, we don't have to do that. We don't need to have any such policies because the local areas are doing it for us!" The government relies on local programs and incentives to implement its messages to procreate, care for the elderly, and thus support the future of Japan. Indeed, the future of the nation is at stake, but the nation cannot dictate a course of action. The awkwardness of the situation only amplifies the rhetoric.

Social issues such as juvenile delinquency, the care of the elderly, women's employment issues, and the foreign labor force in Japan all hinge on the issue of reproduction, to ensure the future of Japan. But getting people to have more babies or plan for the care of dependent parents must be managed through maneuvers and guidance rather than direct injunctions. This task is all the harder when there is an even stronger need to place women in the workforce, and social changes that encourage new accommodations of relationships beyond the traditional extended family or even beyond conventional marriage. Ultimately, what drives families is not rhetoric. Even in the Meiji period, there were no givens in most families, and now it appears that very little is obvious or predetermined. What was once a sure thing (grandmother's pickle recipe or eldest-son succession) was always subject to negotiation and change, even in elite families supposedly closer to the imagined ideal.

Making do is now the "sure thing." In earlier generations an adopted son-in-law might have made up for the lack of a willing and able eldest son, whereas now an only-child daughter might inherit and be responsible for her parents or an elderly couple might move into a retirement community, almost unheard of when they were young. The professional working woman's young son will be in day care, her husband will be living at his corporate assignment in a city far away. Dinner may be reheated prepared meals from a nearby department store food hall. Having the resources to purchase adjustments, the couple will meet the household's various needs. However far they appear to be from the normative model, they are still a family and not a mere collection of individuals sharing a household. And the response from the private sector marketers of goods and services supporting ordinary people doing ordinary things helps (and perhaps exploits) the family's needs but also runs counter to the state's demands for conformity to Family.

At three critical moments in Japan's history—during the Meiji period, the postwar Allied Occupation, and the postboom period of the last dozen years—official Japan prescribed deliberate and organic images of Family. Being constructed for reasons of national security, the images include awkward contradictions. That what is assumed to be "natural" must be shaped by administrative guidance is itself puzzling. That families need to get in step with national agenda when it remains implicit is equally hard to explain. Finally, the fact that people acting "rationally" in their own interest do not necessarily achieve the goals of a free market society even as it caters to those who can afford to take advantage of it is peculiarly awkward. But families just trying to get by cannot hear calls for a revival of the Confucian family: filiality and older models of domesticity are out of step with their realities.

Families have taken the brunt of declaimed outrage over juvenile delinquency, unfilial treatment of the elderly, and even foreign labor. The response of official Japan is to associate these issues with the declining birthrate. Failure to reproduce, a sign of shirked responsibility by individuals failing to make families, becomes a hook on which to hang other ills. If families were healthy agents of reproduction for the economy and society (q.v. state) and if their members conformed to the roles assigned by the state's version of "public morality," there would be only cheerful studying children, attended by at-home moms, respected and tended elderly, and full *Japanese* employment.[1] Or so the story goes. Conservative public agencies have appeared to agree on a Family that will continue to serve a postwar state much as its nineteenth-century prototype did. And families continue to do it their way.

This book treats the disjunction between Family and families and most particularly, how the latter manage under conditions abhorred by leaders but ignored for the most part by social policy and social services, and undeniably present for almost everyone. Like families elsewhere, Japanese families are organic units, agents in service to their own needs. Japanese families, rather than the elements that make them up, are key units in society and often act as individuals do in America, in planning their futures, developing strategies to achieve them, and contraverting established principles and ideologies. Americans see home and family instead as sources of respite from their solitary campaigns for individual fulfillment or as obstacles in their path toward individuality. Accustomed to seeing only individuals as truly free agents, as able to resist the constraints of bureaucratic or ideological conservatism or oppression, Americans may find it confusing or contradictory to see home as the heart of resistance rather than as the hearth from which, to be free and autonomous, one must flee.

That family life is complicated and fits no particular model is obvious. The elderly are supposed to have a conservative view, or at least a nostalgic view of the "good old days" when the "thunder father" ruled the roost and women stayed in the kitchen. But grandmothers (rather more than grandfathers, it should be said) are pragmatists. One said, "After all, each family has to figure out what can work—a son leaves, a wife dies, someone cannot have children, a niece has to live with you because your own child won't: there's no design to all this." People like this sixty-four-year-old woman in Yokohama say it's all a bunch of compromises and adjustments. They make commonsense accommodations while the normative model revolves around its own abstract axis. Listening to their views is *not* like listening to political rhetoric. Grandmothers have a hard time answering the question, "What is a family?" while politicians seem to have no trouble at all.

Families, in whatever definition, are now taken as both the problem and the solution and their members, whether "selfish women," "lazy young," or "stubborn elderly," are seen both as agents and victims. As in the Meiji period, framing the mission and behavior of Family has become a national imperative, and as in the Meiji period, families respond to or ignore such exhortations. This book attends to the contrivances people actually make, not to get in step with national agenda but to get

along. In addition, we look at how private sector community agencies
and programs, as well as services and goods provided by consumer industries, support families. People who use them may be demonized as
selfish or cruel, but the goods and services exist because they are needed.

GETTING, SPENDING, AND SAVING ON SHOWERS

Reference to swings in the economy, to sweeping measures of affluence
and recession are not enough to define family life. Men, women, and children have all been affected by growth and decline in the period of boom
and bust since the 1960s. Some families even budget shower time as costs
of water and heat continue to rise. How families have coped recently with
an economic downturn has roots in family economic functions in the past
but also demonstrates the diversity and particularity of family strategies.
A successful postwar middle-class family in the 1950s and 1960s was a
producing family, not so unlike the agrarian, trade, and craft families of
the prewar eras, but differed from its antecedents in two ways. First, production had become separate from the household and the division of labor between men and women had become customary. Second, though
family in the largest sense extended well beyond the doors of any home,
for practical purposes the operational family was coterminous with
household. It no longer included members related by blood and marriage
and also servants, apprentices, or "fictive kin," some of whom had an
inherited relationship to the family. After the shift to wage earning outside the home (usually by the husband), a single-earner household contained fewer people and tended to be a nuclear household. The presence
of grandparents at some stage of its life course did not make it a traditional *ie* but kept the responsibility to care for these people within the
new temporary three-generation household, a "nuclear-plus" family. Urbanization and the constraints of space contributed further to the
shrinking of household size, but more significant were legal and economic changes. In all cases, the families of the next century will experience very different conditions from those their parents experienced or
provided for them.

For families now, the high cost of housing and housekeeping as well
as child rearing means that maintaining a middle-class lifestyle on only
one income is an elusive goal and that more women stay in the workplace longer than the conventional two to three years before marriage.
Most women now work outside the home for some time during their
married and child-rearing lives, if not continuously. The care of elderly

parents in the nuclear-plus family constrains budget and schedules and may represent an emotional strain, especially for working women.

The need to ensure the futures of offspring also makes demands on family economics and time, through greater investment in children's educational supports, longer years of co-residence with children (who usually make little or no financial contribution to the household) and through the extension of mother's roles to include that of "home coach." Where children are in their programs for life has made all the difference in family standards of living in the second and third postwar generations (according to one estimate, a middle-class family must pay $623,000 to raise a child from birth through his or her early work years). When a working middle-class family (meaning two earners) has two children rising toward secondary schooling, expenses soar and the dedication needed to fund and support the endeavor is enormous. The dual commitment to work and children commits two parents to occupations that restrict their ability to be home for children whose pressured lives need nurturance and guidance. And it constitutes one of several critical periods in a family's life course.

The next comes when children are grown and their mother, freer to engage in work, travel, or hobbies, finds that her husband's retirement brings him home just when she is ready to "fly." Or she may be a full-time worker, helping the family sustain the postretirement economic crunch but unavailable as a traditional homemaker. As pensions shrink and personal savings are spent down over longer-than-expected life spans, the funds available to care for a nuclear-plus household of longer-living elderly fall short.

The high cost of real estate has meant that even after completing their education, children quite often continue living at home while working, usually until their marriages. A typical urban apartment for a single person will rent for about $1,400 per month, out of reach for a young female worker earning an average of $1,900 per month. Especially for her, living at home is the only possibility. This phenomenon, called "parasite singles" by some, has inspired conservative commentary on irresponsible youth avoiding adulthood, marriage, and childbearing. "Renesting" has in some cases been the fallout from an adult child's divorce or job separation, from the choice not to work at all or to work as a *furiitaa*, or part-time freelancer, or even from a scarcity of corporate jobs owing to longer terms of work for older employees.[2] The smaller the household, the more impact additions and subtractions of members have on relationships, economics, and the experience of space and schedules.[3]

A life-course view of family life provides for changing, complicating factors in typifying experiences and strategies of households. At marriage, the establishment of a neolocal residence by a young couple may represent an increase in privacy but a decrease in comforts and service. For their natal families, the launching of the young into married life often coincides with the retirement of one or both parents. By this time, it is likely that one or more of the grandparental generation will need care of some kind: full-time care in one of their children's households, shared care among siblings, or institutional care plus supplemental family care. More typically it is family-based care with supplemental institutional "respite" facilities to give families time away from intensive care. The current cohort of retirees delayed having children until their late twenties and early thirties, and if they have retired or were forced into early retirement by layoffs and restructuring, their children's expenses may be a large part of their retirement budgets. And if those young people are at home still, the concurrence of paths and contradictory needs for independence and support may produce a crowded and tense household.

Strategies to accommodate this household and minimize friction may include a kind of "time-sharing" use of the house. In fact, a family at this stage of its life course may now be only infrequently gathered together. The more members in a household who are at key life-change moments, especially if they are young, completing education or beginning work, the less the family is likely to dine together regularly or spend predictable amounts of time socializing. Working parents are out late; grandparents may be in charge of the household, if they are able, or involved with organized neighborhood social activities; younger children will be at after-school tutoring classes or involved in their own social lives—some of which may indeed be strategically planned as temporary "exits" from family intensity. One teen managed his home time and space in a crowded household by sleeping when others were awake and waking to study in the middle of the night when others slept, giving him the illusion of being alone.[4]

One teenager said her family was of this centrifugal type, a *barabara* (dispersed, scattered) household, pointing out the high-energy schedules and attachments that drew members of her family away from the others;[5] hers was not the only complaint about what passes for family life, far from the Confucian community that officials and social policies assume as the basis for a strong society.

ACCOMMODATING FAMILIES

The story lines of families included in this book reveal several patterns of getting by. These patterns rarely resemble official models of Family and do not represent most families, yet in their diversity and flexibility they demonstrate the basic principle of family life in twenty-first-century Japan as it has ever been, *accommodation,* rather than adherence to rigid cultural norms. The difference now is that influences from agencies and institutions outside the walls of a household are far stronger than they were in the first half of the twentieth century. Some of these influences seem to persuade families to adhere to an image they cannot easily enact; some to support what they need done to survive.

Certain basic strategies these families undertake to marry, have children, support them in school and work, and care for elderly relatives are the family functions officials see as key to national continuity and most people identify as desirable and necessary for self-fulfillment.

Marrying has been delayed in the life course of most people—not, as conservative critics would say, because of reluctance to grow up and take responsibility for others, but because of new economic and social realities. Women and men are engaging in new designs for young adulthood and making conscious and difficult calculations about combining marital relations, childbearing, and work in a brave new world of self-created independence. For many, economic realities have delayed their ability to implement these designs or have forced them to engage "incompletely." Job security in a large corporation may also mean constraints and restrictions as couples separated by job assignments in different locations struggle to cooperate over household matters: having children in these conditions is a difficult choice to make.

Childbearing choices are further constrained by the high cost of raising a "successful" child, and the standard definition of "success" is hard for parents to ignore. Having babies, when it is hard to have even *one,* let alone the multiple births advocated by commentators and officials, makes for complicated strategies of parenting. In many marriages, wives continue to work now that this has been made possible by law and by social convention. Work has become as central a source of identity for many wives as it is for their husbands, even if it means lowering standards for household chores (no more postdusting white-glove testing of bookcases) or dividing up the chores fifty-fifty. When a child arrives, however, it is a different story because equality and cooperation come up against the resistant culture of mothering and the persistence of the post-war exclusivity of the mother-child bond in popular thinking.[6] Among some young couples such as the Fujimuras, whom we meet in the next chapter, there is an "*our* baby" image of co-parenting that carefully shares responsibility for home care, transport to day care, and other functions. This requires flexible work accommodation, difficult in most full-time work, and a decidedly organized attitude with which to confront the disbelief or perhaps dismay of employers and relatives. Having more than one child under these conditions is almost impossible.

And supporting more than one child with time and money is nearly as difficult. Middle-class couples will not sacrifice the prospects of that one child in whom their hopes and resources are invested, even though their bank accounts are drained and their views of the system demanding this exhausting effort are negative. Education, once seen as meritocratic, is now "pay-as-you-go." You must pay increasing amounts into the private, fee-charging supplemental learning programs just to stay middle class, further ensuring that both parents will stay earning through their child's schooling.

That happy supper table where an aproned Mom serves homemade nutritionally balanced foods has also been "adjusted." Men learn to cook, especially if they are posted away from home, and both husband and wife learn to manage the household with the support of commercial resources. As an example of how consumer industries and services have sprung up beside official Japan's exhortatory rhetoric and inadequate social policies, the convenience store has become a strategic partner in family management. Finally, isolated families must accommodate the blessing and burden of care for aging relatives. Critics assail families who use adult day care, home aides, or other commercially or locally provided services and say that families (for which read "women") are forsaking and abandoning elderly or are selfishly relying too much on outsiders to care for their own kin, and that Japan, soon to be the leading nation in the rate of people over sixty-five in the population, is becoming the "throwing-away-Granny society"—a national disgrace.

Women now work late shifts to be home part of the day with dependent parents, while neighbors, private nurses, and siblings also take turns with the elderly. This is accommodation, and doing what must be done is how people describe their engagement with their aging relatives, *not* "Confucian filial piety." And all of this, officials say, would be unnecessary if people would just have more babies.

"ONE CHILD IS NOT ENOUGH"

As the official quoted at the start of this chapter implied, there is no national campaign now to "give birth and multiply" (*umeyō, fuyaseyō!*), as there was in wartime. Instead we see local municipalities, concerned with depopulation and outmigration, offering young couples bonuses, subsidized housing, and other boons for marrying and staying in the area. For staying and having children, couples are given more—tax breaks, free nursery care, and other more extensive benefits for having second and third children, even university stipends.[7] In one area there was a song competition for a pro-baby song, and the winner was a song called "In Praise of Babies." In Okayama, local officials put up a poster showing a sweet child with downcast eyes: the caption read: "One child is not enough; doesn't your child want a brother or sister?"

These appeals are supported by public opinion polls noting that people really *do* want more children than they have and by statements from professional experts such as the comment in one governmental newsletter, "Instead of seeing children as a private issue, Japan must realize that children are a country's most precious capital."[8]

Schools are also involved in this promotion. In junior and senior high schools there are classes on baby care (electives, open to both boys and girls), and students are sent to work in local day-care centers in short-term internships, to familiarize themselves with young children. Local clinics and teachers encourage parents to have more children. One teacher said that "single children" aren't as emotionally healthy or as well socialized as are those with siblings. Teachers whose classes are now made up of many "only" children complain that these children do not know how to cooperate and share; they resort to stratagems such as limiting the number of toys or supplies in one area of the classroom to force children to share.[9] Smaller classrooms with a lower ratio of students to teachers were seen as nice for teachers, but too "homelike," encouraging too much reliance on the teacher and not enough on peers. Teachers feel these only children already have too much attention from doting parents and should learn self-reliance and cooperation.[10]

Accounts extolling the virtues of large families have appeared in several periodicals. A centerfold feature called "The Fertile Takamuras" appeared in a semigovernmental magazine, applauding the fact that this family has seven children, and emphasizing their happiness, their spirit of cooperation, and their ingenious economies.[11] More explicitly negative stories of birth decline were told in national television broadcasts of programs called "Our Children Will Disappear" and "Japanese Women Who Don't Want Children," where women's apparent refusal to reproduce was first called a "birth strike."[12]

Public discussions of abortion availability do not often link the high rates of abortion to low birthrates, for the quiet but effective lobby keeping abortion the main form of birth control is also a conservative doctors' association, and it would applaud a rising birthrate as well. There is a small antiabortion movement, called the "Respect for Life" movement, whose members have distributed videos and other materials to junior and senior high schools, including a version of the video *Silent Scream*, a strong and frightening American-made antiabortion film (chapter 5 discusses the debates over contraception and birth control, and their relationship to the declining birthrate).

Child boosting is visible throughout Japan, at odds with the direction of family planning in the rest of the world, as has been pointed out by some social critics within Japan. The youth population (fourteen years of age and younger) is the smallest it has been since 1920, at about 19 million young. This statistic would qualify as a great success elsewhere, but Japanese officials believe the nation is at risk at both ends of the population pyramid; the call for more babies is strong. Commentators such as Higuchi Keiko take a larger view, noting that the population problem should be placed in a global, not a national context. She says that Japan as an affluent, consuming nation uses disproportionate amounts of the earth's resources and should not increase its population, further endangering the global ecosystem and extracting resources from overpopulated developing countries. Others point out the irony behind the fact that Japan leads the world in foreign aid and promotion of family planning in developing countries and yet Japan's own family planning provisions are rated very low in the world's programs, lower than reproductive health programs in many third-world countries.

Governmental and corporate economic planners do not applaud the "success" of family planning in Japan. "Who will replace our aging workers?" ask the managers who now must fire workers in unprecedented large numbers in recessionary times. Japanese managers have tried to perpetuate the image of "permanent employment" through the last decade of the twentieth century even as they apologetically ask workers to "retire."[13] The unemployment rate rose from 1 percent in 1952 to 4.5 percent in 2000, matching the U.S. rate, a shock to individuals' lives and to national pride. The unofficial unemployment rate among males twenty-four or younger is much higher than the official 10.7 percent rate.[14]

There are sad tales of families having to move in with relatives and give up their homes, to news items of the increase in numbers of homeless persons living on the streets, to the stresses caused by the extension of job-related separations owing to personnel cuts. There have been terrible stories of suicides and even family murders apparently caused by economic failures.[15] Homelessness doubled between 1996 and 2000. Most homeless people are male and there are still few families with children on the streets. Some young homeless men sleep in their cars, use cell phones to make appointments, and try to maintain a stable work life while saving on rent.[16]

Grim stories about suicides and homelessness outweigh in drama the more prevalent stories of stress in ordinary lives. One businessman who no longer works overtime and whose company no longer subsidizes after-work socializing said that he is home more and does not find this change as relaxing as it should be. His wife is not used to having him home so much and the more they are together the more they fight. He senses that she'd be happier not having to prepare dinner for him every night.[17] Many feel that they have no financial, social, or psychological resources for dealing with the shock of Japan's "failure."

Many people, however, don't seem worried. Young people, especially those living with parents, still seem to spend their income without storing it away for the future and continue to fuel the healthy consumer and overseas travel industries. While unemployment is news, the income gap in Japan is still narrower than in most of the industrialized world. Only 2 percent of households have more than $160,000 annual income, and only 2 percent fall below $16,000. Most earn between $35,000 and $75,000 per annum. Only 1 percent of the population was on welfare in 1997. Some feel that maintaining this equality puts Japan at risk in the future and that high corporate (37.5 percent) and personal (50 percent) income taxes are unwanted subsidies to prop up homogeneity. A 70 percent inheritance tax means most families have to sell parental homes.[18] But the arguments to support more private development rather than public welfare and the deliberate equalization of urban and rural education, public works, and other projects are not likely to win out.

ANGELS ON THE HEAD OF A PLAN

The complicated economics of employment and family life at the turn of the twenty-first century involve contradictions: encourage workers to retire early, encourage older workers to stay on the job; encourage leisure activities and consumption, demand that families save for the care of their elderly; encourage women to work, encourage them to have babies for a future labor force that will need more workers.

Those future workers are the goal of an ambitious 1994 plan to make work and child rearing compatible. Ministry of Health and Welfare representatives noted that the "system" supporting child rearing "is rapidly disintegrating through increase of nuclear families and weakening of the spirit of solidarity in local communities."[19] The plan's informal name is the "Angel Plan," its full name "Basic Direction of Measures in Support of Future Child Rearing."

The plan addresses several convergent concerns. One is that children raised without siblings are slow to gain a "sense of support and sociality."[20] But the plan addresses both background issues in low birthrate and forwards concern over the future in emphasizing the "overall diminishing of vitality in society" caused by an aging workforce. After noting that child rearing is regarded as the "problem of married couples and their families," the plan says the problem (meaning the decline in childbearing) must be addressed by state and local organizations and by public and private workplaces.

The first cause of birth decline noted in 1990 is the delay in marriage among women; 40 percent of women between the ages of twenty-five and twenty-nine were still unmarried, a jump from 20.9 percent fifteen years earlier. The second cause is the apparent reason for the first cause, the trends for women to extend education and "an urge for self-fulfillment leading them to seek work" or, "the feeling of freedom in spinsterhood." And behind these, they say, is another layer of causes among women, the feeling that "child rearing is mentally and physically burdensome."[21]

The children women do have in such an unpropitious environment will take the flak of maternal discontent and in turn weaken the fabric of society in the future, a situation that "can no longer go unattended." The report repeats that childbearing is "the option of individuals" but that the support individuals need "should be recognized as an undertaking [in] which the entire society should be involved."

The Angel Plan itself is a revealing text combining detailed planning for day-care services and health care for mothers and children, consultation with employers on the compatibility of work and family needs, plans to promote good family housing and education free from pressure, as well as the alleviation of financial burdens on families bearing costs for children. It is, after all, a full Family plan, a new "code" of support for families for whom the 1947 civil code has little relevance.

But the measures were not easily or quickly put in place toward the target date of 2002 and so another plan was immediately proposed, a five-year Project for Emergency Day-Care Measures, to achieve limited goals in provision of day-care facilities by 1999. By April 1995, there were 22,513 day-care centers housing 1,593,161 children, 31 percent of those up to three years of age.

The problems are not solved by this measure; as we will see in chapter 4, women using these facilities sometimes need flexible timing and better locations according to their work demands. Private day-care centers are sometimes more amenable to early and late dropoff and pickup hours and provide choice for parents who can afford them. Child care for children with slight illnesses such as colds is also contemplated.

One of the more interesting stated goals of the plan is the training of mothers through their participation in the day-care communities. The day-care centers are intended to educate mothers to make up for the diminishing "opportunities for learning from diverse forms of human relations," meaning extended families. Young women are nervous and insecure about having babies and lack knowledge and feel isolated when they have them, so officials hope day-care centers can act as "community child-rearing support centers" with counselors and "circles" for women. The Angel Plan's "concern for the interests of children" focuses on encouraging women to have them in the first place and then on the "lack of continuity" (that is, lack of traditional family values and child focus),[22] which the plan indicates forces governmental agencies to act as the "grandparental" generation in passing on child-rearing skills in a communal environment.

Ad hoc support environments encouraging young mothers also exist, including "virtual communities" such as an online mothers' newsgroup with over 40,000 members. They engage questions and give each other support in chat rooms and bulletin boards, announcing their baby's first crawl or step, or commiserating with a woman in deep postpartum blues. A pediatrician answers medical questions. As one woman says, "forums like this enable you to build real human relationships. The other members really care about your child, even if they've never met her."[23]

The pressing need for child care has even broken through the bias against home babysitting. The strongly privatistic postwar nuclear family did not usually include nonfamily hired help of any kind, let alone help for working mothers, letting others into their homes to manage what was considered a woman's primary and exclusive task. In 1996, however, through a governmental program called the All-Japan Babysitting

Association, the Ministry of Health and Welfare began to provide discount coupons for home babysitting services. This discount was made available through employers who affiliate with the association, but the complicated bureaucratic procedures as well as low awareness mean few have used these coupons. The Ministry of Labor pitched in to support this program for their employees and the babysitters' association itself is trying to improve service by giving quick responses to short-notice requests and offering dispatch and pick up transportation for the babysitters themselves.[24] Will women who are depicted as too engrossed in their freedoms and self-fulfillment have children, and if they do, will they use these facilities to continue the lifestyle they may be reluctant or unable to give up? Or will their husbands take child-care leave and stay home?

While the Child-Care Leave Law appears gender-neutral, it does not operate this way. On leave (but without income), a worker must still pay premiums on social security. On average, an employed woman on leave pays about $250 per month. In addition, while on leave a worker must pay taxes on previous income. It becomes very impractical for a woman to take a leave rather than quit altogether, and for a man to take an unpaid leave and give his wife a chance to work means surviving on her wages, which are likely to be much lower than his. In addition, the long commutes many workers face make family time very scarce.[25]

Even when children are older, families face tensions. Japanese middle-class families have struggled to have some kind of family life in the face of the demands of the workplace and economic changes. The young woman cited earlier who called her family *barabara* lamented that her father was away so often and home so late at night. Whether married women are working part or full time, they are demonstrably stressed by the double demands of workplace and home. Some have two jobs, one part-time and the other an evening job, perhaps in the service sector. Families hit by recessionary anxieties or job loss thus may not have any compensatory shared family time and support, and doubled stress creates very unhealthy conditions.

RELAX OR ELSE!

In the 1980s, public concern about worker health was heightened by media stories about *karōshi*, or "death by overwork." This was at first seen as the worker's or his family's problem, the result of an individual's choice for workaholism, not as a problem of workplace conditions or the strategies of employers. By the early 1990s, however, companies had begun to lay some workers off, and the rise of reported work-related stress diseases seemed linked to insecurity for some, to overwork for others whose work team had diminished but whose workload had not. As the condition receives more publicity and as some families have sought redress in legal suits and won, the reporting too has increased.

Corporate response included enforcement of overtime rules limiting the extra hours a worker might put in at the end of a day. Reported overtime of course meant higher rates of pay, unlike the informal overtime many workers were pressured into contributing without filing for the extra stipend, and companies wanted to cut expenses by reducing this drain. Avoiding lawsuits by ensuring that workers went home at the end of the official workday saved companies money as well as protecting the health of workers. A five-day workweek has been nearly universal for government workers and employees of large corporations since the early 1990s, but workers at smaller concerns may still have a six-day week.

A national campaign to promote leisure publicized the benefits of taking time off, and the Ministry of Labor created a leisure commission to develop schemes to get workers to use their full vacation time rather than a day here and there added to a holiday or weekend, which was the practice of many in the past. The shift from blaming workers for their own cardiovascular diseases or exhaustion to assuming corporate responsibility coincided with the decline of production and recessionary cutbacks among companies. Taking responsibility for issues related to overtime suited employers who needed to cut back in any case. That employee–family members, both fathers and mothers, could now spend more time at home, was a side effect and did not necessarily represent an improvement. In many cases, the worker who didn't do overtime work for his or her company took another job to compensate and added an even greater strain to personal and family life. Women began to be victims of *karōshi* too, and the first lawsuit by the family of a woman who died from job-related disease was filed in 1991.[26]

There are now two extra three-day weekends planned from the year 2000 onwards, called "Happy Monday" holidays. To fit them in, Coming of Age Day, now January 15, will be the second Monday of January, and Sports Day, now October 10, will be the second Monday of October, to form three-day weekends. Encouraging leisure is supposedly beneficial to the economy as time off may be time to spend money, but most people say their holidays will be "cheap, close, and short." They will eat out, which is the most popular leisure activity, travel to a local amusement, or engage in home-based relaxation such as video games and gardening.[27] In the United States, the labor movement provided the impetus for the creation of the weekend; in Japan, it is a concern of the state and consumer industries.

FOREIGN PRODUCTION AND THE NEW UNDERCLASS

If Japanese workers are overstressed and still not getting the work done, who can do it? While the higher end of the wage ladder is downsizing, there is still work going begging at the lower end. There is an increasing foreign presence at the bottom of the labor pool and Japan has become a labor-receiver in spite of strong cultural and legal forces to the contrary. Especially since 1988, there has been a shift to male foreign labor in sectors such as semiskilled industrial work. Such workers are found in the unskilled "three K" jobs (*kitsui, kitanai,* and *kiken,* or "demanding, dirty, and dangerous"). The Ministry of Labor has created four categories of foreign labor, and illegal laborers, though naturally uncountable, form the greater foreign labor force.

Earlier cohorts of foreign workers in Japan "disappeared" for the most part into entertainment and service industries, and they were mostly women. As such they did not threaten the more visible male industrial labor force. It has been estimated that about 200,000 women per year are brought to Japan as *Japayuki-san,* people going to Japan, a euphemism for young women brought for the sex industry. They come from Thailand, Malaysia, Taiwan, and the Philippines by brokers and recruiters said to have ties with organized crime. Amamiōshima, a small island between Okinawa and the Japanese mainland, is said to be the entrepôt for a regular jumbo jet flight from the Philippines and Osaka, a flight locally dubbed "the gangster flight," bringing women for work in Japanese sex trades. In the Philippines and in parts of Southeast Asia there are Japanese language programs and short-term courses for prospective bar hostesses, and agencies created by returnee workers in Southeast Asia recruit female labor for Japanese contractors. The women are promised schooling or jobs in factories but usually become sex workers or workers in entertainment and hospitality industries.

Not all foreign working women are illegal workers, and some are officially recruited, such as skilled nurses from China; some *Nikkeijin* (Brazilian-Japanese) are also involved in convalescent care.[28] Young women in Japan have shifted career choices away from such fields as nursing, and the increasing numbers of elderly in nursing facilities and hospitals now often receive care from Chinese and Southeast Asian women, who, according to some employers, are ironically called "more Confucian" than today's young Japanese who shun such traditional work. Some recruiters actively seek home-care workers with Japanese ancestry in Thailand, among the children of demobilized Japanese soldiers and Thai women who can demonstrate that they are half-Japanese.[29] Another group some have called "foreign workers" is that of women brought as wives for farmers, especially in remote areas of rural Japan where Japanese women prefer not to settle. One village, Okura in Yamagata Prefecture, "arranged" marriages for ten farmers with ten Filipino women who arrived together, married, and studied Japanese to be able to communicate with their new families. They bring income to their families and all work together at a clothing factory.[30] This marriage brokering is now extending to urban men in Japan, and Japanese government officials have said this is because some Japanese men are looking for brides willing to bear more than one child.

The predominately male foreign labor force arriving in Japan since the late 1980s is far more visible than the young Asian women. Young men from Bangladesh, Pakistan, Iran, and other parts of the Middle East have made an impact on public consciousness. Photographs of swarthy men congregating in public parks on weekends accompany news stories of crimes in which foreigners are the suspects. Threatening tales of child molestation, rape, murder, and drug dealing are featured along with stories of the numbers of illegal foreign workers.

These workers are controversial whether they are legal or not. Some workers are more skilled, some unskilled. Legal workers come often as "trainees," supposedly receiving skill training and certification in a media or high-technology field, but abuse of this category of worker has been noted, as many are given no training at all and are put to work immediately at low-level jobs. Some *Nikkeijin* are in a special category because they are seen as a kind of Japanese. They can bring families to Japan for a few years and their children go to schools where, although they appear Japanese, they suffer from a lack of Japanese language and might be bullied for their differentness. These families are descendants of Japanese who emigrated to Latin America in the early twentieth century, hoping for short term employment. Many of them settled and some became middle-class residents of the large Japanese communities in or near São Paulo. Economic crises in Latin America in the mid-1980s drove many *Nikkeijin* from their Brazilian communities back to Japan, where recruiters had found jobs for them. Many came at the end of the 1980s, the height of economic expansion. Others arrived in greater numbers between 1990 and 1994, at the beginning of a recession but in time to get labor-intensive jobs in industries that have since taken a fall though the migrants (some 200,000 from Latin America as a whole in 1994) remain.[31]

Some arguments against the use of foreign workers focus on dependency issues, noting that their work in Japan does not make a contribution to their home countries, that they gain no skills, and that the work they do in Japan will become even more marginalized and undesirable than it already is—simply by virtue of the fact that it is foreign workers who do it. Some predict a new ethnically stratified workforce, native on top, legal foreign workers in the middle, and illegal foreigners on the bottom, with no mobility from these levels possible. The lowest group may become a "welfare class," they argue, and later high costs for maintenance of dependents and the unemployed will offset immediate gains from cheap labor. These arguments often cite the sad example of women who are not reproducing to provide Japanese workers for the jobs foreigners now take.

WHY BLAME FAMILIES?

As we have seen, to media commentators and politicians the future looks very bleak. While some overpopulated countries may envy Japan its birthrate, to these critics a falling birthrate means shocks to all the systems; negative spins on the birthrate blame it for the rising rate of the elderly, the diversification and shrinkage of the labor force and tax base, and the increase in foreign workers. But, we may ask, are the "throwing-away-Granny society" and the "foreign invasion" linked so closely in fact to the falling birthrate, and is it in fact the choices of women for longer education and work life that have driven it down?

A walk at rush hour, in any Japanese city, would lead a visitor to the conclusion that if Japan has a population problem, it is too *many* people and the apocalyptic doomsayers' forecast (one of several different ones) that from the current 127 million people in 2000, there will be a drop to only 50 million Japanese in the year 2500 and that there will be two people left in the year 3000[32]—if current zero-growth birthrates are maintained—seems patently absurd. Tokyo alone has shown a growth of one million people in each postwar decade, and finding a strap to hang onto in the subway is difficult at any hour of the day.

The stories are important as they cast light on problems identified as key to Japan's future. How they are related—in two senses of related, as

connected and as told or represented—is of some interest. Of particular
relevance is the story making about families and the meanings—as problem and program—given to the baby bust by commentators, policymakers, and others involved with both the realities and the projections.

These topics are as much part of daily consciousness as the midcen-
tury mantra incessantly repeated to visitors in Japan—"We Japanese live
in a narrow island country with few or no natural resources." Taxi drivers, sushi makers, and the man on the street can recite the latest birthrate
figures, cluck their tongues about women, expound on the problem of
the foreign worker and the labor force, and worry about the future of
Japan. The three sources of stability so often cited in descriptions of postwar Japan—close-knit family ties with a sense of reciprocal obligations
between generations, the synchrony of women's life roles with children's
educational and occupational priorities of the family; and a 100 percent
employed, homogeneous adult workforce—are now less predictable. And
who else but families are at fault?

The birthrate presents a vexing problem because an anticipated labor
force shortfall exacerbates the need for provisions to care for the elderly.
As we will see in chapter 5, the problem has shaped an inclusive incan-
tation "explaining" the data. Fears that grandmothers will be abandoned
relate to the fears that governmental agencies will have to rescue them
and can no longer rely on families. Further, fewer workers earning means
there will be little in the social security coffers to support the institutions
needed if the public sector picks up the slack. The short term looks bleak,
whether the rate of persons over sixty-five in the population is to reach
one in four, as some say, or one in five. Women and children, it is said,
need a crash course in filial piety.

While future labor force shortages are predicted even under the diminished expectations of restructuring, unemployment is rising, especially among women, who have experienced a 2.5 percent drop in employment in the last decade and a notable shift to more temporary from
long-term employment. This rise in female unemployment may in part
reflect the fact that larger numbers of women now report themselves
out of work, whereas recently, even in the 1980s, women without work
might have simply retired to marry or gone back to available domestic
roles in their families.

The numbers of young male recruits for large-scale company and factory employment have declined and the shift to temporary, freelance positions seems to suggest that men are dissatisfied with the constraints of
the permanent employment system and have opted instead for special-

ist job definitions allowing them mobility. Companies woo them but often cannot keep them. In 1968, 4.5 percent wanted to change jobs, in 1982, 8.6 percent, and in the 1990s, the rate was up to 14.0 percent.

Even in hard times, employers want both full-time commitment from workers and the flexibility a part-time and temporary labor force can provide. And so they try to tempt retired workers back into the labor force. Flex time, rest breaks, and child-care provision on site are sometimes offered, even when the large benefits packages and luxurious perks that used to be offered to new male recruits have had to be curtailed. Only about a fourth of the workforce is in the sector called "lifetime employment" offering secure permanent work with extra benefits. The greatest shift is to the service sector, with few benefits and no long-term commitment on the part of management or worker. What Matsushita Kōnnosuke and other corporate leaders valued as the *marugakae,* or "total embrace," employment experience is now in a decline, along with the lifetime employment model.

As these topics have clustered in public and policy formulations, the emphasis is on women within their families as the source of these problems and ultimately, and only if they cooperate, as the solution. While supporting the morally and demographically challenged family, official Japan tends to target women for not having more children, putting both the labor force and the elderly at risk. The choice to rear fewer children is characterized as a "woman's," rather than as a couple's. Their offspring are seen as antisocial, selfish "only" children, who will in the future abdicate from responsibility for their own dependent elderly. Yet the so-called Asian family welfare model that relies on kin for caregiving appears to some as the only solution. Is this really the only way to meet the needs of families and individuals, and does this kind of response draw on real experiences and data? Others see institutional and social solutions in a frame wider than that of the family.

WOMEN'S REALITIES: WHAT CHOICES?

First, the declining birthrate is neither an isolated phenomenon nor a matter of women's "choice." Attitude polls indicate that both men and women want more children than they have; while the Ministry of Health and Welfare's goal is 2.64 per family, people on average say that they want 2.18. They cite economic factors rather than social or career impediments in their decision to have fewer children. Women say that they *need* to work—for children's educational expenses, for household ex-

penses, and to supplement a husband's low income. But because of relatively low wages for women and a tax structure discouraging them from
full-time work, their income may not do more than support the child
care needed to allow them to work—especially if they have more than
one child. Delayed marriage may relate more to a higher rate of women
continuing their education and work years rather than a "choice" to delay childbearing through fear or horror of giving birth.

And in fact, it may be "marriage avoidance" rather than a birth strike
that creates this picture. Using birthrate data for married couples rather
than data for all women between fifteen and forty-nine years of age yields
2.2 children per *family* on average, not the 1.34 children per *woman* most
commonly cited. Ministry of Health and Welfare attitude polls show that
young men want marriage; their female counterparts enjoy being single.
More women than men, by the way, say they will never marry and never
have children. The percentage of those unmarried in their twenties is now
nearing 50 percent; nearly 40 percent of women in 1990 said it was better to be married than unmarried, down from 80 percent in 1972.[33]
Among women in their early thirties, 17 percent are unmarried, and the
age of marriage continues to rise.

Because the reliance on "family" as welfare system, as backup workforce, as caregiver to the elderly, as tutor for children in the educational
system, and as support for weary corporate warriors has meant reliance
on women, it is now coming under scrutiny. Public opinion polls show
that people are concerned about decline but do not want a pronatalist
policy, or any policy at all directly guiding personal choices about marriage and childbearing. Instead, they want the government to concen-
trate on improving conditions for work, child care, and marriage. While
the Equal Employment Opportunity Law of 1986, the Labor Standards
Law of 1988, and the most recent revised "basic law" to promote gender equality all look promising on paper and make it appear that women
and men are on an equal footing, the fact is that women still care for
children and elderly. Even in the Angel Plan the responsible parent needing training in child rearing is *mother.* Japanese feminists such as Ueno
Chizuko say that equality in these conditions is not possible until domestic chores are equalized and the workplace "humanized" to allow all
workers "family time."

The not-so-subtle push to get women to reproduce seems to many
women to miss the point. In attitude polls they say that social and economic conditions favor smaller families, and that political leaders do not
pay attention to people's real lives. Women insist that in 1990 the 1.57

birth *shokku* did not shock them, and that the population problem is being miscast as theirs. They resist the label and the practice of becoming
hara no karimono or the borrowed womb, the reproductive agent for their
husband's families or for wartime mobilization, and now for society.

Japan is not unique, and some of the complexities of these issues make
Japan in the near future seem more like us than a casual onlooker would
suspect. While "diversity" in the Japanese population lacks the resonance
and manifestation it has in the United States, and while our reproductive issues tend to be about teen pregnancy and low birth weight rather
than low birthrate, there are similarities. Our debates over workforce
and immigration, our concerns over the care of the elderly, public child
care and the support of single mothers, on welfare or not, are not far
from Japanese considerations. The rhetoric is different, and the choice
of women as scapegoat for problems is different, but parallels exist in
our sense of helplessness about the future.

Japanese institutions and individuals will be forced to confront issues
concerning the elderly beyond what any "Asian" model of aging and the
family can support. They will have to come to terms with governmental
responsibility for welfare and a wider range of needs in the populations
to be served. The irony of Japan's situation, when overcrowding, hunger,
and the destruction of the environment are the result of global overpopulation has not yet made an impact on national leaders, and some
actualized globalization (rather than the superficial "internationalization"
touted as a buzzword by governmental agencies) will allow Japan survival while leading in population control, rather than being influenced
purely by domestic economic and cultural priorities. Conclusions about
this shifting field of influences can only be inconclusive. While the national Family project stalls, however, working families are getting their
jobs done. How they do this has a lot to do with the de facto social service "system" established by consumer services and industries respond-
ing to the needs of families and their members.

In chapter 7 we see how market forces stemming from these needs
have given ground-up incentive for the production of goods and services, in both grassroots entrepreneurial enterprises and huge corporate
endeavors. The private sector supports very different families than does
national rhetoric and policy. Of course, marketing a product works most
efficiently when it can construct a singular mass audience and focus sales
volume. But there is no singular "market family" in the sense that public officials posit a singular national Family. Families employ the services
they need and these proliferate and diversify to suit the many market

niches families inhabit. Child care, adult day care, meals on wheels—even surrogate families portrayed by actors—these, in addition to prepared foods at all-night convenience stores and the many small "bought favors" a traditionally service-oriented consumer society such as Japan's has always provided, all form an ad hoc support system for the diverse needs of families.

Those families who need and can afford these get by well. Those who cannot must use other means, giving up larger proportions of their own time and resources to manage, rather than buy outside services and products. Families of all kinds, whatever their resources, do not become "Family" in this process: in their self-created systems, they reveal the essential pluralism of conditions in families and the emptiness of ideological models. Families after all are not trying to be the Family: they make do and are, as the grandmother said, families still.

CHAPTER 2

Family under Construction

One Hundred Years at Home

THE VIEW FROM MIDCENTURY

> Come in, come in. My husband is not here to greet you; there's no one here; I'm sorry. Please sit down and relax. I have nothing to give you but please eat a lot. Our house is so small and dirty; you must be quite uncomfortable. Can you sit on the floor?
>
> A housewife, June 1963, Tokyo

When I first began to study Japan in the early 1960s, the postwar economy had not yet reached takeoff and the material lives of ordinary people were still modest. In 1963, my hostess invited few guests outside the family into her small and sparsely furnished home that was not yet stacked floor to ceiling with consumer goods as it would be a decade later. Except for radios and the occasional "automatic" washing machine, families had few of the modern appliances then common among American middle-class families. Their Japanese counterparts had no cars or air conditioners and few television sets. Carpeting and massive Western furnishings had not yet replaced tatami matting, movable low tables, and futons. But family life was changing inside and out because of the rise of white-collar employment, rapid urbanization, increased emphasis on schooling as the gauge of life chances, and new consumption standards for the "happy family."

Heightened consumer behavior and aspirations to own a "standard package" of goods characterize a middle-classification of modern capitalist societies.[1] Globalization—a vexed concept—is at work here. Yet consumer societies are all rather different mixtures, demonstrating highly variable blends of culture, capitalism, and personal desire.

A charming film of the 1950s, *Ohayō,* directed by Ozu Yasuhiro, describes the tensions set up in one household when the two young sons go on strike to force their parents to purchase a television set, then a rare and expensive novelty. By the 1980s, televisions, video cassette players, audio systems, and automobiles were considered normal household possessions. Goods and "modern improvements" encouraged a new view of family. Though many families, even "modern middle-class" families, continue to act as arenas of production, including women who do piecework at home to supplement their husbands' income, shopkeepers, agricultural and other crafts or trades families, others appear to be primarily designated as "consuming" households, exhibiting one aspect of Japanese "democratic" lifestyle, the freedom to choose and buy.

Over the past hundred years, state making has involved family making. Not incidental to the playing out of national agenda has been the impact of economic and technological change—state-sponsored or unintended—on the local scene. Families on the ground are subject to local economic changes; they are influenced by national economic and political agenda through policies that trickle down to the grassroots level, often at odds with social and economic realities.

In addition, nonfamily issues and ideological concerns sometimes play out in families. Postwar laws designed for "democratic and egalitarian family life" were an uneasy fit for many families operating on nineteenth-century principles. They turned the Confucian patriarch into a kind of "father knows best" figure, bumbling and beloved rather than respected and feared. The obedient Meiji model of *ryōsai kembo* (good wife/wise mother), now often independent of her mother-in-law's guidance, learned to shape a nuclear family home and lifestyle according to her own budget and choice.[2] Other family members obeyed the schedules and goals of outside institutions: her husband spent few waking hours at home; their children attended to the demands of school, guided by its agenda, which parents had to acknowledge as more compelling than those of the home. Urban families whose livelihood depended on the wages of a *sarariman*— a white-collar salaryman—rather than on a family trade could dispense with their children's labor as schooling became the source of future status and security, not an inherited family role and occupation.

These changes affected all families, but to different degrees and with different meanings, depending on their class, occupation, and location:

there was no uniform middle-class urban family style as a model until the economic boom years of the 1960s and 1970s, allowing consumers the luxury of a standard package of goods, and marketers the ability to create and sell one. The term *lifestyle* came into play (borrowing the English word) to refer to a design of life and indeed was evident more in household furnishings than in the activities of members of a family. One's lifestyle, of course, was limited to what one could afford; a marketed lifestyle could take the place of older conventions and parameters of social class membership.

Whereas Meiji-era laws abolished some fixed class designations and status hierarchies of the feudal era, occupation and class still determined both life and family style until well after World War II. Industrial workers, shopkeepers, families in craft production or farming were far less influenced by either the new education system with its school-to-work success correlation or the blandishments of the growing consumer economy. Since they did not need to invest in schooling to assure their futures, and since more children, rather than fewer, was a good economic choice, they had larger households than the emerging middle class. Their cultures of family derived from older models and local understandings that had long guided and codified relationships in their region, class, or family. These structures and relationships were more likely to be organized around a specific mode of production, trade, or other enterprise than around either explicitly Confucian or Western paradigms.[3]

Traditional occupations, such as craft production and agriculture, also did not produce a singular "traditional family." As family historians have pointed out, the period of time in a family's life cycle during which it demonstrated the full extended family, ancestor–trust manager–descendant pattern was limited.[4] The life cycles of most families included long periods in which only two people lived together, and especially poor families would periodically shrink as members, or nuclear units, would migrate where employment was available. The stem family (*chokkei kazoku*), the family type seen as most stable and ideologically preferred, was more an intention than a permanent fixture, however functional its shape may have been for perpetuating the lineal inheritance of land and occupation.[5] At most, it occurred only as the stage in the life cycle of a family when the eldest son, his wife, and children lived with his parents on the ancestral property (virilocality), his younger siblings having left to establish or be incorporated into other households. And it had been truly functional only during the Meiji period's rapid industrialization and urbanization, not among premodern agrarian families who needed as many sons at home as they could get.[6] In fact, universal virilocality is also a relatively recent phenomenon, only penetrating rural Japan in the Taishō period (1912–26), so references at the end of the twentieth century in social commentary to Japan's "beautiful family traditions" usually refer to practices common or ideologized only in the past one hundred years. However transient or difficult to achieve, the stem family structure became a model for the prototypical national Family.

The first family I introduce here, the Maruyamas, is a "classic" nineteenth-century Confucian household. The second, the Fujimuras, is a contemporary family the Meiji leaders would not recognize at all. They are neither representative of significant portions of the population nor emblematic of ideological constructions of family and thus both are "ordinary" rather than "typical." They demonstrate ways in which families manage or muddle through. They neither accommodate themselves to the normative families of their times nor resist the norms in a deliberate way. The Meiji business family we meet here contains real people with a variety of responses to the "right way" of running an established household, and the solutions put together by the young twenty-first-century couple are ways they devise to maintain family.

MAKING FAMILY FOR THE MEIJI STATE

The Confucian family outlined in the Meiji Civil Code was patriarchal, hierarchical, and absolutist in its control over individuals, more "normative" than "normal." The ideal was very difficult to achieve, a rare luxury; most households could not afford the public performance of status that this model demanded. Large households were able to command more labor power but in urban areas their productivity rarely balanced their expenses. Even among those households, like the Maruyamas, who resembled aspects of the ideal, there was far more diversity than conformity by region, social class, and local or even familial preference.

The Meiji Code of 1898 helped create the illusion of conformity to a new national standard. This samurai-imaged family might now appear traditional to many Japanese but at the time it challenged ordinary peoples' realities and perceptions. It was modern because it was national. Before the arrival of American "black ships" in 1853, bringing the threat of Western economic and cultural colonization, there had been no need for a codified model. But exposure to influences from overseas provoked leaders in Japan to create a modern nation state with all its trappings. This meant a range of novelties from a flag and anthem and new notions of citizenship to a railroad, a national education system, and a proper family. A proper and *modern* family would provide continuity and stability and would not offer any toehold for social upheaval: this Confucian family would keep its members in check and in service to nation building.

The question of that proper family's configuration drew the attention of officials. Teams of officials sent by Meiji leaders around the country to conduct research and guide land reform found what seemed to them extraordinary, indeed shocking, diversity of practice and convention in family matters. They uncovered cases of unmarried women and men living together, casual alliances producing children raised in either the mother's or the father's home, divorce at will (usually the woman's) and at high rates.[7] They also observed seemingly random unofficial adoption and succession. Worse yet, they found local customs of matrilineality and matrifocality—in which inheritance lines and residence were based on the principle of female, not male, descent. Family shape and behavior were governed by local custom and the exigencies of land use and production.

Bureaucratic centralization and greater communication with the hinterlands still had not brought the values and customs of the powerful center to the attention of the more remote regions. Local customs in fact were hostile to the coherence of culture and society that leaders wanted to present to the outside world. Meiji officials had to construct a shared "Japanese culture," complete with history and tradition. The idea of "tradition" itself came into existence as a neologism, *dentō,* when Meiji scholars began translating foreign writings and retrofitting Japanese social culture to the imagined past.[8]

Foreign influences were used selectively. The Iwakura mission of 1871 and other official fact-finding missions of officials from Japan to Europe and America brought back models of education, civil law, and bureaucratic institutions, and Western missionaries added a middle-class "Christian" layer to these imports. The "Victorian" family structure encountered by traveling officials seemed to fit their notions of a "proper" family and indeed buttressed their desire for the "renewal" of a modern, patriarchal establishment. Paralleling the official recognition of Family was the restoration of the authority of the emperor.

A traditionalized model of family and society appeared in the 1898 Civil Code. The normative extended family household in trusteeship for the lineage was in part an anachronism, a throwback to Confucian models imported from China and Korea to Japan many centuries before. The *ie* was also an elite model, one only the aristocracy and samurai families had been able to maintain and thus, for many ordinary Japanese people, as exotic as a Western Victorian household. It incidentally showed up class distinctions between those who could afford to approximate it and those who could not.

In fact, it recorded the ideology of family in which the elite officials themselves had been raised—glossed with Victorian domesticity, and with assumptions about the relationship between family and state. The novel assumption was that the family was to be the core of the new "family state," the model for relationships of all kinds in a hierarchy based on the emperor as father of the nation. This state, relying on extrapolated Japanese family values, would be strong enough to confront Western cultural and political incursions, even as it assimilated Western structures and ideas. Its values were rational, bureaucratic, and therefore "modern"; they were clothed in the vague assumptions of an eternal and unique Japanese heritage and experience and were therefore unassailably "traditional." The code ordered relationships within the family just as the new system of family registration (*kōsekihō*) fixed households on a local and national map.[9] A census by local bureaucracies set legal affiliations for all households and required the participation of a household head as representative of the family to the state and of the state to the family. Women and children were registered as members of the male lineage households. Aberrations such as divorce became an enormous bureaucratic and legal *bother,* even though in much of Japan there had been few moral or ideological injunctions against it.

The age- and gender-ordered hierarchical establishment of the *ie* took on a moralized emotional tone in the modern middle-class family, one that turned the *ie* into a *katei,* an intimate domestic unit, as opposed to the official nature of the *ie.* You would not call an *ie* "cozy," whereas the notion of home as source of comfort and solace is indicated in the word *katei,* combining a private domestic space with a moral ideology of home.[10] The notion of a domestic—even "sacred"—haven (popularized in Western media of the time and extolled by Christian missionaries in Japan) permeated the relationship of husband and wife. As families felt the growing effects of work and school and urban bureaucratic institutions, as well as urban crowding, home became a safe refuge from the world. Women's magazines in Japan instructed their readers in the organization of family time and space so that observance of patriarchy was part of a moral act engaged in by household members.[11] A new focus on the mother-child relationship, fueled by sentiment, somewhat miti-

gated male dominance. The parent-child relationship continued to provide the main axis of family, enhanced by new ideas of love reckoned in
blood ties.[12]

The elements of this modernity—exhortations of Victorian domestic
privacy, modern production goals, and Japanese morality—seemed at
odds. The end of the rigid feudal social order promised more mobility
in the next century, and industrialization and urbanization offered new
options to younger sons in particular, yet urban branch families were
less stable and often less strongly affiliated to the main household, mutual support and loyalty less reliable. Landowners could rarely manage
the transition to urban middle class in one or even two generations. Even
so, modern didn't have to mean urban. In the Meiji era, 80 percent of
the population still lived in rural areas, though the means for making an
ie into a *katei* were more available in cities.

The new national homemaking was part of an attempt to codify an
official, stable, and predictable social structure. The forces of modernization also gave families the means for material change, making them
both more various in their options and more "uniform" as they sub-
scribed to the tastes created by the growing middle class. Many not born
to elite status could attempt, as their income allowed, to emulate at least
the material and social cultures of large households or develop new urban family cultures.[13]

The luxury of a "corporate" household simulating elite manners and
possessions was available to such establishments as that of the merchant
family of Osaka, the Maruyamas.[14] Several generations of rising prosperity enabled the Maruyamas, a mercantile family of the end of the nineteenth century, to embody both elite traditions and new family values.
By 1898, the year of the civil code's passage and the third generation after the family's occupation had shifted from that of feudal servants to
urban trade, the Maruyamas demonstrated how existing social and economic tendencies prepared the ground for significant changes the code
would imply for the next generation.

Their household worth had grown steadily in the thirty years of development since the Meiji restoration. The Maruyamas' prosperity now
allowed them to take on some of the mores of the upper classes, though
merchants would scarcely mingle socially with those above them. Under
the Tokugawa class system, the merchant class had inhabited a niche below peasants and artisans and well below the aristocracy and samurai
at the top of the class hierarchy.[15] By the time the Tokugawa shogunate
collapsed, however, many merchants had become wealthy and urbane,

even cultured beyond the level of many samurai, the poorer of whom could barely afford the two swords they were entitled to wear, let alone purchase elite education for their sons or keep their objects of virtu that were now falling into the hands of merchant-connoisseurs. Osaka was the archetypal "merchant city," where the culture of shopkeepers had evolved into a coherent set of values based on mercantile success rather than Confucian ideology: the greeting on the streets of Osaka, *Mokkari makka*—"How's your bottom line?"—is part of urban lore.[16]

In the process of "samuraization," wealthier merchant or peasant families followed a higher social order's practices as they could afford them.[17] Thus such families kept their young daughters at home and sponsored expensive banquets and funerals, although the Tokugawa sumptuary laws forbade the display of material accumulation by merchants (leading some rich families in this class to line their plain cotton jackets with silk). More significant than the display of wealth for the Maruyamas in particular was the household and family style they were beginning to create for themselves.

THE MODERN CONFUCIAN FAMILY

The Maruyamas' family occupation was retail sales and their income came from what would later be a large department store chain but started as a small drygoods shop catering to an increasingly affluent population of townspeople and samurai families. They were merchants and thus engaged neither in agricultural production, as peasants did, nor in cultural production or spiritual culture, as aristocrats, priests, or samurai did.

Merchants were middlemen, and in the past their identification with commerce and money meant lower status than did the honor of leadership or the honesty of production. Fukuzawa Yukichi, the nineteenth-century social philosopher and founder of Keio University, experienced the bias against mercantilism when he was a child. As the son of a samurai family, he was chastised by his outraged father, who caught him studying mathematics with the sons of local commoners: "Numbers are the tools of merchants!" his father apparently exclaimed.[18] The curriculum of the samurai child was Confucian social ethics, instruction in the demands and responsibilities of leadership, and the way of the sword, a course of study that, however less useful than numbers, was especially encouraged when the values of the old society were so palpably at risk.

Maruyama Ichihirō was the eldest son of a family thus ambiguously located in the social hierarchy of the late nineteenth century. Born in 1856 to a family of small shopkeepers, he had no more education than it took to read and write and manage the financial side of his parents' small shop. This shop, however, selling cloth and sundries, had the benefit of its strategic location as it was near a neighborhood of upper-class homes and later—though this would be after Ichihirō had grown—near a significant train station debouching hundreds of customers daily.

By the time Ichihirō was twenty, he was married and his wife, then sixteen, was brought to live in his family as the *oyome-san* (the new daughter-in-law) with his parents, unmarried brothers and sisters, and their paternal groups. He was the eldest son of an eldest son and was thus in line to inherit not only the family business but also the responsibility for its maintenance and the prosperity and harmony of the household.

Ichihirō had been prepared for this, of course: his position as eldest son gave him pride of place with his siblings while his studies focused him only on what would be useful to his future role. Study for its own sake was not encouraged in a shopkeeper's merchant family, and the period of indulgence in his childhood was limited. His father's reprimand to the five-year-old for taking a ripe persimmon from the kitchen was a new and unpleasant experience: his mother and grandmother had always given him everything he wanted. His father took this occasion to note that from this time forward, discipline and responsibility must govern his actions; from that moment Ichihirō's mother had much less to do with his training than did his father, a shift that was difficult for the young boy.

His grandparents seemed more relaxed, less frightening than his father, and more apt to sneak him treats. They were not educated people and could neither read nor write. His grandfather had been a hereditary servant for an aristocratic household and his grandmother, a country girl from a tenant-farmer family living on lands owned by the same household. At the dissolution of the house where the grandfather had been employed, they had moved to the city and, with the help of family members, set up shop on their own and began to raise a family in the rooms behind the shop. Their eldest son, Ichihirō's father, expanded the business, building more rooms for stock and living space, and adding a tile roof.

When his father died in 1879, Maruyama Ichihirō became head of the household himself. All his younger brothers but one were married and had left to seek work and form their own households; they were rarely at their natal home except for critical events or major holidays such as New Year's celebrations. His grandfather had died, leaving his grandmother managing domestic affairs for some time until she passed the ceremonial *shamoji,* or rice paddle, to her daughter-in-law, Ichihirō's mother, as symbol of the transfer of power between the household's generations of women. Just as there was only one male of a generation in line to assume leadership, so was there only one female line for domestic management. Shortly thereafter, his own father died of influenza, leaving him a young man with a young wife and infant daughter, in charge of an increasingly prosperous household.

He was at the time twenty-three, young to be head of a household, but then any eldest son had to expect to take on this responsibility at almost any age. His wife, Chieko, was only nineteen and already a mother—though of a girl, whose birth did not fully legitimate her in the eyes of her mother-in-law and the world. A boy was required as evidence of her suitability as the wife of an eldest son; she had to produce a descendant. While in theory her position should have become that of head woman in the family with the death of her father-in-law, in fact her mother-in-law clung tenaciously to that role, citing the youth of her daughter-in-law, the lack of a son and heir, and her own skills as manager in maintaining the household. She herself was considered on the edge of retirement, being forty-five years old.

What needed managing was increasingly complex. The family itself was more than the collection of people inhabiting the house. It included the store, which took the first floor and an annex of their house. It was also the apprentices, the servants, the ties with the branch families, and community relations with local officials, customers, and suppliers. It was "face," that important commodity encompassing status, behavior, reciprocal relationships with other families, and "knowing one's place."

By the time we meet the Maruyamas in 1898, well after the transfer of power to Ichihirō, the placement of individuals in families was more clear-cut than the social order beyond its walls. As we have seen, the fixed class system had been officially abolished and geographic and class mobility were now possible. In addition, the new universal school system created compulsory primary schooling for all children—at least for all boys—and offered some possibility of social mobility through the development of personal skills. Industrialization had changed the nature of work for many, and a rapidly urbanizing population created new demands, new social services, and an extension of responsibility for people's welfare beyond the family's domain and capacity to provide. This transition from familial to institutional frames of support proved to be a continuing source of conflict in values and issues of distribution, and an uneasy accommodation between sources of identity and author-

ity for individuals. The demands of work outside the home kept employees "hostage" and homemakers more "enclosed" in domestic functions, and children under the schedule of school.

Support for institutional social services relied on governmental funds
and on the new flows of resources between individuals, families, enterprises, and government. Even before there was a fully developed consumer society, generations differed markedly in their expectations for
goods and services and in the acquisition of status through material possessions.[19] Those with the wherewithal acquired both skill in the no-
longer-exclusive arts of court and social capital through educating their
sons in the means of modernization.

The prospering Maruyamas in 1898 included Ichihirō, age forty-two,
the head of the household; Chieko, age thirty-eight; a daughter, age nineteen (married and living in Kobe with her husband's family, now *her* family); sons, ages seventeen, fourteen, and eight and a daughter, age seven.
Grandmother, as she was referred to by all members of the household,
was now sixty-four, retired at least officially from her role as household
manager. Her daughter-in-law had finally, after many years, become *okusan*, the mistress of the house, rather than *oyome-san*. Grandmother was
still, however, the reference point for domestic rituals and arrangements,
as in the management of her granddaughter's dowry and the observance
of domestic rituals. She oversaw the placement of rice and incense on the
family Buddhist altar. She held pride of family uppermost in her considerations, and it was she who invoked the honor of the household, the
"face" of the establishment, when issues of community relationships and
the behavior of the children arose. In this she acted as reference point to
the past and resistance to change. Chieko managed the servants and
planned the meals also overseen by Grandmother.

There were others too. There was Ichihirō's younger brother, still unmarried and unlikely to establish an independent household as he had a
gimpy leg from birth and a "weak" mind as well. He was childlike in
some ways and was given only simple chores in the family business. Also
the three hereditary servants, some of whom had "come with the house":
their families had served and lived with the Maruyamas for two generations, from the time the Maruyamas' shop had begun to prosper, and
were far more permanent than today's "permanent employment" salaryman. Indeed they were seen as belonging with the family as an ongoing
household corporation, not as servants to the business or temporary in-
cumbents. The two women servants were mother and daughter, the young
male servant an apprentice in the store who also ran errands and was

general factotum to the family. The line between family chores and work for the business was a fuzzy one. As a late-twentieth-century-family shop head has said, "if it's called 'family' we can work late without paying people extra and we can take a day off when we please." Getting apprentices to perform domestic chores such as shopping or cleaning was also completely appropriate.

There were also staff who worked exclusively in the store, young people for the most part from merchant families. They were apprenticed to the Maruyama store as training for their future responsibilities in their own families' businesses. This was a common practice: training in another family's establishment was seen as a place to acquire more discipline than in the youth's own family, which might be too indulgent. The family sending an apprentice was making a significant investment to gain the future viability of the family's productivity and welfare. They would bank on the long-term benefit though they experienced the absence of the young person as a loss of valuable labor.

The children of the Maruyama household (except the married daughter in Kobe) stayed close to home. At that time the city of Osaka had attractions for the young, luring many youths into the entertainment quarters. The Maruyamas were protective of their girl, admonitory to their boys. The task of youth was seen to be serious training for the responsibilities of the future, not engagement in frivolous pleasures by right or expectation. What was Confucian "moral training" in a samurai family had practical implications in the merchant family.

The boys (Eiichirō, Nobuo, Tadashi) and the girl (Noriko) were primarily engaged in study, though Eiichirō, at seventeen, was also an apprentice to his father in managing the family business. He was not apprenticed "out" to another family but was supervised by the steward of the shop, all but a family member himself. Eiichirō gradually took on the tasks of meeting with suppliers and producers of the goods they sold and sometimes accompanied his father to meetings with local merchants. After the Meiji-period equivalent of a high school education (rather like today's middle school), Eiichirō's future was mapped in the business. His parents had thought for a time he might complete a higher-level education course as well but deflected their interest in higher learning to Nobuo, now fourteen and in high school. His high school, a new one with university-educated faculty, focused on academic pursuits (including entrance to university), rather than on commercial or trade vocations.

Tadashi was still in the neighborhood grammar school, a one-room schoolhouse that had originally been a *terakoya* (temple school) under

the Tokugawa shoguns. After 1872, all schools had been incorporated
into the new national system of education, upgraded and centralized, using texts approved by the new Ministry of Education and modern methods adapted from European schooling; teachers in the new elementary
schools were beginning to emerge from the new normal schools that
churned out "scientifically trained" teachers.

Schooling changed a great deal in Ichihirō's lifetime. In his youth—
under the Tokugawa's ranked hierarchy of schooling according to distinctions of birth, Confucian texts and primers for commoner children
gave them the basics of reading and writing—schools were where you
were meant to learn virtue and self-restraint (along with reading and writing), but also where you made friends and enjoyed whatever number of
years your parents could afford to keep you out of productive labor. His
children now were attending school by law and with new goals. As the
Imperial Rescript on Education, hanging in every classroom and recited
at least annually by every school principal, dictated: "There should be
no family with an illiterate member."[20] Schooling had become the building block of national development and the measure of a person's life
chances. The clock of the school governed the family's days. Even girls
attended school—sometimes high schools as well, and many young
women from respectable families attended normal school and themselves
became teachers. His own elder daughter had not gone further than elementary school, though they'd hired tutors in samisen (a stringed in-
strument) and calligraphy to increase her chances at a good marriage.
The younger girl, now in primary school, would finish high school if her
mother had anything to say about it, though Ichihirō felt there wasn't
much use in education for girls except to promote the education of their
own children (Noriko did, going on to a Normal School that trained future primary school teachers).

Mornings were busy times in the household. Children were packed
off to school, Chieko would send a servant to the market for the day's
fresh produce and fish. Grandmother would somewhat grumpily over-
see the chaos and, silently broadcasting resentment, retire pointedly to
pray at the family altar after laying out the day's offering to the ancestors. The apprentices would appear in the *genkan*, the front entrance hall,
and bow to their master to receive the day's directions before opening
the store to the public at around nine. The behavior of hired help toward
employers still resembled that of family retainers in the feudal period,
the kind of family retainer Ichihirō's own grandfather had been.

Ichihirō, however, espoused the new thinking. His desire was to run a modern, up-and-coming, even "Western" establishment, and the larger the business became, the more he was interested in "scientific" management, anticipating the later influence of Frederic Taylor in Japanese organizations. When his father was alive, there seemed to be so little change and the routines seemed so cast in stone. Ichihirō's ideas of progress, such as a new accounting system and written records of purchases by regular customers, had seemed to his father irrelevant at best, rebellious at worst.

At the moment we find the Maruyamas, the domestic issue is Grandmother, or Chieko, depending on your point of view. She and Chieko have never been friends, and their relationship seems to have deteriorated with the older woman's retirement from household power. Her informal attempts to control Chieko and the grandchildren had increased as her formal power ended. One day when the greengrocer's cart came by, Chieko ran out to inspect the vegetables and place an order for the day—something Grandmother had done previously. Grandmother was at her heels and loudly criticized her choices as well as the overall quality of the goods offered. Chieko felt publicly humiliated and also worried about her relationship with the vegetable seller. She did not want to bring such trivial matters to her busy husband's attention, the more because it might force him into taking sides between her and her mother, so she tried to downplay the scene in her mind.

It had been even worse another day when Grandmother was heard muttering to neighbors about the children's misbehavior, saying that they had no proper home training. What did she mean, inventing such stories and broadcasting them to the outside world and criticizing Chieko for damaging the family's "face"—particularly when she herself had taken charge of the children's training? When Chieko had first moved into the family, her father-in-law was alive and kindly disposed toward her and his influence helped mitigate any tensions she might feel. It seemed ironic that now that she was a full member of the household, she felt more put upon than when she was a struggling outsider.

She wanted her younger daughter, Noriko, to have a different life. She and her husband had agreed that the child should finish high school, and here too the mother-in-law criticized their plan, saying that education was wasted on girls and that the girl would bring shame on the family if she weren't into marriage and out of harm's way early. The elder daughter, well married to the son of a government official, had been the apple of Grandmother's eye and her marriage the result of the older woman's negotiations. When Chieko bought books for the younger one or exulted over her good work in school, Grandmother murmured dire imprecations.

In spite of this undercurrent, stability and predictability seem to characterize the Maruyama corporate household. The civil code institutionalized the very pattern they were already living: a samurai-style Confucian structure. What it added was the relationship of the family to the modern nation state: the family in service to the construction of a new national ethos, prescribing behaviors and obligations of members of the family to its head, the responsibility of family through its head to the state and other extra-familial institutions. The code flew over the heads of most rural peasants and quite a few less prosperous townsmen, who, unlike the Maruyamas, could not aspire to the new "national" family—even to a makeshift version of it.

The second family we visit, one hundred years later, also has strong ties to the state, but the influences on its self-image and behavior are more complex in origin, less driven by law but still embedded in its members' community and consciousness, and the family's resistances to the demands of society, while unobtrusive, are still clear.

THE DEVOLVED FAMILY, MARKETED FOR JAPAN

The family is the basis of human society and its traditions for good or evil permeate the nation. Hence marriage and the family are protected by law, and it is hereby ordained that they shall rest upon the undisputed legal and social equality of both sexes, upon mutual consent instead of parental coercion, and upon cooperation instead of male domination. Laws contrary to these principles shall be abolished, and replaced by others viewing choice of spouse, property rights, inheritance, choice of domicile, divorce and other matters pertaining to marriage and the family from the standpoint of individual dignity and the essential equality of the sexes.

Article 18, Section 3, Constitution of Japan, 1947

The postwar family observes no such culturally encoded hierarchies and roles as existed for the Maruyamas. By 1947, officials of the Allied Occupation (1945–52) had worked out legal terms that would let postwar families loose to attain a "democratic and egalitarian family."[21] In place of a normative model of the good family were constitutional laws promoting equality and individual rights that vied with social and market forces in a new understanding of family.

The new America-modeled constitution included laws that would influence family life strongly. "Individualism," its planners believed, was as a necessary precondition to "democracy," and new laws would promote freedom within families: they would specify equal inheritance among all children, reduce the power of the household head to control the younger generation through arranged marriage, and establish equality between men and women. In practice, however, families adapted these measures to existing understandings of the primacy of families over individuals. Especially where land was to be inherited, junior siblings often gave over their "equal" rights to inherit to the elder brother, or to one sibling, in order to avoid breaking up the already small parcels of land into pieces too small to farm efficiently. In practice, too, families retained an interest in the marriage choices of their children, though increasingly in an advisory rather than dictatorial way. (More recently, the older generation is delighted to be consulted at all.) Equality between spouses became a matter of separation of spheres of influence—a consultative rather than a role-sharing or companionate family.

Less abstract models than those contained in the new constitution were available too: as Takie Lebra has shown, the imperial family itself was reconstructed to be a modern human role model, rather than a shuttered, exalted, but vaguely outlined reference point. The representations of the imperial family evolved into a modified nuclear family in the current reign of Akihito (1989–) and his empress, Michiko.[22]

Nonaristocratic realities are less ambiguous only because they are less explicitly encoded. While the normative presence of the *seken* still operates to judge and measure individuals' and families' performances by communal standards no longer firmly attached to peoples' real lives, most middle-class urban families seem to be in a free fall, making do and understanding themselves as families in very personal, less socially prescribed ways. The Fujimuras are without question a real family and unhesitatingly put family first in their priorities.

The Fujimuras belong to the second postwar generation, several generations removed from the agrarian family of their origins, and strikingly different from the Maruyamas and other corporate households of the Meiji period. They are a household of three: Aya, Gorō, and Mitsu. Aya is thirty-five, a computer programmer who received a master's degree from an American university. Gorō is thirty-seven, a cartoonist for weekly magazines. Their son Mitsu is just turning five and is in nursery school preparing to attend kindergarten in the spring.

They live in Tokyo, near a subway station convenient for Aya's daily commute to her workplace. As a cartoonist, Gorō works mostly at home and is the parent responsible for picking up Mitsu at his nursery school to which Aya brings him in the morning on the way to her company. This arrangement is the outcome of several attempts to rationalize the fam-

ily's schedules, and it hasn't always been easy: Gorō and Aya are struggling to make their lives work in concert with Mitsu's and, in his toddler years in a day-care center, the fragile patchwork of split-second timing they had constructed pushed them nearly to desperation.

Each member of this small household has strong constraints imposed
by the demands of institutions beyond the walls of their tiny apartment.
Schooling is the priority of this family; Gorō and Aya both had elite educational experiences, and their desire for rewarding work and fiscal
stability also forces them to make accommodations to the schedule and
demands of inflexible organizations, in their case, Aya's company and
Mitsu's schooling arrangements.

Aya has worked since she graduated from college. She and Gorō waited
until she was thirty and secure in her current job to have their child who,
they say, will be their only child. She took only the minimum maternity
leave her company offered. Mitsu was still an infant when she returned
to work. She requested part-time work at first, granted as a major con-
cession on the company's part. The career trajectories of full- and part-
time workers do not converge. She managed to segue into her previous
full-time position after Mitsu entered nursery school.

Neither day care, supposedly tied to work hours, nor nursery schools
accommodate a full-time work schedule. Only after several tries did Aya
find schooling to fit their schedules—and of course Mitsu's personality
and potential. Day care for infants is scarce, and parents must research
the options thoroughly. There is little supervision from the Ministry of
Education, and day-care training and surveillance by the Ministry of
Health and Welfare provides only minimal standards. For a family like
the Fujimuras to find an environment that was convenient in terms of
time and transport, adaptable in schedule, and above all loving, stimu-
lating, and understanding, took time. Their situation was easier than that
of most young working couples, because Gorō's work gave him the freedom to do the school pickups. Other working couples rely on a grandparent to provide the backstop, which is more likely to receive community approval. Teachers and neighbors frown on paid babysitters. Teachers
might tell a parent that her child suffers from being tended by too many
unrelated adults and exhort the mother to find work that allows her to
be the primary caregiver of her child. Whatever she does, she will be
assumed to be available to the school's schedule and demands.

Gorō has never been a "company man": in a sense, his work pattern
is more typically female and his wife's more typically male. He has been

a freelancer most of his life, and his status as a cartoonist has allowed him the freedom (or isolation) of a private workplace. His name is known among readers of weekly comic magazines, though he isn't quite of "star cartoonist" status yet. He works in intense spurts, often late at night, and has more daytime hours than does Aya to play with Mitsu.

While some of the older generation might fault Aya for putting work before her tasks of raising children and maintaining the household and would cluck about Gorō's luxurious homebody life, their families support their somewhat unusual lifestyle. Aya's parents live nearby and although her mother works in an office, her father often comes by to play with Mitsu: Aya says this is good for her mother too, getting "grandpa" out of the house. Gorō's parents eagerly and uncritically take Mitsu to Tokyo Disneyland or some other attraction when Gorō and Aya are very busy. They agree that this is a family, not a collection of accidentally contiguous lives. Its configuration took energy and strategy to create, allowing both parents the work that gives them sustenance and fulfillment, allowing them also the joys of parent and couplehood.

At the time of the last interview, they were planning a family trip to Indiana, taking Mitsu along. Aya's former teacher in Bloomington has invited them, and her home will be the base for the family's driving trips through the American heartland and to Chicago. They will be gone two weeks, a long holiday for a Japanese family: most take a few days here and there, adding to weekends and taking short excursions rather than extensive trips. A salaryman working for a large company will not want to put his workmates out by longer absences or, if he is at a crucial point in his career, jeopardize his advancement by being away from the action for long. He will also not want to be seen as giving priority to family over work. A longer trip is also easier with a younger child, as an older one may be occupied with school or vacation study. However, Aya realizes that she will have to "pay" on her return with extra work, and that she'll have to accumulate many *omiyage*, souvenir gifts, for her fellow workers and superiors.

So far, then, the Fujimuras have bucked the system, but with considerable effort. They are living a life they have chosen, using available facilities and options, but with some evident strain. For example, when Mitsu was a toddler in day care, the caregiver seemed quite disapproving of Aya, saying that day care should only be used when mothers really had to work, and that it didn't exist for the use of women pursuing careers for their own satisfaction. Aya had trouble dealing with the turmoil and guilt this caused her. She was surprised to hear criticism from a woman whose own work as a day-care provider depended on women like her. And of course, she knew there was another strike against her at the day-care center: Gorō was the one who picked up Mitsu at the end of the day, the only father surrounded by critical mothers and grand-mothers. Their family honor, in its modern manifestation of community approval, was at stake in this out-of-role task he'd taken on.

They'd laughed, ruefully, at these things, joined in their determina-tion not to yield to the social influences affecting them, clear-minded about the *nyū famiri* they'd fixed on being. They had resisted the pres-sure to have more children, the pressure that included exhortations about the shrinking birthrate and dire predictions about Mitsu's psychosocial development as a lonely only child. They had maintained good work en-vironments. They had become even more bonded as a couple through their desire for something different from what their parents had had. Gorō was adamant in his determination not to let the community gossip get to him; Aya was practical and worried that the problems would increase, as Mitsu grew and her own role as mother became more intertwined in a complex fashion with the institution of school, other families, and the inevitable demands of the entrance exams, a prospect she says she dreads.

The Maruyama descendants today include units called families that are as small as Aya and Gorō's. They still have a *honke,* a main house-hold, though the store was sold after the war and the eldest son (now retired) of that generation became a businessman whose middle-class family was, like those of many corporate workers, centered not on the authority of the oldest generation but on that of the "earning" genera-tion. The household remains a nuclear family with add-ons, not a patri-archal Confucian *ie.*

Still, Aya and Gorō's family appears skeletal in contrast to the Maruyamas. Small in size, not joined in and by economic production, without a corporate ethos buttressed by tradition, the Fujimura family may appear like a fragile vessel. Yet even less traditional units count as families: couples, for example, who have decided not to have any chil-dren; single parents with one child or two; widowed fathers living with one child; gay or lesbian couples. This diversity has always been present, along with struggles to accommodate the acceptable to the exigencies of daily life in Japan, but now attention to the family has taken on a criti-cal tone of mission similar to that of the Meiji period. Constructed to treat the demographic problems facing Japan's labor force and aging pop-ulation, this view demonizes small families like the Fujimuras. It invokes pathologies such as the "only-child syndrome," mother-son incest, violence against parents in the claustrophobic middle-class pressure-cooker home, violence against peers—even murder. Children are in this reading not just victims but victims who act out under stress unmitigated by family support. Selfish working women abandon husbands, children, and dependent elderly in search of careers, and the nonprocreative wife-not-mother is an unnatural horror. The official view evokes nostalgia for a golden-age family that smoothed any rough edges or eccentricities—or had none. As in the Meiji period, diversity of families has once again become a threat to the nation. The promotion of a multigenerational, multichild family echoes the political and economic agenda of the late nineteenth century.

The families described in this chapter are bookends on the century, but they are not types. They scarcely cover the range of historical change the hundred years between them has witnessed or, in fact, the diversity of experiences and households of their own eras. The Maruyamas, being city dwellers at the end of the nineteenth century, were distinct from the 80 percent of the population who belonged to rural agrarian families, and, being prosperous, did not represent most urban Japanese of the time. They did not have elite social status but were relatively wealthy and privileged beyond the means of many. The Fujimuras, a century later, are part of the more than 80 percent who are urban, most of whom have more than one wage earner in the home. Their education and employment put them in the upper middle class, yet they are unusual even among dual-income households. Confounding postwar normative expectations for role performance and economic participation, Aya is the full-time salaried worker, Gorō works at home.

Within the hundred years that separate the two families—without revolution or even small acts of rebellion—families have done more than react to economic and technological change in the postwar years. Patterns of proactive change have emerged but they are not as easy to depict as are the norms, role prescriptions, and expectations that are, by their very nature, "characterizations."

The Maruyamas and the Fujimuras demonstrate some of the forces affecting family life in its varying relationships with social institutions and policies. In both periods the effects are visible, more strikingly in the postwar period when work, schooling, and the law shape family life. At the same time that these forces homogenize family experience, other forces such as consumer industries, foreign and global influences, and a range of new personal choices diversify that experience.

Social programs to support equality at the workplace, child care, and the care of elderly are in place. However, they are scarcely able to manage the gap between needs and services: a lack of community challenges each family to manage its own needs for space and time and resources. Grandparents needing care must be housed in or near the household and teenagers may want separate spaces of their own. From within the thin walls of the home, the call for help in fulfilling the functions assigned to families has become clamorous.

CHAPTER 3

Families in Postwar Japan

Democracy and Reconstruction

Kanda Michiko lives with her husband and two daughters in rural Gumma Prefecture. Her husband's family left them their land and an old farmhouse that her husband, Masa, a contractor and carpenter, has been renovating. Most people, he says, would have torn it down and built a completely new house, but he loves working around the old structure, admiring the craftsmanship and adding, supporting, and replacing. He has expanded the ground floor, added an extra bathroom, and above all, to the visitor's eye, reveled in craftsmanlike decoration. He is an expert in filigreed wooden screenwork and he has created detailed openwork carving above doorways, in windows, and in waist-high partitions between rooms.

They have no sons, but their elder daughter, at twenty-seven, is marrying a local man who will come to live with them as their adopted son-in-law. Michiko is very pleased that the young man has agreed to be the heir and successor. He is in training to Masa in his contracting business but, as Michiko says, the younger man doesn't have the obsessive passion for carpentry her husband has.

The Kandas explain that they care more for the happiness of their children than for the family's continuation. In a traditional family with no son, the eldest daughter would be required to marry a man who would take her family's name and act as its eldest son, an old custom meant to ensure the patriline. The Kandas combine traditionalism with an easy and relaxed, even democratic, style in their family relations. They never expected their daughter to bring a husband home. The parents support and approve their daughters' extended education and work (both have office jobs), and Michiko herself is far from a traditional rural wife. She serves visitors elegant French sweets with tea, dresses in a trendy Italian mode, and drives careening her van down the dirt roads. Her husband's passion is renovations that put past craftsmanship to modern uses. Characterizing this family as "rural," as a traditional patriarchal *ie,* or as a postwar middle-class family does not help us understand their essence. The Kandas, like most families of any era in Japan, confound descriptive categories.

Hence we survey the past half century to trace the ways that history, economics, and postwar social and political changes have amplified plurality even as leaders and institutions increasingly attempt to buttress the facade of a mono-culturally normative family. In the postwar decades from 1947 to the present, a "democratic" but strongly gender-role-determined unit has taken the patriarchal household's place. This family is designed to be capable of expanding engagement with a consumer economy even as it protects the future of its dependent elderly or its children, perpetuating older concepts of effort and "family values." What has commonly been taken as "the postwar family" now shows up clearly as a series of historically situated "family events," spanning several eras in the last half century.

As time passes, the unit of a postwar "generation" is only somewhat more useful than "decade" in the analysis of social trends. The consumer industries use these categories in mapping, and thus to some degree, creating the markets for their products and images (as we will observe in chapter 7). Families contain by their very nature at least two interdependent generations during some point in their life cycle. But in another sense, a generation means a cohort with distinct historical experiences. Prewar, wartime, and postwar cohorts are particularly characterized by their historical references to war, and the subsequent generations are said to lack a toughening experience, to have become "flabby" without a challenge. Can a family, however, be so summarily described by a decade or era? Is not each era, even one marked by an all-absorbing event such as war, experienced differently along lines of social and economic diversity? Though contested, the idea of "the postwar" is a common trope for policymakers who hope by invoking an era to mobilize private families into service to something larger than the household.

Such tags as policymakers and consumer experts may give to population segments do not survive tests of relevance at ground level. Ochiai

Emiko denies the existence of a postwar family, particularly noting that "democratization" is an inappropriate characterization of family patterns that show more continuity than ideological or structural change.[1] Even powerful images of consumer marketing may give a false sense of homogeneity in the audience they seem to epitomize. People who purchase goods may not, after all, be purchasing a lifestyle.

Each decade's "generation" roughs out the portrait of the postwar period and helps fine-tune the historical variety of family life. The families of the 1950s and 1960s were both the first "consumer" families and the recipients of Occupation-driven ideas of equality and individualism. Images of the 1970s included ideas about alternative cultural styles and family diversification and popular recognition (if not acceptance) of *uman ribū* (women's liberation). In fact, families experienced the further differentiation of women, men, and children as separate units within the no-longer-corporate household. The affluence of the 1980s did not "trickle down" to homogenize consumption. Not everyone could keep up with the ads in women's magazines, the trends for furnishings and leisure. The exhortations to consume homogeneously only revealed basic differences in families' capacities to fulfill consumption goals. Another feature of the postwar Japanese family is said to be its commitment to children's success in the educational system. Disillusion with the failure of this "meritocracy" to provide equal opportunity according to "merit" is another dimension of difference over the past half century. Effort and merit are not enough; funding children's climb up the ladder through expensive extras such as home tutors and after-school cram classes (*juku*) became equally important.[2]

Wealth—either personal or national—may have helped a child succeed in high-status occupations but did not produce comfort or satisfactions in the 1980s, when "affluent poverty" characterized many middle-class lives.[3] Even among those families with resources and property there were very low "satisfaction" rates in Japan compared to American rates for wages, jobs, housing, and life in general.[4] One woman said that by combining her and her husband's savings they had managed to buy their condo in Tokyo, a country home in the mountains, and a property in California, all of which were filled with new furnishings, but they very rarely visited their two leisure homes and rarely even ate together in Tokyo. People with much lower incomes complained of similarly stressful discontinuities between what they could manage to own and what they could enjoy.

Media and marketing set and amplified consumer norms, what one should be and should buy, constructing "diversity" in a semblance of choice among consumer goods and lifestyles. Consumers were typed by age and gender as well, so any family could be targeted both as a consumption unit as a whole and by its individual members' tastes and desires. In order to maintain a high level of intensity of consumption, new products had to replace ones that had saturated the audience, and the audience itself had to be disaggregated, yielding microsegments, diverse consumer "cultures."[5] A young person's choice of clothing then became a choice among a range of "styles"—am I Shibuya? Am I hip-hop?—rather than a choice between particular items. By the 1990s, marketers were scrambling to catch up with consumer realities, which had outstripped the diversity constructed by the consumer industries, as households had themselves found new ways of being diverse and centrifugal and, increasingly, frugal.

THE AFTERMATH OF WAR

The end of World War II has been called Japan's second opening to the West. It was a time of many openings, to domestic as well as foreign sources of change and plurality. The late-nineteenth-century "opening" of Japan was organized by central social agencies aimed at defending against political or cultural colonization. During postwar reconstruction the changes were influenced more by economic than by political and social modes of organization, even as legal codes and the social order they represented were created under the direction of alien conquerors.[6]

The Allied Occupation (1945–1952) promoted a most unfamiliar family as one able to resist the Confucian antecedents of patriarchy and militaristic national ideologies as well as the threat of communism from the Asian mainland. No longer a self-sufficient unit, the new middle-class family had many tasks and functions beyond its walls and was dependent for its status on employment and education. Children were in service to the demands of schooling; adult workers worked long hours and committed themselves to the task of economic reconstruction. During the war the family was to produce soldiers; family now was to produce democratic citizens for peace and prosperity.

Families had taken the brunt of wartime devastation. Many urban households had broken up not only because their men had died or been lost in the war but because near-starvation and the loss of lives and homes in the firebombings had forced people to scatter to relatives in the countryside. Many children had been sent to the countryside during the war to protect them from the devastation of the cities, just as were their British wartime counterparts.[7] Survivors' stories of wartime scrabbling for a few grains of rice in the bottom of sacks and barrels, learning from country cousins which wild plants were edible, going without shoes or heat in classrooms, forgoing lessons for "conscripted" war-related work in elementary school buildings, filtered down to their children and grandchildren as tales of the horror of war.[8]

The Occupation at least officially created new priorities for families, loosening the hold older generations had on the younger, and buttressing new images of family relationships with laws replacing those of the Civil Code of 1898.[9] The power of grandfather's authority was reduced to his war stories. He and grandmother became babysitters. Daughters-in-law were released to work outside the home, though their wages were brought home to the household and did not represent economic independence. There was a readiness for change among the war-devastated population, and the fact that Japanese families and society had never fully engaged the models of uniform patriarchy and Confucian norms the official version had touted as necessary for the war effort fit the conquerors' priorities as they rearranged Japanese society.

The attempts at wholesale change during the seven years of the Occupation—in an unprecedented moral, political, and social overhaul of a whole nation—represented a zealous new kind of social engineering. The Allied reformers hoped to create a democratic, peaceful society out of a country that in war they had characterized as its opposite: fascistic, authoritarian, and demonically destructive. Education was to be the device for creating a new democracy in Asia, families were to be the bedrock of egalitarianism. As in the Meiji era, families were impressed with the duty to replicate the goals of the new state: husbands and wives would be equal partners, children would be nurtured without the constraints of hierarchy, and grandparents would be cared for out of love, not Confucian filial requirements. American officers used the American Constitution as a model but some went further to incorporate explicit rights and freedoms, especially for women, that had never been considered by America's founding fathers.[10]

The first postwar model of the family was intended both to stabilize and to shake up conventional experience of the time. As Samuel Coleman has shown, the standardization of life was an aspect of postwar society: the timing of family events, such as births of children (closely spaced, limited in numbers), the split between male and female chores with clear demarcations of tasks, the allocation of identity along with one's work, were all new phenomena in Japanese life.[11] This family was vaguely American-style, a "new middle-class" image of a household with a father working outside the home, a stay-at-home mother, two or three children, and perhaps a grandparent—but well in the background, more like a family pet than a revered or feared ancestor. The model was supposed to be "democratic," though the Japanese version did not include equality in the sense of full role interchangeability between men and women. Families were to take part in community life as an aspect of democratic "civic responsibility" as individuals, rather than as households represented by the eldest male. Membership in parent-teacher associations (PTAs, a very American concept) was required, women were given the vote, and women's organizations recruited housewives to engage them in consumer activism and other "womanly" sorts of involvement in the wider arena.[12]

DISMANTLING THE *IE*

In the documentary film *Farm Song* (John Nathan, producer and director), the story of a four-generation rice-growing family in northern Japan in 1978, the grandfather pointedly says, "No one can live here who wasn't born here."[13] He refers only to males; women live in the house but they don't "count." They marry in but were born elsewhere, and daughters "marry out." He expresses a prewar understanding of the patriarchal, patrilineal *ie* in which women functioned to work for the male lineage and provide heirs for it. This bedrock concept of family in the Meiji Civil Code had ordered people's lives—for the Meiji-era Maruyamas and the "home front" family promoted in wartime—and made predictable their duties and obligations. It did not look in the least "democratic" to the Allied authorities.

The patriarchal household, and the *ie* system itself, was to be unmanned by destroying primogeniture, by which the eldest, or a single, son inherited the house, land, and responsibility for the older generation. In the new postwar constitution, modeled on the American one, inheritance was to be equal among all children, including daughters. This division of property was supposed to loosen parents' hold over the young and permit financial independence. But the already small lots of land, though legally partible, were not so in practice. One child continued to inherit, parceling out compensation of some kind to the others.

The key to the *ie* system was the *kōseki*, or family registration. During the Meiji era more and more information, binding and codifying the *ie,* was included in each family *kōseki,* usually kept at a ward office or town hall. From its creation in 1871, the registry included all citizens, registered by family, for census, tax, and military conscription purposes. By the late 1880s, a family was recorded as a permanent residence, a genealogy, and a rendering of the line of inheritance through in- and outmarrying young. The Occupation policymakers recognized the *kōseki* as the key administrative nexus between family and state and replaced it with the registration of individuals, not families, permitting the registration of new nuclear households. Now anyone could establish a new *kōseki,* which would verify his or her status. Away from the main house, nuclear families could act as freestanding units without fiscal or social responsibilities to the *honke* or, even more significantly, establish autonomous legal households on their own. In practice, census takers and the local ward offices still recognized only one person as household head, and where they recorded a married couple, the household head tended to be the husband.

In addition to the change in inheritance patterns, aiming at equalizing the relationships between siblings, the Occupation hoped to provide women with rights that would establish their equality with men. Beate Sirota Gordon, a young woman of twenty-two enlisted to help draft the 1947 constitution for Japan, contributed a section on women's rights that in many ways provided more constitutional support for women than American women enjoyed—at least on paper. It was Gordon who wrote sections against primogeniture, against prejudice against illegitimate children, and in support of equal opportunity for all children in education, as legal elements in the support of women. She and other Occupation workers organizing Japanese women to support their political and legal rights found that these did not necessarily change the social and cultural frames of their lives, but it was a start. The Shufu Rengōkai (Shufuren, or Japan housewives' association), created in 1948, was at first militant. Its campaigns against price fixing and against unsafe products, and its involvement in savings promotions, gave rise to slogans like Workers in the Kitchen or the Voice of the Kitchen.[14]

Deeper changes came with greater prosperity, but the immediate postwar struggle for survival also created opportunity, releasing people and families into a de facto diversity of practices. These new accommodations to necessity—single-parent households, working grandmothers supporting disabled husbands, women and men cohabiting without marriage to pool resources and real estate—were unaccredited by law or culture. Most families found it hard in practical terms to measure up to the prewar model or engage fully in the American model of a "democratic family."

Families in the Occupation period (officially 1945–52, but extending throughout the period of reconstruction as well, into the mid-1960s) were struggling to normalize themselves, and the norms themselves were in flux. Each household would likely include a grandparent or two, usually in the care of one son or daughter. If the caregivers were not the eldest son and his wife, then some accommodation between siblings would be made. Well beyond the end of the Occupation, families were so strapped for space and resources that the care of the elderly, now officially the obligation of all siblings, produced a *taraimawashi* (passing around) situation in which elderly parent(s) would be shuffled through their children's homes. Sometimes it would be the parents who would stay in the ancestral home, with a son and his family who would return as needed when the parents became dependent. In *Tōkyō monogatari* (Tokyo story), a film by Ozu Yasuhiro set in the 1950s, an elderly couple move from one of their children's homes to another, seeking a comfortable living situation, but they feel unwanted until they arrive at last at the one-room apartment of their widowed daughter-in-law, who demonstrates true love and filiality even without the demands of blood relationship. As in many of Ozu's films of the period, a woman's love and steadfastness keep "family" together and demonstrate the importance of true human feeling as a source of stability in chaotic times, as the reconstruction period was.

The postwar urban home was essentially a nuclear family with add-ons, rather than an extended family with omissions. Activities and contributions to the household economy deviated from both the pre- and postwar norms, and economic and educational demands dominated priorities more than obligations for filiality. The wife might work outside the home, but for middle-class families, the value placed on the woman's role as "home coach" to the child increased as education became the measure of a child's potential. Even a mother's engagement in full-time wage work would not diminish this responsibility. Many families, especially during the first decade of the postwar era, were just getting by, and ideologies and norms for "correct" family life were a luxury—whether they were "feudalistic" or "democratic." The following family portraits, though labeled by decades, obviously fail to represent all families of their period. Nor are these decade markers useful as more than conveniences in encapsulating the style of an era: especially in the 1970s and 1980s, though this kind of imaging helped style merchants frame the public's consumption habits and thus may have more than symbolic value.

THE 1950S MIDDLE CLASS, OR *OZZIE AND HARRIET* JAPANESE STYLE

In 1956, Miura Akio lived with his wife, three children, and mother-in-law in Ōta-ku, Tokyo. He was then thirty-six and worked for an insurance company, to which he commuted daily on a bus and train. His wife and her mother took care of the children, and his wife also worked part-time as an accountant for a small electrical goods company near their home.

They had a house—old and very small—that had escaped the firebombing of the war. It had two downstairs rooms and one upstairs room, bath, toilet, and kitchen. Two older children shared the upstairs room and Grandmother had one room downstairs. The youngest child slept with her parents in the tatami room that by day was the family's eating and general purpose room.

They just got by: Grandmother had a small pension as the widow of a railroad worker who died in the early years of the war in Manchuria. Akio is a younger son and his elder brother was in the countryside with his parents, so he was free to support his mother-in-law. He said that taking her pension felt shameful and he half-jokingly referred to himself as a *mukōyoshi*—an adopted son-in-law brought into the family to act as heir in lieu of a son—but he had little choice. Indeed, his wife's mother cared for the children while his wife worked. They had a radio, a bicycle, and finally bought an "automatic" washing machine (requiring several human interventions in its cycle to enhance its "labor-saving" function). They were constantly at work just to provide for their daily needs— much like farming families of the time.

In the 1950s, the premises of the rising middle class began to dominate the dreams and material expectations of Japanese families. This middle-class ideology was at least in one way like that of the suburban family in America: it involved a new private and independent two-generation family.[15] It differed from the American image by virtue of the fact that the husband-wife relationship focused on the rearing of children rather than on the sexual and emotional fulfillment of the couple, and relationships with other institutions shaped schedules and performance of family functions to a greater degree than in the American case.

Of course, only a degree of self-sufficiency was possible, given the preference for a sense of privacy in service to the "face" of the family, and the family's increasing dependence on consumer industries, schools, work-places, public transport, and other institutions outside the home. School and workplace too measured individuals' participation and commitment, not private family work or rituals. Education and employment were as they are today, "greedy institutions" demanding the involvement of all family members, not only of the students and workers who were direct participants in these organizing establishments. For a mother, service to the school was important, from sewing the nursery-school child's smock,[16] to helping an elementary school student do her homework, to arranging *juku* and paying for the high schooler's practice exams in addition to com-pulsory PTA participation. The corporate warrior husband, whatever his personal proclivities, had to participate in after-hours socializing with em-ployers and workmates or lose credibility in the company. A wife's work, hobby, and social life—activities not directly related to the care and feed-ing of the family—were restricted by time and neighborhood watchful-ness (the powerful constraint of the *seken*, or the normative presence of the social surround). One woman felt she had to wear an apron when she went out, to demonstrate that she was tied to the home as a "housewife": she removed it at the station before getting on a train to meet her friends. A wife's struggle to make ends meet by working outside the home was of course legitimate, but rewarding professions or careers were not.

In the postwar middle-class family in Japan, the emotional intimacy between husband and wife or between parents and their children were secondary to the commitments each had to work and schooling, directly or indirectly. It was not only institutional greediness that created this con-straint. In traditional Confucian households, the husband-wife relation-ship was "scripted" for control and discipline on the husband's part and obedience and reverence on the part of the wife.

"Vertical" intergenerational relationships still obtained. The 1950s lex-icon did not take the concept of marital sexuality beyond the needs for reproduction, and in any case, the space available to families at home allowed very little privacy for couples: the "privatization" of family re-ferred to its separation from other larger units, not to internal privacy for individuals and couples.[17] "Privacy" in this sense was lacking in ru-ral families where a houseful of relatives precluded conjugal isolation or freedom, and in the cities where even a large apartment complex could not offer anonymity.

Urban lifestyles are varied, as they have been through the history of cities in Japan. Ronald Dore's *City Life in Japan* describes the *yamanote* and *shitamachi* styles of urban life in the 1950s.[18] The first was an elite "uptown" life with its origins in the aristocracy and yet available to technological innovation and the blandishments of consumer marketing. The second was the traditional style of shopkeepers or tradespeople of "downtown" Tokyo, the "old middle class," continuous in culture and practice with their forebears who had lived as thrifty and conservative working families in the same neighborhoods and occupations for generations.

The life-chance-conferring aspect of educational and occupational tracks operated more strongly for the urban than rural, and among urban, more for the *yamanote* than for the *shitamachi* households in determining family priorities and investments. The children of traditional trade and craft families had their own ladder, destined as they were to follow the family occupation for which the new middle-class credentials were irrelevant. The Miuras needed to create those credentials for their children through education, having no status they could pass directly to the children. Distinctions between *yamanote* and *shitamachi* would soon give way to more bureaucratic understandings of status and the good life in the middle class as described by Ezra Vogel in the early 1960s. His book, *Japan's New Middle Class,* describes families guided by the demands of modern institutions, organized into the "separate spheres" their gender-driven roles indicated, in service both to work and school and to the productivity the nation needed.[19]

There was little synergy between the goals of the Occupation and the popular yearning for a Western lifestyle on the one hand, and the experiences of ordinary families on the other. The two-generation family in Japan was in the 1950s still an exception, and the separation of work and family had only just begun to characterize people's lives. Neither law nor economics drove Japanese family culture toward the American suburban model. White-collar work in large-scale corporations was on the increase, but until the late 1970s most work took place in more traditional small-sector organizations, and most family life took place in homes where the educational system and white-collar salaried worker schedules were not the only imperatives.

THE BOOMING 1960S:
WORK, HOME, AND THE GOOD WOMAN

"Farm boy makes good" could easily describe Kitazawa Jōji—"George." He moved to Osaka from his family's home in the tangerine-growing area near Shizuoka, after a job with the U.S. Occupation forces near Misawa Base. By 1958, he had taken the name "George" as more than a nickname (but less than a legal name, since it lacks the appropriate *kanji* or characters for legal registration), left to marry his childhood sweetheart whose family had come from Shizuoka, and set up in business for himself in Osaka.

His English ability was what he planned to bank on: he started a small import business with his wife, Mariko, and he managed it *fufu* (mom-and-pop) style: he took care of the customer contacts and she did the accounting. He shook hands, read English-language papers, and tried to get his wife to cook American foods—at least at first. His *Amerika-boke* (America-crazed) style was "normal" for some Occupation workers, though those more removed from American influences saw such behavior as undignified. As a family, however, traditional Japanese understandings influenced their lives through Jōji's wife, whose family now lived nearby. Mariko herself was neither fluent in English nor much exposed to American ways, except through her husband and the radio he kept tuned to the Armed Forces radio station. Their two children spoke little English but were studying it in school.

The Kitazawas lived in a "semidetached" style: they were almost an extended family household since Mariko helped tend her aging uncle whose senile dementia was more than her aunt could handle. Typically she would be at her aunt's house almost every day and sometimes several evenings each week—and her cousins reciprocated by dropping by with their children constantly, forcing her to be hostess whenever she wasn't being nurse. George's view of married life, influenced by American base life, magazines, and movies, was less extended and more private, but he accepted her family as his own and even cooked supper and breakfast for their children as necessary, when they visited their Kitazawa cousins. The young Kitazawas, however, were more influenced by school and friends and were amused (or embarrassed) by their father's eccentric domesticity.

"America-yearning" reached a peak during the Tokyo Olympics of 1964, which appeared as a signpost of success in the hard work of reconstruction, the evidence that Japan and its booming economy would not be left in the dust. Subway construction, large-scale building, the rapid urbanization of this period seemed focused, highly energized, and positive. Storefront English language academies proliferated and a Westerner would be greeted on the street with enthusiastic requests for "practice English." There was unbounded optimism—and the growth of large-scale enterprises during this period began to surpass even the family-held conglomerates of the prewar years. Even small companies like George's could prosper in this atmosphere.

Secondary and higher education in the 1960s also experienced a boom, along with a rise in expectations among families for their children's progress along its track. High school began to be a bottom-line goal and some form of higher education became a desirable credential.[20] Vocational or specialized education was less valuable than the generalist liberal arts degree for "good" jobs. While George wanted to send their son to America and their daughter to an international school, his wife hoped for a local public college for the boy and a junior college for the girl.

George's lack of ultimate authority in his own house was an indication of the compartmentalized nature of their household—and of his family's own particular configuration. His wife's participation in the family enterprise did not in itself make them a traditional urban shopkeeping family.[21] In some ways they were also the "new" middle-class family, working to support and nurture its members, whose main identities reflected their roles in school and workplace.

Increasingly, women at home symbolized the good life. The late-nineteenth-century Western "cult of domesticity" cast its shadow over postwar Japan and America alike. In suburban America, the woman at home signified peace and prosperity. In Japan, a latter day version of the Meiji period's good wife/wise mother colored images of the properly managed nuclear family too. Husbands who could afford to keep their wives out of the workforce, as in the American expression, "My wife doesn't have to work," were judged to be successful. In addition, families who could manage without children's labor could keep them out of work and in school to study for their own independent futures or maintain the lifestyle their parents had achieved and, sometimes, even to support those parents in their old age.

As Suzanne Vogel has demonstrated, the compensation for a woman who stayed at home was the glorification and "rationalization" of her role as housewife.[22] And staying at home was a rational economic and social choice, as the trade-offs of work within and without the family produced a hard-nosed calculation favorable to the definition of woman as housewife.[23] And, indeed, popular culture romanticized this choice. The taste of mother's miso soup was celebrated in sentimental songs that were sure to bring tears to the eyes of drunken businessmen:[24] mother's domestic skills were not only scientized—as they had been in the American "domestic science" movement[25]—they were also a means for emotional validation.

Consumer economics set the shape of and rationale for the postwar family. The postwar consumer boom created the atomized but savings-focused, securely compartmentalized, "suburban" Japanese middle-class family. As culturally supported form followed economic function, the two-unit, mutually supportive but role-divided household became normative by the late 1960s. The good man fulfilled his role as worker, bringing the pay envelope home to the good woman who handed him his monthly allowance and picked up his underwear from the floor of their small company-subsidized apartment. The wise mother consulted not her husband but her children's teachers, backed up home study with snacks and coaching, and, if she needed to work, kept "mother's hours" and was home to greet the children after school. More and more families had radios and even televisions, and nearly everyone read newspapers and magazines. The messages got out to an audience waiting to be molded.

There was little else to know about this family than what was obvious in advertising (mom in an apron, dad in a dark suit and white shirt, two children with school knapsacks) or in the children's academic performances, the husband's contribution to corporate productivity, or the wife's home economies boosting the rate of personal savings. Or was there?

In fact, just like families of the Meiji era, families in the 1960s maintained their diversity and, by the end of the decade, sometimes their active resistance to the growing universalization of the "good family" model. Women bucked the trends and developed professional careers, sometimes going to extremes to do so: one woman "divorced" her husband on paper so as to be able to publish under her own name and travel for professional reasons (married women who did work-related travel were flying in the face of the Labor Protection Laws); another woman, without benefit of any sort of divorce, moved her children to her mother's nearby home—both because it had a better school district and because then she could create a home studio in her own small apartment for her freelance cartooning. There were men who left their jobs (in what was to be called the *datsu-sara* movement of the 1970s [flight from salary, from *datsu* and *sararii*]) to go out on their own and take the risks of independent work. These cases do not typify the 1960s: instead, they presage the 1970s.

CONSUMPTION AND CREDENTIALS IN THE 1970S

Takamura Nobuo and Masako married in 1972 and their life together was continuous with their lives as university students. Their apartment was crowded with stacks of books and long-playing records; they listened to American and British folk and rock music. Unlike George, they did not identify themselves exclusively with American culture but saw it rather as one location among others from which to draw new cultural elements, ideologies, and material goods.

One of these elements was feminism, and while Masako did not consider herself a radical feminist (to her, radical feminist meant man-hating extremist), she did imagine that she and Nobuo could "balance" their roles in a "fifty-fifty" family life, sharing tasks and decisions, an emancipated "companionate" marriage. Thinking of family as focused on a *marriage* between two sexually and emotionally bonded people, rather than considering the husband-wife relationship only as a precondition for procreational and economic family building, was a new idea. Judging the family's success by the emotional tone of the spousal relationship was even more radical. Nobuo and Masako, coming out of the student movement of the late 1960s, felt a political need for a cooperative family style and to that added their own romantic idealization of a love relationship.

We see them in the mid-1970s now planning to have their first child and advised by her mother that their lifestyle and the urgent demands of child rearing will not mix. Masako's mother said, "It's all very well to have a husband help out [her phrase, not Masako's] with household chores but men simply *can't* care for babies."

New models and options for family building in the 1970s preoccupied urban young couples and seemed to demand choices. Student revolutionaries of the late 1960s and early 1970s like Nobuo and Masako were not the only ones hoping to make changes; the strategies of men and women who wanted to resist the system (at least for their own sake, if not for society's) were more generalized and "normalized" in 1970s urban culture, and the new consciousness drew in some from the rural areas too, as media disseminated urban practices to the whole nation.

The most publicized cases of course were the most aberrant: "normal" is not news. In the early 1970s, reporting on family focused on oddities: stories of dual-income/no-kids or lesbian or gay couples (in this period, more lesbians than gay men cohabited openly), retired elderly living in communes, even celibacy as a feminist political strategy to protect a woman's autonomy.

To be defined as a couple-family rather than a procreative family was itself anomalous. And even couple-families seemed sometimes to be households of two individuals who scarcely touched home base as a couple. One 1970s husband and wife were more separated than usual, as he was a traveling troubleshooter for his company and seemed to be on the road at all times, while she managed a small dressmaking concern and was always at home. Another was a two-career household, in which neither person was home during the day to give definition to the apartment as "home." One pair could not be defined as a "couple" at all, made up as it was of two unmarried women whose cohabitation in a lesbian relationship could not yet be recognized even by their relatives. Finally, a single man who had lived on his own for more than ten years, an economist working unpredictable hours in an international think tank, was under siege by his employers and family to get married and even he wasn't sure why he hadn't.

Statistically, of course, people engaging in these "deviant" practices were in a small minority. Their eccentric forms of family were not always deliberate choices, and there was little crossover dissemination of new "family cultures" to the majority of the population who may have been diverse, of course, but not classifiable as "trendy." What probably influenced more people was media-driven, consumption-oriented "nesting."

Maihōmushugi (my-home-ism) rather than radical action or even Nobuo and Masako's idealism better describes the aspirations of most people in this period.[26] A focus on "my home," the single-family residence inhabited by a nuclear family, shaped consumer desires as well as the emotional tone of many people's lives. *Maihōmushugi* got families buying, and marketing to nuclear households meant a larger audience for domestic goods, with more establishments needing these goods. It too was a media construct: the images of such a family included Dad putting on a miniature green in a minuscule backyard, Mom happily puttering over a gourmet meal guided by a television in her white-tiled kitchen, a puppy leaping to catch a ball thrown between two children, a girl and a boy.

Images of the good family move fast in Japan: behind every consumption fad is a transitory notion of the good life fulfillable through the purchase of the item in question, and if you are not alert, both the trend and the chance to realize the dream it implies will pass you by. The consumer verities of middle-class family life of the postwar years must be seen both in freeze-frame and in fast-forward. The units in which people operated were the merged dyad of mother-and-child, the institutional connection of child-and-school—and the corporation-identified father. The family who played together in the ads did not always sit down together for dinner. The ironies of postwar consumerism included the contradictions between family-focused products emphasizing a family-anchored consumption program, and the small nuclear unit whose members were divided in time, space, and function.

Dower notes that "Japan appears to be a country of formal marital stability but de facto 'single-parent' families where the mother-child relationship is emphasized almost to a point of unnaturalness, while the father is virtually an absentee parent."[27] For corporate employees, it was out of the question to say, "For personal reasons I won't be able to work late," and so the elaborated establishment of the home with its microwave and electric bread maker and other technologies was merely a symbol of the "private castle" that homes were supposed to be.[28] That organic, integrated family of the ads for food processors and home entertainment centers in fact rarely ate those delicious meals Mom made in her state-of-the-art kitchen together, rarely sat in the same room to watch the sumo tournament or the dubbed 1950s *I Love Lucy* reruns on television. Mother (and Lucy) in the house maintained a faint, flickering image of the traditional home as an anthropomorphized place needing a person—a "housetender," or *orusuban*—to keep it from being "lonely."

Maihōmushugi reached a crescendo of domesticity in home decorating magazines, department store sales of large-ticket appliances, gourmet cooking schools for housewives, and American-style bunk beds—and in very Japanese-style home study desks for children. All models of this estimable piece of furniture had a front and two sides enclosing the studying child, fitted out with shelves, lights, calculator, pencil sharpener, and even—in one high-end model—a button to push to summon Mother for help or a snack.[29] The home study desk perhaps characterizes and encapsulates the family of this era more than the "suburban American" image of the home as playground for its members.

In the 1970s, the full force of the academic credentialing society, the *gakureki shakai,* had struck families. That child playing with a puppy in the yard in *maihōmushugi* advertisements was more likely to be studying or at *juku,* grabbing a bowl of instant ramen instead of mom-made miso soup. The belief that effort counted more than ability inspired middle-class families to get their children to work hard. By the 1970s consumer industries were active in promoting products to support the struggle: correspondence courses, tutoring, practice examinations, and cram classes would give a child an edge. And most of all, the physical and symbolic presence of Mother (as in that button on the study desk) at the core of the campaign to succeed.

Most families at this time had at least two children cramming for the

entrance exams to high school and college, and parents would spend almost the same amount for girls as for boys, even if the career goal they
had for daughters was still ultimately the good wife/wise mother ideal.
A girl's marriage credentials depended in part on her education; the rationale was that through her schooling she would be better qualified to
act as a motivating home coach to her own children. In the Meiji period
a seventeenth-century Confucian tract by Kaibara Ekken, *Higher Learning for Women,* was touted as curriculum for the good woman that also
philosophically justified gendered education in the nineteenth century.[30]
And by the 1970s, another rationale for higher education urged her along
the monolithic, narrowing educational track, to prolong her schooling.
Even without ideological support for it, women were entering the workforce, where their credentials mattered. Married women began to consider
more than stop-gap work. (Now, more than 50 percent of working women
are married, and up to 68 percent of married women work. The gap between image and reality, between women's commitments and time available, is thus very great.) During the 1970s, participation in the labor force
by female graduates of high school and college became almost universal
among women. The M-curve charted women's work lives (see chapter
5) and served as a life-course predictor as much as a statistical gauge of
women's career patterns. During the 1970s and 1980s, the dip in the chart
of women's employment during the years of early child rearing represented a near-mandate to leave work to engage fully in family roles. Later
the dip flattened out: fewer take more than the maternity leave to which
they are now entitled, and now, bell-like, the curve has almost become
an inverted U, demonstrating that there are more women who must, or
do, take work as continuous in their lives.

Young women in the 1970s fully expected to work for some period
before marriage or the birth of their first children, and to return to the
labor force when their youngest entered full-time schooling, or later,
depending on the family's needs. They began to want work that was
interesting and that defined them more. Most young women lived in
their natal homes during their bachelor work years: employers did not
want to hire unmarried women who did not live with their parents, seeing them as potentially unstable or "wild." Young working women with
few expenses fueled the economy by their spending. Female consumers
would lead the boom of the 1980s and tended to participate in the culture of affluence by their purchases, the media that led them and their
uses of leisure.

BUBBLE AND BOOM IN THE 1980S

Muta Haruko, a young office worker in the early 1980s, left her parents' home by 7:45 every morning to catch a bus, then a train to work. She had often stayed up late the night before and, trusting to a trained reflex, slept standing up holding the strap, waking just in time for her stop. At the end of the day, if she was lucky, her employer wouldn't stay late and she too could leave work in time to reach the department stores before closing. She says she almost never returned home without spending money on the way, at least for cakes or fruit for her family, but more often for clothes, music, or supplies for quilting, her hobby.

Haruko was also saving money for her wedding. By the 1980s a young woman's wedding was her family's largest expense next to housing and work before marriage provided her contribution.[31] Haruko had a bank savings scheme to help her plan for big indulgences such as trips to Hawaii and Hong Kong (for her trousseau and household items for her new home).

Obviously, Muta Haruko was not the free-spending Japanese traveler depicted in Western media. The Japanese tourists and investors overseas who snapped up Louis Vuitton luggage and Hawaiian real estate indeed had become the image of Japan's economic success in the 1980s. As the bubble of land values swelled, more Japanese did in fact look abroad, either to spend on more transient pleasures there the savings no longer seen as adequate for the purchase of even a modest home or condominium in Japan or, taking a lump sum payoff for early retirement, to purchase for investment or retirement a larger unit on the Gold Coast of Australia, on Waikiki, or near a golf course in California.

Of course, offshore investing was not possible for everyone, nor was travel. Haruko herself complained of deprivation: as she and others who lived in the "affluent poverty" sketched above said, they lacked time and space for all their schemes. Many of course did not have the luxury of such "poverty," without the assured salary and benefits of the middle-class "corporate slave." During the 1980s most young women were encouraged to leave the workforce at marriage age (and sometimes summarily fired as a nudge toward the "correct" role). Thus for Haruko, marriage was an economic as well as a social necessity. The dream of the single-family home had become harder and harder to realize. Even without a known prospective spouse—like many other young women, she was saving and accumulating for an establishment whose male inhabi-

tant was only at the moment lightly sketched—Haruko figured her first
married home would be only a tiny apartment with two "living" areas
and a combined kitchen-dining area, plus bath and toilet.[32]

The fact that time was the missing element in people's lives compressed
amusements into either telescoped or virtual getaways. Tokyo Disneyland became in the 1980s the most favored dating destination, as a safe
and easy escape into a contained adventure.[33] Even if consumers could
afford the (Mercedes) "Benz," or a vacation in Europe, overloaded work
schedules meant the full enjoyment of such luxuries was almost impossible. Social requirements also intruded on "off-duty" recreation. On a
week's holiday in Europe, 1980s tourists spent on average 3.5 days shopping for the compulsory *omiyage,* mementos owed to family and colleagues at home in exchange for their absence: Haruko estimated that
she spent about $1,500 on gifts during one trip to Hawaii. Vacations
cost, in more ways than one.

Ritualized shopping and relative deprivation, the soullessness of accumulation and the emptiness of ambition also characterized discussions
of lifestyle and morality during this period. If there was one tendency
that characterized most Japanese editorial commentary in the decade of
the 1980s, it was malaise about the present and doubt about the future,
amidst the security and plenty that supposedly insulated them from the
troubles of the West.

Young people in particular—youth in bloom or in orbit, out of touch
with reality—were the media's target in discussion of the "new breed"
of youth. Complaints focused on their ultra-materialistic self-centered-
ness, their disavowal of the values of hard work and thrift that had fueled Japan's engine of postwar economic success. These people were the
"grasshoppers"[34]—not saving, but hopping from job to job, spending
on novelties and fashion rather than looking to future family-building,
home owning, and elder care. They were afflicted with the "three Mu's":
mukandō (immovable); *mukyōmi* (no curiosity); *mukanshin* (no motivation).[35] The market created them; the media decried them.

Of course, these young people, together with the elders who raised
and condemned them, were not a uniform "breed." Some of those who
had finished their schooling by the early 1980s (whether they were among
the 60 percent of the age group whose terminal credential was a high
school diploma or the nearly 40 percent who completed some form of
higher education) did not have the choice of job-hopping, goods-grazing,
and jet-setting.

The life chances of rural youth, for example, were still considerably

different from those of their urban age-mates. Farm-raised boys were educated in the same national curriculum and, if their parents could afford
to lose their labor power *and* pay for their fees, they too went on to some
sort of college or university. But if the family—farm, shopkeeper, restau-
rateur, trade, or craft—owned its own source of income, there was likely
to be considerable pressure on a son or daughter to take on the responsibility for its continuance. Eldest sons of farmers particularly were subject to this pressure even if most farm-bred youth took modern-sector
employment in nearby towns. As long as they lived on the farm, they
were farmers, and their wives were farmers' wives.

In the 1980s, even women in the countryside had a chance to become
new-breed young women with an interest in freedom, luxury, or at least
a delayed commitment to marriage. If the choice was theirs, these young
women and their urban counterparts would make their marital decisions
independent of the needs of families, theirs or their future husband's. They
coined the phrase *baba nuki, kaa tsuki,* meaning "without grandma, with
car," describing the desirable future husband. Mothers-in-law represented
the oppression and immobility of the old-style family; cars represented
the free-wheeling youthful style of the modern couple. Many farmers or
eldest sons of any trade with an intact three-generation household often
resorted to using bride-import services from Southeast Asia and the
Philippines, to bring young women willing to marry and live in large families, work hard, and have more than the 1.57 children per woman of reproductive age (the well-publicized birth *shokku* of 1990).

The effects of Japanese media and marketers' constructed diversity
began to show in families of the 1980s even before the recession at the
end of the decade demonstrated its fallacies and limitations. People knew
what they didn't have and denigrated what they did have. And the gap
between the haves and the have-lesses became much more apparent. Further, the promise implied by the "meritocracy," engaging people's energy and will through the notion that hard work would yield success,
seemed empty to the many (most) who couldn't squeeze onto the "lifetime employment" track, guaranteeing a cradle-to-grave package of
benefits, security, and promotion. Those who did were far from wholehearted about its benefits, constrained as they were by its limitations.

It was in the 1980s that stories in the press began to appear about
karōshi, "death by overwork," in which salaried workers would literally work themselves to death through long hours and stressful jobs. This
phenomenon would not in itself have reached public consciousness if a
few families of dead or disabled workers had not begun to protest and

even sue companies. *Karōshi* became a legal corporate issue, and not just a matter of family bereavement, and companies tried to enforce family leisure time to show their worker-friendliness and reduce legal costs.

Lifestyle issues became matters related to economic prosperity, even to national security, not just topics for private off-duty examination and concern. What happened in the private space of family life, in the *uchi*, in essence a space outside the rules and critical focus of society, seemed now to be subject to invasion by policymakers. What would lie ahead in the 1990s as issues for public concern would make Muta Haruko's life look conservative and predictable.

MATING, MARRIAGE, AND DIVORCE

Shock headlines contrasting the greater number of divorces now than twenty years ago still do not place Japan in the high-divorce category. In the immediate postwar years, divorce declined even though legal access to divorce improved for women. By 1988 the rate of divorce per 1,000 persons was 1.26 and Japan as a modern nation ranked very low indeed compared to the United States. By the end of the 1990s, there was a rise to 2.00 per 1,000 persons, still half the rate of the United States (figures 1, 2).[36]

The rising rate of both informal and legal divorces has been attributed to changes in arrangement and expectation: what people want from marriage, especially what women want, is changing. Young women say they are looking for men whose life skills—meaning earning power and stability—are good. The "new" man, who will share chores and child rearing, may be a women's magazine ideal, but realistic young women set a high value on a stable and prosperous household (independent of other relatives, however). Some women in their twenties say they want an exciting romantic relationship in marriage, but by their early thirties, financial and social support becomes their goal.

Among most young people dating is common but is not seen to be a preliminary to marriage. Many young women spend more time socializing with female than with male friends. Boyfriends are not usually fiancés but may be amusing companions, good sexual partners, or glamorous accessories, depending on a young woman's point of view. Fiancés are another matter.

Getting to marriage means more organized research and a commitment more to the institution than to an individual, according to those

Figure 1. Marriage and divorce rates, 1970–
99. From Ministry of Health and Welfare,
Statistical Handbook of Japan (Tokyo, 2000).

now delaying marriage to their late twenties or early thirties. There are now about five thousand "marriage information services," which offer alternatives to traditional connections leading to *omiai* (arranged meetings of prospective spouses), which families or close friends might provide. Like some American dating services, the services are often computerized and personalized with individual interviews (and often videotaped for customers).[37] Men are said to need these but to feel some stigma in using them, as it means some kind of "arrangement" that may seem either feudalistic or evidence of a person's social inadequacy. Women are more matter-of-fact, saying that using them is modern and better than using family connections. Expressing one's preferences freely within the sphere of family may lead to friction. Turning down a computerized image is easier than saying no to the son of one's father's colleague in front of assembled relatives.

The ways individuals can meet and contract marriages are highly diverse now, as are the various formations that count as family.[38] If a couple living alone is a "family," the older generation's views of suitability matter less. If a woman's earnings are substantial, the earning potential of a future spouse may not be quite as important. If, supporting herself and living alone, a woman does not want children, she can take lovers or cohabit with a boyfriend or lesbian partner. The choices are many and

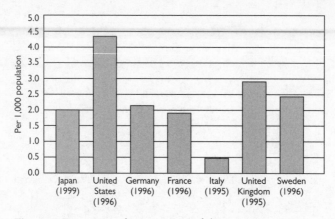

Figure 2. International comparison of divorce rates, 1995–
99. From Ministry of Health and Welfare, Statistics and Information Department, Minister's Secretariat, Summary of Vital
Statistics (2000).

are, it seems, in the hands of women who engage them more fully: men
appear still to want a more conventional match, and their employers expect them to marry.

Weddings have changed too, both because younger generations can
make choices for themselves and because the range of choices has increased
with postwar economic changes, including current recessionary options.
Prospective spouses themselves can choose because they have made contributions to the cost of the wedding from their own salaries, and because
pleasing the young is now a priority of families as well. The use of wedding halls and hotels is most popular, employing efficient and experienced
professional staff who deal with the complicated details and protocols involved. Families without in-house experts (grandmothers) on wedding
decorum feel more comfortable with a predictable and acceptable package of ritual, meal, and guest management that meets social expectations.[39]

Weddings are far from cheap, even under the recession conditions of
the 1990s, and a young woman's calculations of style, location, and cost
often precede her choice of a spouse. Like the "hope chests" of young
American women in the first half of the twentieth century, in which they
lovingly stored linens they embroidered toward marriage with still unknown bridegrooms, the savings accounts of young Japanese women receive regular infusions toward the ceremony with a man who seems only
an accessory to the event. A typical Japanese hotel or wedding hall ceremony in 1990 cost on average about $35,000 for some one hundred
guests. This outlay would cover ceremony, reception, the rental of wed-

ding kimono and other bridal party apparel, as well as the small gifts given to guests (though the total can go much higher, the money gifts given by attendees help offset it).

There are more choices to make: the most expensive is a Shinto wedding in full kimono with priest and attendants, a sake-sipping ritual (three special flat red lacquered cups of sake, swallowed in three rapid sips each) with a full ceremonial Japanese meal. More popular now for romantic and budgetary reasons is a Christian ceremony. Most wedding halls or hotels have both a Christian chapel and a Shinto hall, and the Christian one comes with a minister and perhaps a three-woman choir. Other lower-cost options include shipboard ceremonies on cruises, or weddings in Guam or Hawaii. Some entrepreneurs offer full videotaping so that those left at home can "participate" later.[40]

NARITA RIKON, OR THE HONEYMOON'S OVER

Divorces are as various as marriages. The rise (or media hype) of "Narita" divorce in the 1990s, the separation of a newly married but already disillusioned couple as they land at Narita, Tokyo's international airport, exposed the problem of motivation and commitment in marriage. In particular, as the bride usually initiated the dissolution, it questioned young women's commitment to the idea.

An unmarried woman in her late twenties said that several of her friends had recently divorced after very short marriages. Their parents pressured them to marry and, to relieve this pressure, they did. Their divorces were releases from the bargain, she explained, for now they were free to find a better match themselves, since their parents now saw them as difficult to place, "damaged goods." Waiting until the early or midthirties to marry was about on a par with being a divorcée, in the marriage market. She herself felt sad for these women and a little shocked at what seemed a cold arrangement and simply hopes her family will give her no grief over waiting a little longer.

Why marriages end is an unanswerable question, and some say women are to blame, both because they have nurtured romantic illusions about a relationship with their husbands and because they have too little commitment to the institution of family, preferring to focus on themselves rather than on others. The separation of men's from women's roles within the family has been blamed as well, since it forces women to be more independent. Their distinct role assignment allows women a sense of authority they might use outside the home as well.

The impasse in communication may create a de facto divorce: not a legal separation even, but what is called *kateinai rikon,* or "in-house divorce" in which spouses have almost nothing to do with each other and may even live separately. For understanding and sexual companionship, men have long turned to bar hostesses or perhaps a younger woman from the office. In the 1990s, it became apparent that women were seeking these things outside marriage as well—but in their case, usually as solace during or after the dreadfully pressured years of seeing children through "examination hell" into college. Companion bars and dance halls have sprung up where women (usually middle-aged) might spend time with a young man hired there as a gigolo for the evening. Women mentioned that they had had affairs outside marriage as well, sometimes with co-workers, sometimes with old flames.

Divorce is far from the common, almost "normal," experience it has become in America.[41] There has been a rise in Japanese acceptance of divorce in unhappy marriages, according to opinion poll responses. In 1984, 65 percent said that divorce was unacceptable, with more men (73.2 percent) than women (66.9 percent) opposed to divorce. In 1998, however, approval of divorce for unhappy couples rose to 54 percent. Overall, and continuing today, the older the respondent, the more opposed to divorce. The stigma for divorcées has been somewhat reduced, particularly for middle-aged women who have done their job of raising children and supporting husbands at key points in their careers. In fact, the number of divorces occurring after twenty years of marriage has doubled in the last twenty years. But even a woman who initiates a late divorce (*jukunen rikon,* or divorce at maturity) may be blamed for the failure of her marriage. No-fault divorce is rare, though the laws seem to permit a version of this. Divorce proceedings themselves are difficult or humiliating, demand long separations, favor mediation and conciliation, and have contestable interpretations for divorce that include abandonment, incurable mental illness, and adultery. These in part were established to protect women from arbitrary or whimsical deprivation of economic support but can keep them in marriages that produce hardship and anguish.

While the core of a Japanese family is *not* the husband-wife relationship, but the parent-child bond, divorce represents more than a break between spouses. A divorced woman with children is seen as putting her children at risk, as they will be stigmatized, bullied, and isolated by schoolmates, assumed by teachers to be doomed to failure, and possibly passed over by top companies for hiring. At the very least, it is assumed that a divorced mother, almost always a working mother, will not have the time or energy to help her children succeed in the educational system. Many women interviewed reported a period of their marriage in which there had been a strong possibility of separation or divorce, but most had stuck it out "for the sake of the children." In spite of this, there has been a rise in mother-headed households amounting now to 2 percent of all households in the past decade. The tie between husbands and wives is seen as fragile without the motivating presence of children. *Ko wa kasugai* (children are the bond between husbands and wives) may be a factor in the relatively low rate of divorce in young families.

A TAXI DRIVER'S SPIEL ON THE 1990S

Driving a Tokyo cab is not the high-adventure, risk-prone, cowboy activity a frightened rider unaccustomed to Japanese taxi rides may think it is. It is a job based on information and communication, from memorizing the Tokyo street atlas to listening to garrulous drunks. Cab drivers need to know everything and, according to Hamada Goichi, he himself is the most encyclopedic of them all.

Goichi is a fine commentator on the families of the 1990s: he came of age in Tokyo in the 1970s but his parents' roots were in the snow country of Aomori and the Kansai countryside. He says he is an "instant Edokko"—telescoping into one the (minimally three) generations of Tokyoites it takes to be a genuine child of Edo.

His perceptions of change over the past three decades and of the diversity that now exists in family shape, experience, and values give us a better view of these confusing times than can any one family. The families of the 1990s are as hard to categorize as those the Meiji officials came across when they tried to create a unitary Japanese family from the variety—or chaos—of the times.

Goichi's grandmother in Aomori had been divorced and remarried— rare for the times but tolerated in the small village where she lived. Goichi's father didn't get along with his stepfather so he left home at fifteen to go to Tokyo and didn't return. His mother was the third of three daughters of a grocer in rural Kansai and, according to her, was lucky to marry at all, as her family had fallen on hard times in the war and had no dowry money. A cousin knew Goichi's father, who was a shop apprentice in Tokyo, and off she went as a bride to this unknown man in an unknown city.

Both Goichi's background and his job make him tolerant of the many ways there are to be a family. He has little in common with textbook middle-class families, who, he says, are "boring," but in any case, a "normal" family is unusual: they all have odd bits and corners that don't fit the mold. He points to in-house divorce, which leaves women in early middle age emotionally dependent on their kids and sexually starved. He counts among his passengers some middle-aged women who regularly patronize "gigolo" bars where male escorts "make them feel like women again"—and a few young "office ladies" who prefer the transvestite bars where women dressed as male hosts are "real gentlemen."

He also knows a couple who go by different names, as the woman has found a legal way to revert to her maiden name for career purposes. This woman like others has a paper divorce when she needs it, to handle the problem of overseas travel or other times when she needs to use "her own name." He knows a lesbian couple who, he says, quarrel like any older couple comfortable enough with each other to gibe and parry publicly. He knows young men who play the field—but come home to mother. He says young women these days are more out and about than the young men, who, he says, have no street wisdom about women and are often shy and uncomfortable. He worries that they can't be serious about family building because "they have no confidence."

Goichi himself is a man about town in many senses: he is well versed in the town—his job and self-identity tie him to Tokyo—and he is everywhere; his knowledge of high and low and in between knows no barriers. He tells you not to believe the fancy images of family life created by television and advertising: no one lives like that, he says. And he warns you equally not to believe the downside stories, the horror stories about family murders, incest, victimization of the elderly. He says they are just like the ads: to sell you something. What Goichi cannot begin to sum up as a "family of the '90s" is a collection of accommodations and expressions of familylike feeling. These may show up as diversity, deviance even—and a set of media sound bites trying to make coherent images out of messy realities.

In 1989 the recession officially came to Japan. Recessionary thinking colored most people's lives, encouraged by the cultural habit of deliberate self-diminishment and the public discourse associating scarcity with motivating and productive values such as hard work and thrift. Those who had been worried that materialistic youth were going to the dogs in the 1980s could at least be hopeful that they'd have to tighten their belts and get to work.

Japan was becoming more like the rest of the world as it experienced the shocks of economic downturns, downsizing, and unemployment.

Mainstream employees might be at risk, but those most strongly affected were at the economy's margins. The inhabitants of the Sanya area of Tokyo and similar day laborer doss-house quarters in Osaka and Yoko-hama are where the bottom has dropped out. Goichi knows several of the older men in Sanya by name. These are people, he explains, with no real name, men who lack family, lack a place in society, lack a roof over their heads, and ultimately, lack a self. And, as James Fallows noted, no women and children turn up in homeless shelters and soup lines.[42] The men are invisible and hidden from middle-class view. Many Japanese are not aware of the existence of the homeless and the areas that are for the most part managed by organized crime and Christian missions rather than by governmentally funded social services. They owe their lack of visi-bility, it is said, to their lack of family.

But for the successfully employed young family, the 1990s made less difference. Following a predictable life course, a young couple marry and leave their natal homes to live on their own; they have a few two-career years and some "togetherness" as a couple. Then when their single child is born, the wife takes at least a maternity leave, and two-role parents replace a two-career family. Whatever equality or mutuality had existed in the couple's performance of household tasks before childbirth tends to disappear when the woman becomes a mother and the man a father.

There has been little change in attitude about who is responsible for homemaking: over 90 percent of respondents in the prime minister's office annual poll for 1995 said that cleaning, washing, cooking, and cleaning up after meals are women's responsibilities.[43] Over 80 percent called household finances and shopping the wife's chores and well over 70 per-cent identified child care too as a female activity. In spite of this "pref-erence" there was a slight rise in men's housekeeping activity between the 1980s and 1990s in both dual- and single-income households, but there was also a rise in women's reported housework time in dual-income households, so it appears that a rise in men's time on these tasks did not mean a lessening in women's. New consumer products have been created for the woman who must perform her cleaning chores at night, including "quiet" washing machines and vacuum cleaners that will not disturb anyone's rest.

SEPARATION—IN ROLE, NAME, AND LAUNDRY

In the 1990s other separations exacerbated this role division. *Tanshin funin,* or job-related separation, created two-household nuclear families in which one member, usually the husband, lived on his own in a remote city on a job assignment (which could last years) while the woman and child lived in the original city, instead of moving with the husband. The usual reason given was the family did not want to interrupt their child's educational experience, even though the existence of a national curriculum, giving all students at any grade level across Japan the same study plan and even textbooks, should make school-to-school mobility more rather than less possible.

The intensity of the mother-child household is said to be dangerous to both parties. The isolation of the husband is pathological for him as well, perhaps triggering stress-related illness and even death. The requirement to split the family destabilizes it: the system arranges, the system disarranges.

A seemingly trivial home appliance, the washing machine, capitalized on the distinction. The creation by Hitachi of a two-chambered washing machine, marketed in 1989, makes it possible to wash two loads of laundry at the same time, and advertising demonstrates that it should be used to separate the husband's dirty underwear from the laundry of the rest of the family. "My husband's underwear? First I scrub [each piece] thoroughly with a brush and then I throw them into the washing machine . . . of course, I would never wash them with mine or my daughter's because his are so dirty." In some of the commercials for this machine, a housewife is shown picking up her husband's underwear with long chopsticks. According to Nakano Osamu of Hosei University, these were popular in the 1990s as women could not accept things associated with maleness, like drinking, smoking, and sweating.[44] The *pantsu wake arai ronso,* or "issue of separate pants in the laundry," became a concern about the distance and "dissing" of men within the family. Other forms of verbal rather than physical separation may be equally symbolic and less trivial.

WHAT'S IN A NAME?

Takegawa Sayako applied for a research grant in the name she had been using for years as a research psychologist and scientific writer. She won the grant that would take her to England and duly sent in her paperwork to the Ministry of Education, responsible for disbursing the grant. The documents included a photocopy of her passport in her married name, Iguchi Sayako, which she did not use in the application. The ministry noted this discrepancy and refused to issue the funding until she legally changed her name on the passport *or* registered herself officially in her married name for all professional purposes. Both are untenable options in her view, and she has hired a lawyer to help her before the term of the grant expires.

Family separation of a symbolic sort also began to appear in the 1990s, as some women in these *nyū famiri* decided to keep their maiden names, a practice relatively rare in Japan. The two-surname family is called *fufu bessei* and flaunts both tradition and law, as Japanese family law forces both parties to a marriage to have the same last name—not necessarily his, but *one* only. *Bessei* or "separate names" are a real hassle, as the woman's employer may harass her, passport officials may deny her documents in her maiden name, and her health insurance may remain inaccessibly in her husband's family name. In 98 percent of registered marriages the husband's family name is listed as the official name of the couple—but more and more couples are unregistered, or cohabiting. An unregistered marriage leads to other problems. A child born to the marriage, for example, will have difficulty registering for schooling or will have a discriminatory note on the application. This difficulty may in part account for the very few, less than 1 percent, of births outside legal marriage.

The two-surname family is seen as a "women's issue," but it is part of a wider concern over the *kōseki* system, family registration, as noted above. The *kōseki* register becomes a legal document cited or referred to for passports, job applications, or private investigations into the background of prospective spouses. In the 1990s and earlier, protests against the ubiquity and availability of these records focused on the discriminatory uses to which the documents might be put: families of *burakumin* (former outcaste community) origin, for example, were subject to background searches for work and marriage. By 1976, *kōseki* were no longer public record and could be used only for official purposes, but this regulatory change was not enough security for many.

NEW WORDS FOR THE NEW FAMILY

In contrast to the constraints and images of the old Family, the new ones have inspired language and imagery—trendy words and phrases that have been created in media and marketing and have become part of the popular discourse surrounding family change. The *fukugan shufu* (many-faced housewife) is one of the milder coinages, describing the housewife who does not stay home but instead has created a busy collage of a life of activities. She is also called *soto-sama* or "outdoor lady," the opposite of the traditional *oku-sama* meaning "indoor person." Such an individual is also a *tenuki okusan*, a "no-hands" housewife, who, after her day of work, tennis, pottery class, or lecture series, stops at a department store basement food hall to pick up a range of prepared meals or foods for her family's supper. These caricatured women are usually not wage earners, but of course the prepared foods work equally well for those coming home after a full day of work; they are not only for the women derided for their lives of "three meals and a nap." The foods are often, as some women say, better than they could make themselves; their families know they are treats, not a stopgap.

Other linguistic evidence for men's separation from women's lives came in trendy phrases like *Gorby teishu*, or "Gorbachev husband," good at handling diplomacy away from home but poor at domestic life. Men reviled in this way can scarcely be blamed for staying away from home, with *kitaku kyohi-shō*, or "home refusal syndrome" coined as the adult male equivalent of *tōkō kyohi*, or "school refusal" demonstrated by children who have become averse to the pressures, academic and social, of school and therefore play truant. Such men stay at the office, engage in more after-hours *nomunikēshun* (from *nomu*, to drink, and the English word communication, hence communicating through drinking), even rent a capsule room in a capsule hotel night after night. Such behavior may be understood as part of the job and may not immediately signal dysfunction within the family.

Retirement may reveal hidden dissatisfactions too. Advertisements for Japan Rail in the 1990s showed elegantly attired youthful older couples standing next to a bullet train about to take them to rural Japan for a second honeymoon, but more often couples' lives are just as separate at home as they were before retirement. The language used to describe the hapless homebound and dependent retired male says it all: *sōdaigomi* (big bag of garbage), or wet fallen leaves, clinging and sticky. "Retirement-pension" divorces allow the woman one-half of the pension and her freedom, a flight into "woman's heaven" or *onna tengoku*, that period of a woman's life when she has neither children nor husband to care for. A middle-aged woman with financial freedom and good health can indulge herself in those hobbies, travel, and the companionship of other women that her younger prototype, the *soto-sama*, has only on a part-time basis. This image of womanhood has led a significant number of older men to state in public opinion polls that they wish to be born women in their next incarnations.

WOMEN WHO SAY NO

Younger men too seem to be suffering from women's flight from marriage: they complain that women refuse marriage in the first place, that many "just want to have fun." Men's view of marriage tends to be tied to serious responsibilities, and indeed many employers urge young male employees to marry as soon as possible as an indication of their own seriousness of purpose and willingness to take on adult commitments. If a man reaches thirty unmarried, the path up the corporate ladder may be limited and his family and employer may put pressure on him to find a bride. One bachelor, in his early forties, found himself accused of homosexuality or of "marriage-phobia," a condition more often seen in women than men; he is being backed into an arranged marriage to prove his maturity and sexual identity—or, he says, he will have to leave Japan.

To help the young men along, personnel managers hire "office ladies" with an eye to the young unmarried workers' future family lives. They position suitable OLs (who wouldn't be hired if they weren't suitable as future brides) in clusters of three and four at desks near suitable young men, assuming, they say, that a young man has no time or imagination to think beyond the women sitting near him in considering a future spouse.[45]

Young women are now delaying marriage as long as possible, especially young working women in large urban areas. The intent of the 1986 Equal Employment Opportunity Law (see chapter 5) was to provide women with equal access to jobs and salaries equal to those of men. While the law has no teeth in it, its template for employment conditions for women encourages women to stay at work and discourages employers from placing discriminatory pressure on women to leave the workplace for early marriage. The "*croissant* syndrome"—leading women to choose the glamour of a career over the responsibilities of family[46]—attracted many women now in their late thirties who, like their cartoon counterparts in America, are said to wonder why they "forgot to have children."

The one major concern keeping women to their traditional roles and family duties is the increasingly likely fact of caring for their, or their husband's, elderly relatives. What David Plath has called the "Confucian sandwich" affects women most particularly,[47] and the wide female readership of the best selling novel *Twilight Years* by Ariyoshi Sawako is evidence of the engagement and distress among women attempting to fulfil the "sandwiched" roles of nurturer to the young, nurse to the elderly. As we will see in chapter 6, in many families a new bilateralism means that senior parents of either the husband or the wife or both may demand their care. Most families still hope to avoid institutional care for relatives as long as possible, and yet there are long waiting lists at the best nursing facilities. In the late 1990s, particularly, there was a rise in nursing home building, but it is not keeping up with the demand.

Mobilizing families in the early twenty-first century to function as organic integral units, as sources of solace and support for their members, is supposed to diffuse the burden on social service agencies. That there is no one postwar family to reform and cajole into fulfilling these functions is eminently observable; not only is the target moving, it is multiple and idiosyncratic, requiring particular strategies and supports to engage each family, rather than the Family supposed by policy and ideology, in its unique and increasingly difficult task.

The protean Japanese family at the beginning of the century parallels its prototype one hundred years ago. The Japanese government has relied on families to nurture and prepare the young to be citizens, and to give the elderly a safe haven and support. And once again the government is mobilizing to support—or insist on—a predictable, compliant, and singular Family out of plural families whose behavior has often been unpredictable or at odds with public images. In chapter 4 we look at children whose lives are diverse and changeable, as unlike the official version of the Good Child as are the official Family and the families we have seen.

PART TWO

Containing Elements

Elemental Families

Starting with Children

Ken-chan is the center of our life. He is a mirror of our family and our marriage. Sometimes I feel it is very hard to be a mother. But still, without his happiness I cannot be happy. It is always difficult to live as a mother who longs for wings and fly to the sky. After all, we all three are fine.

A professional working mother, 2000

A reporter from a Japanese news magazine asked me, "Why do Americans who are having their first child say they're *starting a family*? In Japan, having a child doesn't start a family: family goes on, it's all around you, backward and forward—it's like the air."[1] To her, this suggested that children must be more important in America than in Japan. She said that Americans without children must feel they have no family but also that if it takes the birth (or adoption) of a child to begin one, the American notion of family is shallow and impoverished. Family to her means her great-great grandmother of whom she's only heard stories, her siblings' in-laws, a cousin from Osaka, most of all her mother and father's home. Furthermore, family does not depend on a couple's—or a woman's— decision to procreate.

There is no question that children are important in Japan, the more so for the assumption that you will have them, that it's "like the air"— natural, expected, needed, elemental. But children don't *start* a family. Rather, they continue it and help focus and shape relationships within the household. They also influence the virtues and values that shape a sense of family beyond its walls. Further, having children is not part of a dream of individual happiness—and apparently, neither is getting married—or at least so the representations of young women's dreams would indicate.

Of course, the existence of children identifies, validates, and gives meaning to life for people in Japan. Declaring children to be the future of the nation is a common and effective political strategy. Children *are* elemental to family and crucial to the establishment of nation-as-family within official discourse. They are, above all, the most "perfectly Japanese" ingredient in the constructions of family after the war. The appeal to have more children is at the core of the twenty-first-century family crisis drawing together some strands of rhetoric and some issues raised by new social and economic conditions.

Why children are both elemental and problematic in Japan today is a question with tangled roots. It appears paradoxical that bearing and raising children could have both institutional and social approval but not have structural support. This contradiction, unpacked, reveals the gap between ordinary families' realities and state agenda.

Why does the priority placed upon reversing the falling birthrate seem to separate this issue from the care and welfare of children in families? As we have seen, women, not couples or families, are seen to put the nation at risk by their failure to reproduce. Even without the admonitions of policymakers and officials, women's occupational, marital, and reproductive choices are becoming increasingly complex.

The difficulties of combining reproduction and career help explain declining births. The family roles, whether as wife, mother, or caregiver to the elderly, are designated as fulltime identities.[2] Workplace roles for men offer little flexibility to the person who must combine a full-time job with family roles. As women have entered a complicated labor market, whether as "full-time temporaries," part-time housewives, or professional career women, they must make their lives contingent on other people's paths and plans as well as fulfill their multiple roles. Before the 1980s, the assumption was that wholehearted performance of her scripted roles would make a woman feel fulfilled. In Ariyoshi's 1978 novel *Twilight Years,* the heroine finds resolution of her family crisis only when she lets go of her job to devote herself to her senile father-in-law's care at the end of his life.

There is no single understanding of how children fit into this busy landscape. Most people say that without children life is incomplete, but young people have other priorities and do not worry about national goals. National leaders and institutions invest children with very different meanings than individuals do, as parents and as participants in other social institutions. An explanation for this perfectly Japanese tangle of meanings requires a longer look at the personal and the public meanings of childbearing and child rearing.

Ken-chan's mother is one woman trying hard to merge her roles or at least to straddle and guide them in parallel, like a team of horses yoked together. And she is ten years older than the young and still childless reporter. She saw having a child as necessary, important, and inevitable—like the air. She is also a career woman and took only a brief maternity leave when her son was born. Her focus on both work and family is very sharp and very complex. Her sense of professional accomplishment is parallel to her sense of the magnitude of the responsibility of motherhood—both are "elemental" to her identity, as is her consciousness of the conflicting realities of her complicated life. It can be almost too much for her, sometimes.

While in the past having children was like breathing, "like the air," the choice to have them and the demands of child rearing are now more fraught with complexity. As we have begun to see, prewar traditional family values have been condensed, distilled, and institutionalized outside the home. As ideology goes bureaucratic—mandating what might be personal concerns—it also becomes vague in its justifications: extolling the virtues of good motherhood means little if a mother simply needs child care. Policies attempting to bridge the gap often stumble on their own rhetoric. Such policies include the Angel Plan (encouraging more births among working women), the Golden Plan (giving institutional support to the ideal three-generation caregiving family), and the Family-Care Leave Act (promoting family based care with partially paid leaves of absence from work). These programs encourage the notion that there is a Family responsible collectively as an establishment for the care of its own, while in fact it is people in families, to wit, women, who are the caregivers.

Parenting in Japan has not always been an official concern, but it has been the object of media programming. Even as far back as the late seventeenth century, child-rearing manuals have specified parental practices, including the notion of *taikyō* or learning in the womb. The belief that children absorb their mother's feelings and activities even in utero underlined the idea of a mother's unique role in enhancing her child's character and abilities. A mother was responsible for prenatal as well as postnatal environments for her children. Motherhood was promoted as the virtuous activity for any woman, and among elites, a woman's "special" wisdom and virtue seemed designated for motherhood.[3] Families needed children, especially males, to continue the lineage and to produce and support the elders. And yet a child-based agenda and rhetoric had no place in official society until urbanization, industrialization, and the breakup of the rigid class system made the newly created Meiji universal school system the standard measure of a child's and his family's future prosperity.

Is Japan now a "child-centered" society? Do families, schools, and other institutions begin with children? And if so, what vision of the child governs their view and actions? The postwar image of the middle-class child, cosseted and supported at home to ensure high academic performance, dominates most discussions. Within this view, mother is portrayed as home coach, father as interested but mostly absent from the intensity of the mother-child relationship. This two-unit household, mother-child as one element and father as the other, is divided by the demands of occupation and education but functional in sorting roles and spheres of authority. Choices and decisions in such a family are clearly "child-focused."[4] "Child-centered" in this case, however, represents a reduction in the scope and timeline of family concerns from the Meiji period lineage household. The late-twentieth-century family reversed the temporal focus from sacrifice for the sake of the long line of ancestors behind to sacrifice "for the sake of the children" yet to come.[5]

The child's potential as learner—or perhaps, if we envision school as a matter of scoring high on tests, as "scorer"—is at the foreground of such a landscape. Institutions such as schools and cram classes have created choices and costs for parents. Organizing a regime suitable for the particular child's ability and financing it tends to be the mother's job. Time is similarly budgeted: family events such as vacations, or even weddings and funerals, must give way to the study schedule and school events. Maintaining the principle of "effort = success" means supporting the *input* side of children's time and demands adult interventions of time and money to ensure payoff on the *output* side.

Pressure to succeed has its downside. Those who do not or cannot participate or who do and fail may suffer an early loss of options. Nearly all of the 60 percent of the age group who do not make it to higher education are forced to understand their lives as either failed or deviant. The pressure has produced pathological outcomes. In the late 1990s, commentators, psychologists, and politicians associated social and psychological issues, some highly sensational and tragic, such as the murder and beheading of an eleven-year-old by a fourteen-year-old in Kobe in 1997, and other problems such as drug use and teen prostitution, with distorted experiences of education. Though the pressure to succeed comes from the system of credentialing that has grown up alongside schooling (with its narrow and flawed measures of academic success), the critics did not indict the educational system. Ultimately families drew the blame for abdicating their responsibility to instill "values" along with skills in the pressured race for credentials. Children do nothing but study, say child psychologists, educators, and family clinics in criticizing families, and parents measure their own worth by their children's test scores. What drives families' child-centeredness, then, is their need to reproduce their social status by means of their children's achievements.[6] Furthermore, a focus on children posits the optimistic notion that all children start from an equal takeoff point and are fully engaged in the effort model of success.

The effort model's form of meritocracy does not work for everyone. Ability and hard work together may propel some young people upward beyond their points of social origin into occupational niches that spell success. But not surprisingly, parents' varying abilities to place their children on the ladder to success parallel differences in child-rearing ideologies. Harold Stevenson has shown that middle-class mothers who can spend time on their children's homework, go to PTA meetings, and arrange *juku* classes or any other necessities to get them through the rigorous exams, tend to believe in effort and family mobilization as key to a child's future.[7] Meanwhile, working-class mothers, who work full time outside the home or who themselves lack an educational background that might support children's study, tend to believe that it is genes and luck. For them, a child is either born with smarts or not, is given a chance or not.

Families may not all do it the same way, but they all engage in promoting their children's futures. The family's child-centeredness is one matter: the institutionalization of a focus on children is another. Why families are having fewer children, so few now that the population of the next generation will be well below replacement level, has less to do with families' love for children than it does with the power that schools and workplaces have to confirm or deny access to status. If success must be purchased, it is better to have fewer children so as to be able to invest more in each one's chances.

This chapter looks at engagement in childhood during a less than golden era in Japanese family history, when families are often reduced to their most basic elements and when family strategies to function must operate either within systems constraining their potential or outside them with greater risk of failure. The elemental family can indeed place children efficiently on a track to success in societal terms, but its choices can put children at risk. Within a small household with limited social and emotional resources, a narrowing of choices puts pressure and responsibility on (neurotic) isolated mothers and on (alienated) detached fathers. Thus when parents' emotional problems have an impact on children, they get attention, but attention that demands solutions from those already burdened and pressured. Yet official Japan implicates parents as significant servants of the nation and, as Anne Allison notes, the work women do as mothers becomes the production of young workers for a capitalist labor force. Those fond (but neurotic) mothers are then perpetuating state ideologies as they coach their children and pack the perfect school lunchbox.[8]

There is a distinction between children's lives as ideologically significant (as in, "children are the nation's future") and children's lives as given shape by ground-level cultural and institutional definitions, in families and schools. The trickle-down from adults' lives, constrained themselves by institutional demands such as out-of-town job postings, 200-percent role overload, and the multiple conflicts of a postpatriarchal three-generation household, have profound effects on children, as we will see. The critique of family has most publicly focused on its effects on children, including the influence of parental "absenteeism," or the intensification and distortion of parenting created by the examination system. Less discussed are the influences of peer culture, marketing, and new media technologies. Dangerously, these technologies place children outside the safety range of family values.

Here we consider the lives of children framed by families. The size of modern families may relate directly to the high value society places on children. Indeed, one reason families are small is that each child is an important and unique link to the future of household and nation (the number of children in modern families and the contested meanings children bear come up for discussion later).

At their birth, children redefine all members of a household, who thenceforth are called "father," "mother," "grandfather," "grandmother," "aunt," and "uncle" as well as (older) sister and brother. This naming from the child out is so ingrained that couples without children may have to invent terms self-consciously for each other or use terms they had created themselves during courtship or avoid using any terms of address for one another—and may refer to their in-laws as "uncle" or "aunt," at least until a grandchild comes along. The phenomenon is evidence of the identity-conferring powers of bearing and rearing children, which may for many be the main rationale for marriage.

Young women wanting to have children eventually may wait to marry until biology determines the date. To them, the decision to marry has little to do with marital companionship, romance, or even sex and more to do with the sense of incompleteness they might feel without a child. In a survey conducted in 1993 by the Economic Planning Agency, 19 percent of those polled said that "child-raising is part of becoming a full-fledged adult" and 11 percent said that childless couples "were unfortunate in not experiencing child-raising."[9] In 1999, in response to the question, "should married couples have children?," 20 percent of women ages eighteen to thirty-nine and 10 percent of men of the same ages said no.[10] Though a young Japanese woman may not say "I want to start a family" as her American counterpart does, she usually sees childbearing as closely connected to marriage. In spite of the above opinions, almost all people marry by the age of forty and most eventually have children.[11] The majority have their first child within four years of getting married. In the Japanese case, it is not necessarily even the young reporter's idea of continuing an ancestral line, but having a child in the most role-defining, personal, ego-enhancing sense. Having a child gives them cultural value, a known if difficult set of fulfilling tasks, and of course love and companionship.

Not having a child then means not only a lack of cultural "place," role, and task, it also means very serious personal experiential loss. In spite of this, more people, singly and in couples, are choosing not to procreate and the no-child condition is only one of the ways in which some contemporary families deviate from the norm. Before examining further the still anomalous experience of no-children, let us return to the normative experiences of child rearing.

IKUJI AND CONSTRUCTIONS OF MOTHERING

An only child raised in a small household represents to older people a great distortion. *Ikuji*, the Japanese word for child raising, implies the whole environment of child nurturance that in the past included a larger household, more adults, and other children—siblings or cousins—with whom a child had contact. No child-rearing expertise or official information outside the family governed interactions between children and elders. While the immediate community did have power to guide a family, in general, a child's experiences and relationships were a private matter.

"Self-reliance," now a curricular goal, was achieved in such a family when a child was left to make his own way in the neighborhood or with responsibilities for the care of a younger sibling, for example. Today self-reliance must be more deliberately created. Professional expertise has become a sought-after commodity.

Authorities on child rearing whose information helps organize the regimes of children today themselves decry mothers' reliance on their pronouncements. They refer to this as "child-raising neurosis" and say that too much attention to professional advice makes young mothers insecure in their autonomous roles as caregivers. They fear that young women avoid childbearing (or avoid having more than one child) because of their lack of confidence. Raised in a household where their mother did everything for them and where they had no sibling care responsibilities, they may indeed not know what to do with a child. Or they may have a distorted view of the burden if their own mother was particularly possessive. If she took on exclusive responsibility for the household, she did not encourage children to do tasks. The education mama may be a subtype of mothers completely involved with child rearing. Yoshie Nishioka Rice describes the *kosodate mama,* "a mother who totally devotes herself to rearing her children as her exclusive, singularly important responsibility."[12] While the *kyōiku mama* was committed to her offspring's educational credential-gathering, Rice's "child-rearing mother" connected a psychosocial framing of child development to the institutional framing of successful endeavor later and saw emotional and psychological merging as the source of a child's healthy development. This stay-at-home mother bonded with her child through *skinship* (the Japanese-English coinage meaning close physical contact) and nonverbal merging of mother and child in *ittaikan* or one-ness and balanced, positively valenced dependency.[13] The common thread running through descriptions of Japanese women in the 1960s and 1970s suggests that women received as much as they gave in total commitment: they gained a strong core identity from child tending. It is far from the image of anxiety and lack of confidence used to portray the insecure young mother of the late 1990s.

The older model of training through *wakaraseru,* "getting the child to understand," meant a patient long-term strategy of anticipation and understanding of an individual child's proclivities. Ezra Vogel describes this method as engaging the child in her mother's goals through avoiding opposition.[14] It requires confidence and trust in one's ability to anticipate sensitively the child's responses. But the young mother today, thought to lack that confidence, would neither be able to use *skinship* as child training nor have the internal resources and support to use discipline. The result, it appears, is the withdrawn child, fearful and clinging. An absent father and no siblings amplify the negative effect. Older children in such a family, according to Suzanne Vogel, may "act in," staying out of school, developing psychosomatic complaints and possibly acting on their anger and anxiety with physical abuse against their mothers. Unlike American young people who may take their frustrations to the street, "acting out," Vogel says Japanese children bring them home.[15] In Japan, violence within the home more often means abuse of parents than of children. The yielding, unconfident mother is not the *skinship* mother who can, through her own fine-tuned awareness of the child's dispositions, set limits for the child without setting up barriers between her and the child.

Tatara Mikihachiro, a child development specialist and psychoanalyst, has discussed parent abuse syndrome and associates it with educational pressures and frustrations more than with maternal inadequacies. He says that abuse of parents rarely occurs in families not engaged in the competitive entrance examination track.[16] The association of child pathologies with parental failings, particularly those of the mother, is a recent one and there may well be a relationship between this association and the general blame placed on families—for not having more children, for not raising them in a traditional home. Families, heretofore watertight inward-looking units, subject only to village or neighborhood influence, are now the objects of public policy. Commentators refer to social and ideological touchstones and outcomes of child rearing such as filiality, virtuous behavior, and commitment to work and "community." Postwar interest in psychology has given critiques of child rearing a different tone, as parent-child relations are examined, syndromes and pathologies totted up as the failures of families. While most of the attention given to the psychopathological problems of children seems to be focused on women—on "education mamas" such as *kosodate mama* or *kyoiku mama*—men too may be invoked and blamed.

FROM THUNDER FATHER TO SUNDAY FRIEND

In both America and Japan the minimal definition of family has become "mother-and-child"—in America because of the high rate of single-parent families, in Japan because of the exigencies of fathers' work life. Japanese fathers are deeply involved with their children, but those who work away from home, whether on a daily, monthly, or yearly basis, see their children much less than do American fathers. Lacking proximity, they maintain a strong image of what it means to be a father—and engage cultural ideologies of parenthood, as we will see, more than do the present mothers.

Many Japanese psychologists and educators have bemoaned the relative absence of the father from active influence in the environment and rearing of children.[17] From a conservative perspective, the patriarchal household represented a moral framework in which the "thunder father" exhorted and controlled children's behavior through virtuous example and strong discipline. This image is drawn from Confucian texts and from the reported, remembered behavior of elite fathers in the past.[18]

In many families today, father is more an idea—but not a Confucian one—than a present reality. Assigned to another city or out late every night, the once-a-week Dad has been called the Sunday friend.[19] Psychologists now worry that children raised without the regular attention of a father will be overindulged, self-absorbed, and too dependent on mothers. The intensity of mothers' involvement, it is said, undiluted or uncorrected by the presence of another adult, can lead to these psychological and social pathologies.[20] The absent father syndrome represents a key problem among middle-class families: the conflict between family needs and career expectations. However, often commentators and psychologists say fathers are needed at home, blame for the "syndrome" resulting from their absence seems still to land on mothers. At least she is supposed to buffer the child from the worst effects of it.

ARE YOU MY FATHER?

Kawamura Yukio is one of these absent fathers. He is a white-collar worker in his early forties, with two children ages eight and ten. His career in a general trading company began when he was a new recruit just out of college; he felt lucky to have landed a place on the permanent-employment track just before the energy crisis of the mid-1970s created job insecurity for many, though his degree from a prestigious private university in Tokyo would have won him a good position in any case.

The role expectations of the white-collar world and family are nowhere more at odds than in the timing conflict between career and child rearing. For a man on track in family building, the early thirties is the time to marry and have a child, or children. For a woman, the appropriate moment is in her late twenties. Those who have more than one child tend to space them about two years apart, as did the Kawamuras. Doing it on schedule doesn't make it easy, for these peak child-rearing years are also critical years in the career trajectory; the confluence of these two most crucial and demanding streams of responsibility—and valuation—raises the bar high for parents. If both parents work, timing grows even more complex when the demands for cooperation between family and school enlist mothers in school activities as well as home support and strategizing for a child's academic success.

Yukio's company transferred him to their Osaka office for two years when the children, both boys, were five and seven, but the two-year term went by and he is still in Osaka. In this *tanshin funin* (separation because of job transfer), he is not alone: such "broken" homes are the subject of television dramas, advice columns, and many late-night bar conversations between lonely men.

He talks to his wife several times a week by telephone, especially about the children—now about a plan to move the elder to private school for junior high school to try to avoid the worst of examination pressure later. He feels these matters are her decisions and that he is just getting updates from her. She doesn't seem happy on his once-a-month visits home when he brings the laundry home to her. Even at home, he isn't "present": he is so exhausted that he sleeps the weekend away or plays computer games with his sons. She recently told him she's considering going back to work, and not just for more adult companionship—though her autonomy in domestic matters doesn't please her either—since they are running two households, they need her extra income for a retirement nest egg.

When his wife announced her intention to work, Yukio naturally (considering the potential effect on his own work) consulted with his immediate superior in Osaka, who warned him that this is a critical moment and that he should take a tough line with her against this threatened move; Kawamura's own position will be in jeopardy if his absent wife dilutes or doubles what the company sees as her supporting roles because they feel he will become even more stressed knowing she is not totally available to the children. The job transfers most businessmen experience are routine on the usual promotional tracks. Occasionally, however, they mark points at which the worker is judged ready for return to advancement in his "home" city or for more permanent marginal exile. It is a time of anxious ambiguity.[21]

The effect of absent fathers on their wives is less attended to than the problems they create for children, and in any case, seeing women as victims of their husbands' socially approved mainstream career tracks would call into question the structural bedrock of the Japanese economy, its capacity to drive workers' lives. Looking at children creates a more acceptable critical focus, both negative (see what has happened to our children!) and positive (do this for the sake of the children!).

But the children usually feel the strain much less than the parents. *Tanshin funin* creates stress for women: they suffer loneliness, anxiety, and poor physical health. Most of their anxiety is said to be related to children: separated wives felt that children's school performance, problem behavior, and overt delinquency were caused by the absence of fathers. An even clearer correlation exists between absence and mother's anxiety than between absence and children's problem behavior.

Tanshin funin is a very common experience among middle-class families, at least for some time during children's schooling since it results from parallel concern for a continuous career (in school or in an organization). Separation adds to the already considerable strain felt in families about school and work. A functionalist approach to the middle-class Japanese family would emphasize role separation and the independence of husbands and wives from each other in the spheres of domestic and wage-earning work. It might help them manage work and family responsibilities. However, *tanshin funin* experiences belie this, or at least show that role separation does not mean that physical separation will be any easier. But with such an approach, even where its members are experiencing high stress, "family integrity" appears to be undamaged.

As in most families, the Kawamuras need an extra income for their present comforts and future security. The tendency among managers and commentators to call working mothers "independent women" puts them in a category of antisocial "selfish" persons generally decried in Japan. The gap between economic realities and the norms for personal and familial behavior means that even women who *must* work for their families' sake must also bear the burden of defending this non-normative "choice." There are few institutional supports such as after-school programs, or child care. Use of such facilities may be seen as evidence of selfishness, seen as damaging to the child where the proper care of children emphasizes the inseparability of mother and child. The fact that this same inseparability is blamed for the excesses of *kyoiku mama*'s narrow emphasis on credentials, the lack of self-reliance among children, and the perpetuation of antisocial selfishness among the young is an irony not lost on women.

Some companies are now engaging in more family-friendly solutions for the absent-father problem. In some cases, an employee is allowed to forgo the transfer for family reasons, but he must accept a slowdown on promotions in exchange (with the implication that his contribution, if not his work ethic, is limited): in other cases, a certain number of transfers may be rejected, depending on family responsibilities (as for families with more than one small child or with responsibility for an invalid or elderly relative).

Not all fathers who are "absent" see themselves as uninvolved with their children, however. In fact, more fathers than mothers see themselves as bonded to their children. As mentioned above, *ittaikan* (merging, one-ness) of mother and child was taken as the norm and the goal of Japanese mothering by observers for much of the postwar era. More men than women apparently see "one-ness" as valuable in child rearing, and among men, those who participate in child rearing tasks the least value it the most.[22] Togetherness, as imagined by fathers, is not a physical or geographical engagement. They feel close, even merged, without proximity, whereas for mothers, the standards of closeness to children appear to be high and to relate to the *skinship* of physical closeness.

Closeness and merging as a culturally valued aspect of child rearing now seem less matters of philosophy or choice than of history and social structural change, products of the shift to nuclear families, the intensification of the educational process in the 1950s and 1960s, and the lack of attractive extracurricular options for women in those years. "Working mother" families cannot demonstrate such a value, but as in the family-like values created around the middle-class suburban family in the United States, the observed phenomenon of one moment in history becomes the value for the next.

EDUCATION MAMA TO *TENUKI OKUSAN*

Kawamura Yukio's sister-in-law, Yamakawa Masako, is a married career woman with one child. Her husband took a year off in 1993 to care for their child when she went back to work after a year's maternity leave. She seems like a superwoman to her older sister but she says that every day is a struggle. *Their* mother was a full-time housewife and neither of her daughters wanted to take on that role: the older sister always thought she'd go back to work in a sort of J turn—not all the way back in a U to a full-time job, but to a job allowing her to be available to her husband and children; the younger sister thought she could do it all. Neither ever thought of not marrying or of not having children.

Yamakawa Masako is a very organized worker and mother. She is definitely in charge of household schedules and tasks. Her husband is more involved than any man they know in child care but he does little cooking or cleaning. Neither of them has time for PTA meetings and they get regular calls from officers encouraging them to participate. Masako says that if she even went to *one* meeting she would be hounded to take an active part in projects and committees and she'd feel even more guilty. In any case, she says, they are applying to private schools for their son now that their joint income permits.

The role of "no-hands" housewife is neither a joke nor a guilty confession in their house; *tenuki okusan* is just a job description, a fact of life. In fact, very little of the conventional housewife role describes her—neither mothering (she has, since her husband's year off for parenting, become the leisure-time parent or Sunday friend) nor homemaking (although she is responsible for the evening meal), nor representing the family to the community (thus her avoidance of the PTA).

The meals she provides symbolize her style of efficient engagement and of departures from tradition. On Sundays, she makes two or three large and freezable "main" dishes (the idea of a central dish in a meal is a Western concept) such as pasta sauces, stews, and soups and stores them in three-person meal-size portions in the freezer. They have pizza delivered on Friday nights. Western foods, she says, are more conducive to freezing: Japanese foods are labor-intensive and must be served fresh. Perishable items, and ingredients for school lunches, she buys several times a week on the way home from work at a large supermarket. In doing this, she appears to avoid the social aspect of housewifely shopping at small neighborhood-based produce and grocery vendors where everyone is known by name; she also ignores the injunctions of magazines and experts to shop daily as an act of nurturance for the family by serving up high-quality fresh foods. Buying a large American refrigerator-freezer from Sears symbolized her household management strategy. So do her visits to the prepared foods sections of the department store food halls, frequented by *tenuki okusan*, young working women, and men who are away from home on job transfers. She says she would like her son to be like his father, a self-sufficient adult reasonably free of the constraints of gender-role typing, but she also worries that somehow he is being deprived of the indulgences a *really* good mother would provide. For another contemporary mother, raising a daughter this way seems even more problematic.

FROM MOTHER'S HELPER TO *LOLITA*

Daughters *are* different, at least according to Sawako's mother. Sawako is twelve seemingly going on twenty, and she is the youngest of three children, a large family these days. The two boys are in their midteens. Her mother has gone back to work part-time and Sawako is her chief worry.

Until she turned twelve, her mother could rely on her to run errands, wash the rice for the evening meal, and be at home to help with supper when she returned from work and a bit of food shopping. But in the six months since Sawako entered the sixth grade, things have changed. The sixth grade is the last year of elementary school, a significant watershed year presaging more "serious" engagement in junior high school, preparing for high school entrance.

The two older boys are in junior and senior high school and apart from a few incidents in school, in which one of them was bullied by classmates and the other left school in the middle of the day to go to a movie, they have caused no trouble. Sawako's teacher, however, has told her mother that he worries because her school performance is dropping and associates this with her friendships with a "fast" set of girls who, according to the teacher, "dress strangely."

Sawako's school has no strict dress code but her mother knows what "strangely" might mean—skirts too short, socks too loose, pins, and other illicit decorations added to the regulation shirt. Unlike other schools, especially junior high schools, that prescribe hair length and styles, her school has only an informal recognition of acceptable hairdos; though Sawako occasionally streaks her hair with a bleached orangy-brown color, she can wash it out for school. "Fast" girls like her friends have tight-curled permanents or waves covering half their faces, and permanent brown or blonde streaks, not the cellophane gels that allow temporary transformations, "part-time delinquency." These friends never come to Sawako's home. A close friend who does come home with her is not part of the "fast" group, and Sawako's mother heartily approves of her.

The two boys share a room but Sawako has her own. The walls are pinned with music posters, the mirror ringed by small photo-stickers of herself and friends taken in automatic *purikura* (print club) photo-booths, and a bookcase crowded with more stuffed animals than books. Sawako looks genuinely very young for her age but in front of a mirror she practices what teens in the early 1990s called a *burikko* or "false-innocent" look, wide-eyed, with her lower lip thrust into the pout of the *ganguro,* the aggressively made-up girls now stalking city streets. She no longer returns home directly from school and leaves the table quickly after supper to close herself in her room or talk on the telephone.

It isn't clear what Sawako's friends are up to, but her mother worries about *enjo kosai*—teen prostitution or "sexual dating for money." Young girls—not many as young as Sawako, but in junior and senior high school—meet men after school at locations known to both as pick-up sites and get into men's cars or go to love hotels with men often older than their fathers. Girls in school uniforms are said to receive higher fees than girls in street clothes, though an orthodox uniform less often signals sexual availability than a "modified" one (shorter skirt, hair permed, makeup, and, in the trend of the year I met Sawako, exceptionally "loose" white socks, glued to the right height on the leg).

In telephone booths throughout urban Japan printed stickers advertise phone sex in *terekura* or telephone clubs, and they recruit young girls. Many have photographs of provocative or not-so-demure "schoolgirls," some with only a skirt on, some with shirttails out and legs spread. Youth is the draw;[23] laws banning either production or possession of child pornography are weak or nonexistent. A study showed that 97 percent of bookstores and convenience stores surveyed in 1996 sold pornographic portrayals of children in either photographic or cartoon form.[24] Citizens' groups have lobbied to criminalize the production and possession of this material, but there is some reluctance to "legalize morality" and some resistance to establishing legal rights and protections for children.[25]

Though protest groups claim that there is a connection between pornographic output and teen prostitution, it is hard to prove. And when a case does come to trial, the print media themselves manage to reveal (and market) its more lurid conclusions. Accounts of the case of a solitary type obsessed with virtual internet relationships, the owner of a large collection of child pornography and connected to the murders of young girls, drew the public's attention to the larger issues of protection of children. As in the United States, this case also created a discussion focused on the technology-generated isolation and poor socialization of youth in families where "no one is at home."

Sawako is probably not yet at risk for prostitution, though she seems to be aping the dress of girls who look the part—and she says the girls she knows who have gone with men aren't "professional"; she says it's a kind of "play." Her friends say it's interesting: they get money for clothes and gear, and (she thinks) they don't usually have intercourse.

She says what they do is disgusting to her, watching men masturbate or just listening as men say *iya na* (yucky) things to them, but as she, a self-conscious preteen, explains, "you don't have to take off your clothes."

In today's atomized family, teens' secrets can be kept when no one dares ask. Deviance is part of the new public construction of adolescence. Sexuality is a topic families do not commonly undertake to discuss. One grandmother said that "in the countryside before the war everyone knew everything by the age of seven. Here in the city everyone is so modest and secret about sex and kids have to learn from each other, and they are pretty ignorant." Home is now a location of private secrets. Boys too, like Sawako, have secrets and try on "deviant" selves behind closed doors.

AN *ESUTE* FOR *BOTCHAN*?

Without the strong presence of parents of both sexes in the household, children are more vulnerable to fads created by peers and the media. Those include some trends involving gender-bending distortions of earlier images of the good male or female. The media decry the sexualization of young girls—just as they both encourage and decry the fashion to "feminize" young men. Boys, they say, are moving away from "macho" personal styles to the use of cosmetics, facials, the shaving of body hair, and the frequenting of *esute* salons.[26] *Esute* (from French, *esthétique*) salons are multipurpose, full-body beauty salons—on a European model—where until recently only young women retreated to have facial and body hair removed, skin toned, and cosmetics "prescribed." Advertisements on television in the early 1990s made such personal care all but compulsory: one ad featured a young man telling a young woman that their relationship has to end—she responds with "Give me thirty minutes," rushes to an *esute* salon, and has a full makeover, returning to the young man who immediately vows eternal love. In another ad, the young man kicks a slatternly looking young woman out of bed and sends her to an *esute*. In the late 1990s, young men began to engage in self-improvement through elaborate body care.

Gender identification is strong as an aspect of social role playing and place in society, but now specific personal and psychological identifiers of gender are more fluid. Though trends appear to be crossing gender lines, it is not a unisex model of personal style or gender identity that prevails: trends continue to stress distinction. Thus, character and attributions of "manliness" in the Western sense are less important than the

positioning of males in institutional structures. Ideas about dependency
and autonomy for example, as gender-tagged, are differently related to
masculinity and femininity in the United States and Japan. A man physically and emotionally dependent on his wife, or a boy on his mother,
will not have his masculinity called into question in Japan—and though
"mother's boy" may be an epithet in Japan, it is below the threshold of
name-calling. There is no question as to who wears the pants, at least in
the public sphere.

Conventional wisdom in Japan says that girls learn their future role
and tasks from their mothers, boys, especially eldest sons, from fathers.
Traditionally they learned by direct observation the trade or occupation
they would inherit. In child-rearing manuals of the eighteenth and early
nineteenth centuries, parents were told that at the age of "reason" (about
seven years of age) boys should be placed under the direction of males
in the household, to be disciplined and taught what they needed to know.
In some parts of rural Japan, the lessons would be taught by older boys
to the younger in a community "youth house" where boys lived together
in an age-based hierarchical social world of their own.[27] What growing
up for males now means in Japan may not be related to obvious markers: turning twenty years of age, at Coming of Age Day, means little. Getting a job still does not imply full manhood. Marriage has power to confer adult status, but fatherhood has more.[28]

On the way to job and fatherhood, there is school. Study is indeed the
lot of many urban middle-class children, and to boys especially, attending a *juku* (to cram, along with others) may allow them the only social
life they have away from home. At home, mother's presence—patrolling
the child's studies or not—may be all there is, and the atmosphere can
be socially and perhaps developmentally limiting (depending on the theory of self-development).

As boys grow up in Japan, with relatively low self-sufficiency and independence, they may strike an outsider as psychosocially retarded. In
Japan, however, the classic image of the *botchan*—the slightly irresponsible, boyish, protected son, a person in the child position whatever his
actual age, happily careless in his habits, knowing his mother or wife
will pick up after him—doesn't denote an unmanly young man. This image persists but has given way to a knowing, cosmopolitan style—at least
away from home. Shifting from dependency at home to responsibility at
a workplace is not as striking a shift for a Japanese man as it would appear to be for an American. A man at work is responsible to others and
cooperates in a wider dependency web of relationships—what Jeannie

Lo notes as the *shigarami* of workplace relationships.[29] The personal assertion of male leadership and authority are even less relevant to contemporary married life, where the division of labor, though gendered, is largely uncontested and where being at home means being dependent, unless you are the woman of the house.

This configuration of the male role leaves a lot of room for personality differences, including attributes that in America might be seen as "unmasculine." Older people may scorn as "trend slaves" or as "decadent" the young men who engage in "feminizing" uses of *esute* makeup or skin treatments and who shave their chests smooth. They are not, however, expressing concern about the young men's sexual orientation.

BONBON BOY

Dai Kimura is a nineteen-year-old college student attending a private university in Tokyo. His father is an insurance company executive, his mother a freelance writer. He is sandwiched in age between two sisters, the elder of whom works for a marketing company. Dai does not yet know what he wants to do after college; he assumes he'll get a job but so far has no preference. Like his father, he enjoys rock music; like his mother, he writes; and like his older sister, he designs his own deliberately ripped, patched, and generally eccentric clothes. But there the affinities stop. He spends little time at home, going to rock clubs with his friends, writing science fiction in a coffee shop near his college. The clothes he makes (clumsily but with passion) are interpretations of his fictional outer space characters' garb, for *kosupure* or "costume play" in the vernacular of youth; not exactly daily streetwear. On weekends he spikes his hair with beeswax and gel, stripes his eyelids with color, and dons blue and silver nail polish.

Like many college students, Dai lives with his family—or at least changes his clothes, stores his gear, and mostly sleeps at home. He doesn't eat with his family but sometimes with his older sister, who often comes home as late as he does. *Botchan* doesn't quite describe him, although his family is reasonably well-off and he seems removed from the practical side of life. A current colloquialism may apply better: *bonbon* refers to a son of wealthy family, equivalent to the "suburban prince" in America, someone who, if not born with a silver spoon in his mouth, is not preoccupied with finding a promotional path. Far from a careerist, Dai appears to feel entitled to his pleasures.

His sisters tease him about his clothes and makeup. They don't have the same freedom to experiment and express themselves in public as a young man during the college years has, before the responsibilities of life kick in. The higher the status of her family, the more the young woman is constrained by the *ojoosan* (young-lady-of-the-house) or *hakoiri musume* (daughter-in-a-box) models of deportment: as women of my mother's generation and protective Japanese mothers today might observe, "Girls have to be more careful."

Dai's maternal grandmother contributes most to his pocket money, enabling many of his aesthetic and sartorial pursuits. She lives in the same household but in a separate wing built originally for her and her husband (his mother is an only daughter and thus the one responsible for her parents' care), but grandfather has since died. Obaasan is healthy and active, cooks for herself and occasionally the children, who frequently eat at her place or drop in on her for treats. She is happy to be close to her daughter and happier by far than some of her peers, who have been called "thrown-away grannies." Dai is the apple of her eye; even with purple eye shadow, he can do no wrong.

CHILDREN FOR FAMILIES, OR FOR THE NATION?

Japanese people value the presence of children. Covert pronatalists may overlook this point as they worry about the low birthrate. The issue is not why there are no children, but why people delay marriage or do not marry. As we will see, the rates of children born to women of reproductive age, between fifteen and forty-nine years of age, are indeed low, at about 1.3 children per woman. But if we look at the rate of children born to married couples, it is closer to the desired rate, at 2.2. Having children is for most people the reason to get married, but marriage itself may be such a constrained state that it itself represents a barrier to the desired outcome of children.

The families that have been dismembered—literally, in which the component members have been separated in function, geography, affiliation, and sentiment, and in which dysfunction and disillusion are said to characterize their current conditions—are, of course, more than the sum of these parts. It would not do to ignore the gloomy negativism of commentators or intimate that harangues about families' responsibility for their children's moral alienation and the decline of Japanese society are just a Japanese cultural habit or political expedient. For the fact is that ordinary people do feel disjointed, guilty, and constrained in their relationships and familial engagement. But they do not appreciate interference with choices and options in family affairs. Daughters-in-law told by local bureaucrats that they'd best quit work to care for an aged parent-in-law at home are rarely pleased to comply with this "social policy"; nor are mothers happily compliant who are told by managers that their children's education will suffer if they take on more than part-time work. Top-down social adjustment has rarely been popular or effective in Japan. What people lack are the means for actualizing choices and options. And they cannot finesse what they do not have into compliance with social policies (whether these are explicit or implied) or agreement with the fundamental ideologies that buttress them.

To return to my exchange with the journalist that began this chapter, the visceral understandings of family in Japan are not fragmented, temporary, or residual: they are extensive, continuous, assumed, inclusive of generations, and larger than individuals. It is children who help focus this family and who engage policymakers at least rhetorically. *Kodomo-tachi no tame ni*—for the sake of the children—gets the policymaker or politician's foot in the door. What is good for children is less clear to policymakers or parents than how important children are. Professional experts offer complicated, mixed messages to guide families in raising successful children. The efforts of psychologists suggest emotional supports for children, whose central place in Japanese families has not protected them from risk, and demand more of families in availability and guidance. The efforts of educators both engage families in the work needed to help children succeed academically and call for family support and solace against the rigors of examination hell. Those policymakers concerned with the shrinking family supply working mothers with daycare facilities; these same policymakers also strongly abhor latchkey children and parental absenteeism.

In corporations, the term *marugakae* (total embrace) means the total package of employee-friendly benefits the postwar model of a large paternalistic organization was supposed to deliver. A similar image of a "total embrace" family with several adults available to children, and explicit values organizing daily life at home and in school and workplace cannot contain the social and economic realities of ordinary lives. To keep up such an imagined family at the turn of the twenty-first century requires the flexibility and options that existed in real families before officials waved images of modern middle-class families before the population, implying but simultaneously denying choices and options for the "democratic, individualistic" family.

Francis Fukuyama, in *The End of Order*, refers to "The Great Disruption" (which, he says, began in 1965) as a starting point for discussing the shattering of modern society. By this he means the collapse of the family, whether nuclear or extended, and he—along with many conservatives—chronicles its demise, associating the fall of the family with poverty, child abuse, crime, and related ills. But unlike more conventional conservative critiques, which lay these ills at the feet of the welfare system and feminism, Fukuyama instead targets reproductive choice and women's entry into the labor market as reasons for the family's demise and the consequent disasters outlined above. His reasoning is that now women can control their own bodies and do not need the intervention of men to have children and support them. Men thus no longer feel responsible for the children they father, and all social and economic obligations enforced in traditional codes fall away.

This is not an indictment of women or men alone, but Fukuyama feels that change for the better can only come from supporting men—and he refers to Japan as a case where such support is available to men. Fukuyama cites wage inequities in favor of men, divorce laws discouraging women from leaving their husbands, and insecure employment for women as factors in stabilizing families. He writes, "If Western countries were to reintroduce discriminatory labor laws that kept women out of labor markets and did not permit them to earn comparable wages to men, then the resulting dependence of women on male incomes would probably help to restore traditional two-parent families."[30] He does helpfully add, "needless to say, this is not a real policy option," and he points instead to American women who engage men to father their children without supporting them as a causal factor in the misuse of welfare, the lack of incentive to men to work and act responsibly. He praises Japanese women, who give men, he says, their place and their responsibilities and thus stabilize both family and nation.

Similar arguments might well be in the ideological background of conservative policymakers' considerations in Japan. If so, they are not explicit. Rather, the vexed issue of children and family in the media and policy circles in Japan stems from the construction of modernity—reaching back to the 1898 Civil Code. It demanded a uniformity of family performance unrealistic, unsuitable, and in fact, impossible to maintain either according to the agenda of Confucian nation-building or according to the postwar ideal of a state based on democratic and individualistic family life. Paradoxically, if family-friendly policies were actually to tolerate the range of realities in which people live instead of demonizing them, people would be able more nearly to approximate the families that policymakers hope to create.

Ken-chan of our epigraph is the center of his mother's life: she has unconditionally and unequivocally put him first since he was born eight years ago. He is a bright child, passionate about music, learning about the world, and studying English. He is, according to his mother, already a "ladies' man." His father is equally available, as he is an academic with a small consulting firm and from the start has cared for his son, cooked, and cleaned house. But within the family unit the relationship between Ken and his mother is still central. Her engagement is not diluted by her career or by her wish "to fly." This tiny unit, the "we all three" household, is an example of the reduced and thus amplified family: the bare minimum of mother, father, child can fulfil family functions as culturally prescribed: economic support to a household, procreation, and social and educational support to a child to reproduce parental status. In emotional terms, this family is close and successful. It condenses these functions and intensifies the third one: Ken-chan is the rationale of his parents' marriage. The three of them translate the reciprocity principle of Confucian "family values" into a twenty-first-century version: parental engagement amply repaid by the ability the child has to validate his parents' marriage psychologically and socially.

Children are wanted, even in a nuclear household of two. Children are not, however, "like the air" as they were once said to be: ordinary, normal events in the life of the extended family and the future heirs to the lineage. They are problematic to the extent that fewer of them will be present in the labor force to support the large population of elderly that baby boomers will soon become. Children are elemental, necessary to the state and to families: on this there is agreement. But what must be done to encourage families, as they try to cope with child rearing and the other demands on them, is subject to debate and politics. In an economy with insufficient resources to inspire reproduction, the cry "for the sake of the children" loses its appeal. Still, it has a more positive ring in families than does "for the sake of the elderly"—which is what the encouragement of childbearing is now, in part, about.

Life Choices for Women and Men

The Bounded Realities of Reproduction

Yanagihara Kazuko, the mother of two sons thirteen and ten years old, sat on a curb in front of the Hawaii Prince Hotel at the yacht basin in Honolulu, surrounded by supporters protesting a yacht race on August 3, 1998. Ten years earlier, Kazuko had been dismissed from the Japanese company sponsoring the race, a manufacturer of audiovisual electronic goods such as video players. She had been working for the company for thirteen years and was pregnant with her second child. Her boss had tried to get her to resign. Finally, the company ordered her transfer to a location necessitating a long commute from her home; when she refused the order, she was fired. Having lost a judgment from the Tokyo District Court, who claimed that she could have accepted the transfer and that she was under an obligation to obey the company's order, she took the case to the public. She recognizes that she is in for the long haul of "bullying" the company through public demonstrations such as this one. Surrounded by banners and supporters—including her husband—handing out leaflets in English and Japanese, Kazuko tries to raise consciousness during a festive sporting event supported by the company that, as she says, continues to harass her and to discriminate against women employees and their families. She says that because of her and the campaign, the company is known in Japan as the "enemy of working women."

Feminist protests in the 1920s against the traditional patriarchal household system of the Meiji era saw the family as the enemy of women's interests. Their counterparts today claim that the race sponsor and companies like it perpetuate the oppressive practices of the Meiji-period family. While the fact that men play a structurally less dominant role in a middle-class household limits familial patriarchy, it has continued to have an effect on women's lives. The classical Confucian model demanded obedience to fathers, husbands, and sons within families; now workplaces, social institutions, and policies reinforce a gender bias. Behind these corporate perspectives, the model for women's lives is not Confucian but middle-class, assuming a functional distinction between men's and women's roles in the family.

This indirect patriarchy institutionalizes a form of family roles that seem socially, economically, and culturally archaic. Employers and personnel managers, not husbands and mothers-in-law, are invoking family ideology. Young women before marriage and mothers reentering the workforce may have no choice but to play along with the hegemonic vision of family life, the office version of the "good wife/wise mother" formula. The employment and family policy agenda of the public and private sectors in Japan focus on women and project an image of disunited, fractionated relationships at home.

This chapter looks at women and men who are not at war with each other in principle or in the details of daily life. Except perhaps for their employers, the women I interviewed for this study almost universally refuse to indict particular men as impediments in their lives. Fathers, husbands, and sons, they say, were either remote and neutral or engaged with them in their struggles. Younger men especially resist at least some of the work code constraining their lives too, and some support full employment for wives and daughters in professions and careers. Mothers-in-law, generally more traditional than their sons, are less powerful now and may even be allies to the young. In this context, feminism targets systems and institutions rather than the intimate relationships of the home. Younger women's mothers and grandmothers may have had a more direct experience in the prewar years of male domination, but these encounters with power now take place for the most part outside the family.

The contradictory understanding that women are the prime movers of family life, and that their very importance to it may simultaneously disenfranchise or limit them, imbues family life in Japan today. Often the only choice is to engage this contradiction and live with the fallout of juggled child care, midnight housework, or "late" marriages without children. Women who are unmarried and childless at thirty-five might be said to have been unlucky, thoughtless, or just "locked out of the marriage market." Only a few have literally chosen between family and career. The two roles appear mutually exclusive: a *kosodate mama* (child-rearing mama) sees her life as incomplete without children and clearly distinguishes herself from younger women still unmarried or choosing not to bear children at all.[1] In contrast, a career woman must meet, to some degree, her organization's expectations or become an entrepreneur and work for herself.

Living away from the parental roof is the first step toward independence, avoiding the dependency of the "parasite single." Mortgages for unmarried home buyers were only available after 1981 and even then, the buyer had to be over forty years old. Now that 50 percent of women in the twenty-five to twenty-nine age group are unmarried, and some are quite well able to purchase or rent single-person housing, things have changed.[2] Real estate companies (some run by women) now focus on the single woman looking for urban apartments or buying "mansions"—condominiums for long-term solo residence.

One of the factors that women consider in the "choice" to marry and to have children is the management of family. It encompasses the organization of family around the demands and resources of institutions outside the home such as workplace needs, schooling imperatives, and the limits of social services for dependent family members. Women are still the managers, doing research on schools, hospitals, and nursing care and they are the ones who provide filial care of the elderly and, now, economic support. Paradoxically, the image-making powers of institutions frame women as mothers sine qua non yet as producers too, thus keeping them single and working longer, having fewer children, and raising the ones they have in often anomalous, countercultural arrangements.

Because the norms and institutions of motherhood diverge sharply from the realities of women's roles as mothers, we look first at examples at odds with official policies.

Mariko is twenty-eight, a part-time worker in an insurance company. She is older than the other women in her section, who are mostly in their early twenties and unmarried. When Mariko married at twenty-two, she had already been working for almost two years at this company, a full-time "office lady" at that time. Most of the OLs the company hired from her generation were, like Mariko, junior college graduates, but now the company is shifting to recruiting women from four-year colleges. Although she knows her employers prefer the younger, full-time clerical workers, there are many more married women in positions like hers now than there were when she began and, in theory, the Equal Employment Opportunity Law protects them. Her husband's mother cares for her two-year-old son during the mornings, and Mariko tends to arrive home by the end of the child's midday nap. Her husband is a foreman in a machine tool plant, the eldest son of a shopkeeping family. They live with her in-laws. The family hopes he will inherit the shop and quit his factory job when his parents retire. Mariko hopes they can live independently of his parents some day, and most of her income goes toward the purchase of an apartment of their own, the subject of dispute within the family.

Shizue is thirty-five, a divorced mother of two, living with her parents and working full time in a fashion design company. She is college educated and has worked for several years as a graphics designer. Her parents have a small house in the suburbs of Osaka, so she and her two children share one room in their house. The children are in school in the neighborhood and get themselves back and forth to school. The elder, a boy, does errands when he gets home and makes tea for his grandmother, who is crippled with rheumatoid arthritis. Shizue hopes her younger child, a daughter, will soon relieve him of these duties so that he can study for exams to enter a private high school, an "escalator" school making entrance to a private university relatively smooth. Her evenings are spent helping her mother, cooking, and coaching her children in their homework. She laughs when asked about her "social life."

The issues these two women and this book address affect the family as a whole but often are assumed to be part of the problem women's choices cause. Mariko and Shizue are not wildly deviant cases. They are two rather ordinary examples of the diverse lives women lead and of the influences that create their choices for them. The dilemmas of policy and behavior surrounding families in Japan come down to the definition of family as "women's domain" and the assumption that responsibility for its success or failure remains in the hands of women. The less institutional support for women in their domestic roles, rather than exhortations to uphold Japan's uniquely "beautiful family traditions," the harder their task.

WORK AND GOOD WOMANHOOD

The epithet "working woman" is scarcely a new phenomenon. The career woman character in the soap opera *Poka Poka* described in the introduction to this book is a recent version of an old story. When work drew young women from the countryside to the textile factories in the early twentieth century, parents supported them (or even sent them), since filial daughters helped their families through their wages. In family businesses, whether tiny food stalls or large factories, women most definitely are needed and can even inherit and run such businesses. The difference is that these women are clearly working for the sake of their families. Professional or career women are different, it seems. They have almost invariably had university education extending parental investment in their independence, have delayed marriage beyond the prescribed timing, and now compete with men on the same occupational tracks. This is not the image of filiality a working woman was in the past supposed to project.

In the late 1980s women spent on average eight years in the wage-earning labor force (excluding piecework at home or nonwage family enterprise work), while women today may spend up to twelve years working after high school and before their first children are born. Most women today enter the labor force after finishing high school, junior college, or four-year college and continue until marriage or, increasingly, into marriage and after the birth of a child. The age groups of women most likely to be in the workforce include women between twenty and twenty-four (for college graduates) and forty-five and forty-nine, but the twenty-five to thirty-nine age group (when women are most likely to be bearing children) is fast increasing in the workplace (figure 3). More than two thirds of mothers are "working mothers"—a rate higher than that in the United States. The types of work these women do varies with the ages of their children. A third of those with children under six work, two-thirds of mothers with children seven to fourteen years of age work and over two-thirds of mothers of children between ages fifteen and seventeen are in the workforce.

Of working mothers it appears that about a third, especially including those with young children, work part-time (part-time workers in Japan comprise more than 20 percent of the total labor force and women are more than 70 percent of this pool).[3] There is an increasing tendency to work continuously, for reasons of choice and necessity, though only one half of women who are married work full time.[4] And the Japanese economy needs women in both roles, mother and worker. Work for

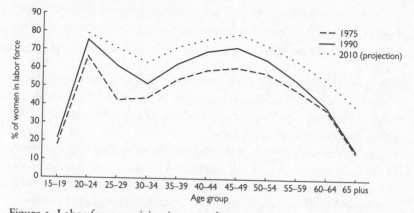

Figure 3. Labor force participation rates for women, 1975–2010: the M-curve. Data for 1975, 1990 from Sumiko Iwao, *The Japanese Woman* (New York: Free Press, 1993); projection for 2010 from *Economisto,* July 20, 1993, 29.

women helps them support the economy as consumers and gives employers flexibility in managing the labor force.

Corporations favor "contingent workers"—part-time working women, defined socially by another role than work—because their "flexible" work lives suit corporate needs. Women still rarely claim unemployment stipends when laid off and in any case do not qualify for most company benefits as part-timers. They are thus low cost and they can be hired in good times and fired in bad.

Women's jobs are for the most part service positions supporting men's work. In spite of the "female" definition (part-time, temporary, non-seniority-based) of their work, it demands serious commitment. The serious commitment may vary, however, depending on the worker, her office environment, and whether she is in a blue-, white- or pink-collar position. As Yuko Ogasawara has demonstrated, many young women workers cannot or do not take their work so seriously.[5] The pink-collar corporate "flowers" who decorate and serve the white-collar premises of most organizations file and perform other clerical tasks alongside men whose tea they pour. The OL's work appears to be an extension of the traditional familial role as service provider but is now rarely part of a woman's nuclear family life, much less an aspect of her relation to her husband than of her relation to men at the office. The work is not meant to be fulfilling or, it might be said, to produce a commitment to continue working. In fact, it is intended to end with a woman's acceptance of her role as wife and mother.

Dissatisfaction on the job will only make the role of housewife look good by comparison and rarely has produced protests, even after the promulgation of the Equal Employment Opportunity Law in 1986. But young OLs may perform acts of subversion, as Ogasawara shows, to show their ability to control men for whom they work, including work slowdowns, leaving the office at critical moments, or on one notable occasion, deliberately spoiling the required chocolates before sending them to their bosses on Valentine's Day.

Leaving the office *exactly* at the end of a workday may be a statement, but it is also an aspect of the separation of male and female work. Women's workdays are short relative to men's schedules, allowing them greater participation in consumption and less in the work that "counts," men's after-hours socializing. The 1986 Equal Employment Opportunity Law nullified the labor protection laws that had prevented late-night work for women and for most noncareer jobs, but the custom of letting women workers leave first continues largely undiscouraged. Women leave first, shop most, and return home to their "second shift."[6]

Shibata Tokue, a commentator and city planner, notes that the gender division in labor patterns is highly visible in the engendered "rush hours" of Tokyo: every workday women tend to leave the large corporate headquarters and governmental bureaucracies at around 5 P.M., a pattern that empties the center of the city of female workers and collects them at the major commercial hubs such as Shibuya and Shinjuku, a few stops out from the center. There they shop or browse at the department stores that cater to young fashionables as well as working housewives— the former cruising the clothing floors, the latter picking up prepared foods in the subterranean food halls. The unmarried ones often go together to restaurants—either among the top-floor array in any department store or smaller, more chic establishments in entertainment quarters nearby. From these hubs the women fan out further. The housewives head home quickly, by 6 P.M., on the next set of suburban trains and buses, followed an hour or more later by the younger ones, usually to their parents' homes with a packet of elegant pastries or some fruit expressing the "guest" quality of their co-residence with their parents. Men follow this path a few hours later as they evacuate the financial and business center of the city. They usually do not shop but add rounds of bar and noodle-stall hopping before the final bus or train home. At the very last station on their path, they may also buy flowers or fruit for their families, perhaps to expiate their guilt at being late. These station-area shops stay open late for the purpose of "family harmony," as one man said. The human geography of the center-periphery emptying of the city is thus predictable by sex, age, and work status. And the consumer and entertainment industries orient themselves around this pattern.[7]

Women consumers are critical to the Japanese economy, even if their power to buy relies to some degree on "doubling" their roles. Before they have children, young working wives are not considered to be "doubling" their roles as much as working mothers are. A woman who works at the cost of ignoring her husband is not as damnable as one who appears to ignore her children's welfare.

Men's work conventionally creates no split commitments and women may encourage its singularity. A good husband is "healthy and absent," as the saying among middle-aged women goes. The "Cinderella Mrs." (as she is called) who rushes back home to scullery duty before her husband's arrival is becoming rare; the wife of a retired man might treat her stay-at-home husband like a "big bag of garbage." The current generation of young men may be more self-sufficient when they reach retirement, especially if they have had independent lives *before* marriage, untended by their mothers. They may know how to cook and clean for themselves and some may even enroll in special cooking classes for men.

Young women today have been educated in a far more "unisex" environment than were their mothers. The rates of completion of higher education by women have steadily climbed, now reaching about 40 percent of college-age people, indicating strong parental support. Higher education for girls may for some amount to credentials for marriage,[8] but the opening of career options increases the value of higher degrees for women. For most women, however, higher education means two-year junior colleges and specialized training schools such as beauty academies or secretarial schools. Women show rising rates of enrollment in four-year schools and, more significantly, rising rates of earlier participation in examination-preparation classes—a hint that parental investment in children is becoming more equal.

There is still a marked difference in the product of this investment. An access and wage gap separates men and women, in spite of the Equal Employment Opportunity Law, which specifies that employers may not discriminate against women in setting a retirement age or dismiss them if they marry or get pregnant. This law requests employers to endeavor to recruit, hire, and promote women equally and, in 1990, backed up its guidance with some penalties for noncompliance. Moreover, women who desire this "equality" must make the same commitment to their work as men do, effectively preventing them from motherhood as it is now configured.

The current "ice age" in women's employment chances refers to the deep freeze for women whose educational credentials are as high as those that gain men access to good jobs.[9] What empowers men in the job market may well have the opposite effect on women. Further, tax laws have discouraged many women from full-time or well-paid work. Often it makes financial sense for a wife to keep her salary below ¥1 million ($9,000) per year. If she does, the couple pay no tax on her income and, in addition, the husband can get a ¥570,000 spousal deduction. In spite of this institutionally imposed ceiling, women are seeking more rewarding work. Some workplaces allow women to move from part-time to full-time work and occasionally from the noncareer track to specialized career positions after a few years of clerical work. The shift to supervisory work may still involve some gender bias, however, as the management jobs women are likely to hold are in public relations, customer service, and personnel, where human relations (good work for women) are part of the job description.[10]

WORKING THE DOUBLE SHIFT

Where job security and a full benefit package within a company are not available to women, they may seek improvement by changing jobs. For men, job changing has been a trend since the early 1990s but shifting jobs might still indicate to more mainstream employers a "nontraditional" work ethic. Women have less to lose and may risk changes for better salary and status, better hours and working conditions, and, as one said, a "better match with my skills." There is some indication that work satisfaction for women depends more on the content of the work itself, for men more on the status of the organization.[11]

In any case, women stay on their salaried jobs—on the *same* job—through marriage and child rearing in increasing numbers. As we saw in figure 3 (page 127), the M-curve has begun to flatten out, as 50 percent of women who work between the ages of twenty-five and thirty-nine do *not* stop working for housewifery or child rearing, yielding an annual rise of 2 percent staying on the job. The age of women who leave (presumably) for child rearing continues to rise, as does the age of those who retire from the workforce. And in contrast to the claim that women in the earlier postwar generation stayed home, forsaking work for pregnancy and childbirth, data gathered by the Ministry of Labor in the mid-1970s noted that only 36.7 percent of pregnant women or women who had recently given birth retired from work: 63.3 percent did not.[12]

WORKING AND CARING FOR ANGELS

The Equal Employment Opportunity Law seems to promise fulfilling work for women; the Angel Plan, established in the mid-1990s, seems to promise to support the working mother: both promises are unfulfilled. The Angel Plan's intention was to create more places in day-care centers for the children of working mothers, but while the earlier stigma attached to letting nonfamily members raise children has faded, the high cost and scarcity of really good child care still presents a barrier to many: what is "good" child care of course undergoes the same scrutiny as "good womanhood" does.

In 1999 additional funding was added to the Angel Plan allocated for child-rearing support; placement of day-care centers near commuter train stations was a priority of this new initiative. Small child-care allowances previously given for children under three years of age were extended to children under five. These ($50 per month for children nos. 1 and 2 and $100 per month for children nos. 3 and on up) are "almost an insult," according to one mother.

Public child care is on the whole quite good. For young children, there are usually three caregivers and sometimes a full-time nurse for a group of ten children. Daily reports are sent to parents including what the child ate, if he or she napped, and something about the mood of the day. Such attentiveness does not resolve structural problems. The center's day is often not long enough for some working mothers, and extending day care beyond the closing time of 6 P.M. is proposed. There are also not enough places for the demand: wait lists for such programs, especially for infants, are very long. And the moral ambiguity involved in using such facilities is sometimes hobbling to mothers who feel the stigma of accusations of "warehousing" their children.

The bottom-line question in the lives of working women is "who will care for my child?" Both Mariko and Shizue have struggled to care for their children. A dearth of child-care facilities that meet the stringent standards women and professional experts share has forced working mothers to construct complicated systems of child-care support. One mother told of her patchwork program for her child: "I take my child to a neighbor's house at 7 A.M. and she takes her, with her own child, to the nursery school at 8:30. At 2:00, the two children are picked up by my sister who takes them home until I get there at 6 P.M. and then I take the neighbor child and mine home to my house and wait for my neighbor to come home after supper, in time to put her child to sleep." If any link in this chain were to fail, some woman's work will be at risk.

The media do create poster women for mothers, however. Matsuda Seiko, the popular singer, did not retire at the birth of her child and took only a short maternity leave before resuming her stage and recording work. A television personality, Agnes Chan, in the late 1980s practiced *kozure-shukkin,* or "taking-a-child-to-work." Meant to point up the shortfall in child-care facilities, her act, like Matsuda's resumption of her career, generated a mostly negative response from the media: in a spate of "Agnes-bashing" she was called a *geinojin* (show business) feminist, and a bad mother.

Women who work and raise children have multiple concerns well beyond the predictable shortage of time and energy or the need to "juggle" responsibilities, compromise, and patch their lives together in the face of unpredictable events. In addition, their work lives are less secure and less financially rewarding than men's, as they rarely earn "permanent employment," or job tenure. Further, mothers of young children are under strong pressure from the *seken,* the watchful community of relatives and neighbors, to do the right thing by their children, meaning, to devote themselves to their children's future as the educational system and social parameters narrowly define it. And finally, where there is a dependent (ill or elderly) adult to be cared for, the woman of the family is the one who must accommodate their needs. The Golden Plan and its later corollaries were established in the 1990s to support family-based care of the elderly. Ultimately, however, these state-sponsored programs depend on the "beautiful Japanese traditions" of family that in turn usually depend on a female caregiver.

Intensifying the stresses caused by employment policies is the bottom-line economic need for most women to work. For many families, it now takes two incomes to maintain a middle-class lifestyle. Ironically, women who leave the homemaker role to keep the family middle class maintain the postwar image that persists in media, advertising, and consumer culture. The double shift is a double bind, for the 1992 Family-Care Leave Act (providing 60 percent of salary for a parent or caregiver who stays home for one year) does not solve a family's economic problems. A few men have taken family leave, and indeed fathers with children are more visible in playgrounds, parks, and zoos (if only on weekends) than at any time in the past. However, fewer than 40 percent of fathers have (ever) changed a baby's diaper—or put children to bed.[13] The Ministry of Health and Welfare hopes to engage fathers through a poster campaign: a 1999 poster read, Any Man Who Doesn't Raise His Children Cannot Be Called A Father. Overall, however, family life is still synonymous with "woman" and her absence from home is still a problem.

In 1983 an international conference on women and work was held in Tokyo. One session included presentations on the attitudes surrounding working mothers in several societies. In mine, I summarized popular attitudes affecting Japanese working mothers, noting that in public opinion polls most men and women said that children would suffer if mothers worked outside the home. On a television news program that evening, a synopsis of my presentation was illustrated by a pair of cartoons. In the first, a child sat at a table in an empty kitchen; the clock said 4 P.M.; a tear is falling down his cheek and he holds a poor report card. In the second, the same child sat at the same table with the clock at the same hour, but this time he was smiling, with a healthful snack in front of him, a good report card in his hand, and an aproned mother standing by. The commentator said that the foreign expert on child rearing (myself) advised that children do better when mothers stay home. My report on attitudes was reduced to a reiteration of the attitude itself, given prescriptive weight by an "expert."

New attitudes, or rather, contradictions within older attitudes, do appear in lifestyle surveys. In the 1998 prime minister's office poll, questions about work and family produced a complicated picture. Responses from men showed that 62.4 percent saw their work taking precedence over family or community. (The report failed to ask whether these men felt work *should* take precedence or not.) More interesting was the fact that 45 percent of women who worked gave the same answer. Combining work and family for women broadcast a mixed message: 86 percent of all adults said that "it is acceptable for women to work *as long as they keep up with housework and child-rearing duties*" (italics mine).[14] And a labor force survey on female employees by marital status, issued in April 2001, shows that the large numbers of married women working include those in their child-rearing years (figure 6). Even with the dip in workforce participation among women in their late twenties to mid-thirties, the rate never falls below 60 percent of the female population between the ages of eighteen and fifty-five. Mothers *are* working.

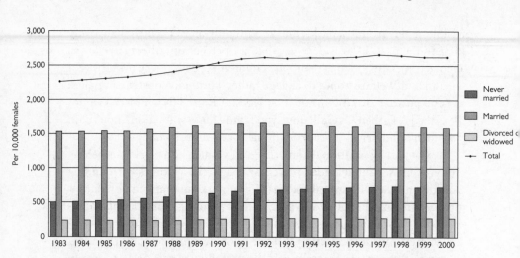

Figure 4. Female employees by marital status, 1983–2000. From Ministry of Public Management, Home Affairs, Posts, and Telecommunications, Statistics Bureau and Statistics Center, Annual Report on Labor Force Survey (April 2001).

THE GOOD CHILD IS MADE, NOT BORN

As we saw in chapter 4, the shorthand version of middle-class child-rearing beliefs is that nurture, not nature, is critical in the creation of a successful child. Environment, rather than innate abilities, makes the difference, and the mother is to provide that environment. By first giving her child physical warmth, safety, and nurturance, then emotional bonding and cognitive stimulation, she inscribes the future on a blank slate. In service to his or her development, no sacrifice is too great. Both Mariko and Shizue are seen as having made choices that put their children at risk by their absence.

You can never start too early: the "Sounds of the Womb," an obstetrician's recordings of the mother's heartbeat and other supposedly comforting sounds heard by a fetus in the womb, was the 1970s extension of the centuries-old tradition of *taikyo*, or learning in utero. With this recording playing from within a stuffed teddy bear in the crib or on a tape deck, a newborn baby could feel secure, as if in the recreated safety of the enclosed womb. In addition to easing the transition from womb to world, new technologies try to ensure the child's successful climb on the academic ladder. The latest is a prenatal English-language learning system, including texts to be read aloud by the mother-to-be into a sort of resonating device strapped to her belly. Women with an older child or a job must struggle to perform such intensive premothering. But the attitude that equates maternal effort and engagement with the success of children is hard to ignore: there is no substitute ideology in the mainstream.

Some women do, however, combine work and this totalistic approach to mothering. Kaji Noriko, a scholar of classical Japanese poetry and professor of linguistics, has one child, a girl. She intends to have no more children, saying that she can barely do a good enough job with Chieko. Chieko at four has a life packed with activities. At two, she was enrolled in a eurhythmics class, a music class, and a playgroup—not to serve as babysitting while Noriko worked, but as part of Noriko's program for the development of social and creative skills in her daughter. She says that the "ante" has been "upped," and that mothers are not talented enough or sufficiently trained to provide such enhancement for their children: they must turn to professionals. Art lessons started for Chieko at three; her works are hung throughout the small apartment. At four, she adds English lessons to the list of *okeikogoto*, enhancement lessons, and she is also in a fine nursery school, to which Noriko applied when the child was born, and for which both she and Chieko were interviewed and tested.

George deVos described what he calls "role narcissism," an intense focus on performance, as essential to the understanding of high standards for both mother and child. Working mothers have to prove themselves and go further, they feel. They are "watched" by their families and peers, by teachers and the wider community, for signs that their work has interfered with effective child rearing.[15] It appears, however, that ideas about effective child rearing have changed slightly. The mother who earlier was noted to be the environment nurturing a child's abilities is now permitted merely to provide (and pay for) that environment. Chieko's talents are handed over to specialists as Noriko works to afford them.

The middle-class postwar model of interdependence and one-ness between parent and child (*ittaikan*) is not the only model of child rearing (see chapter 4).[16] To participate in this model you need to be middle class, able to afford the time and money needed to pay for enhancements, able to be available as coach and support. This is a luxury for people for whom work is a choice, not possible for those who must work.

Harold Stevenson has found that a very different attitude exists among working-class women, who believe less in nurture than in nature—and who tend to see inborn qualities in a child as indicative of the child's future (as we saw early in chapter 4).[17] These working-class women— single mothers, divorced or widowed, women who are raising their children virtually alone because of their husbands' job transfers, or women who have other responsibilities such as the care of a dependent invalid or elderly relative—cannot find enough hours in the day to manage, let alone excel in, the many compulsory agenda in front of them. If they can withstand the dominant ideology, they lighten the burden.

Stevenson's finding is thought-provoking. More data on the class-based conceptualization of child rearing will force us to reconsider the stereotypes about Japanese child rearing ("effort counts more than ability"), class and culture ("Japan is a homogeneous middle-class society") and Japanese mothers ("totally devoted to their children's education"). We must acknowledge variety and diversity in Japan when we consider the lives of women. Middle-class women, who by definition participate at greater rates than working-class women in middle-class institutions such as higher education and the white- (or pink-) collar corporate workplace, find themselves defined, and define themselves, by the standards and measures of these bodies. As Mary Brinton has described them, these women with familial and institutional "stakeholders"—professional experts—to support and direct their lives have a more uniform lifeline and schedule than do women who must struggle to accommodate the contradiction between dominant cultural models and the demands of their socioeconomic niche.[18]

HOLDING STAKES AND FINDING PATHS

To some degree all Japanese women feel the framing power of professional expertise as they struggle to uphold their part at home and in the workplace. There is also a consensus of opinion conveyed in media and institutions delineating and enforcing a path said to ensure the success of life-course events. Unlike the professional experts, this consensus often has no personal connection to women's lives to validate its role. It offers framing concepts that professional experts can invoke and enforce but may also pertain to forces beyond, such as the occupational sector or marketplace. It may surface as the message in magazine articles, advice columns, or consumer advertising. Common sense, in women's day-to-day experiences, may conflict with this message.

At times the exhortations of media and marketers contradict the established expertise of family, community, and workplace. The print media particularly are alert to women's vulnerable identities. Young middle-class women, targeted by magazine publishers as voracious readers and need-to-know consumers, buy and read magazines that cater to their interests and direct their life plans. These magazines see themselves as guides, providing "manuals" with lesson plans for life.

THE *CROISSANT* SYNDROME

Shizuko, a woman in her early thirties, is unmarried. She works in a midsize electronics firm where she has been since she graduated from junior college over ten years ago. She shuns the term "career woman" but, living on her own, with her cat, laughingly says she can't think of what else to call herself. Her parents have given up arranging meetings with prospective spouses, her boss has jokingly threatened to fire her so that she will be "forced" to marry, but he likes and needs her too much to do that. She skis, travels with friends (most of whom are married or planning to marry), and reads a lot. She is *not* a "Ms. Anne-Marie," the slang term for an unmarried women with no man in her life. However, her boyfriend's existence in her life is very low-profile; she referred to him in an interview only once and sees him perhaps once a month.

One example of magazines' influence over young women like Shizuko is the "*Croissant* syndrome." *Croissant,* a women's magazine targeting young working women in their twenties, featured articles on the single woman from the late 1970s to early 1980s.[19] The gist of these articles was that women did not need to rush into marriage and that they might seek other satisfactions from accomplishing professional and leisure goals first—and ignore the pressure to marry. Indeed, by 1985, one out of five women living in Tokyo was still unmarried in her thirties.

Twenty years later, Matsubara Atsuko demonstrated the effect of the message in her book, *Croissant shokugun* (*Croissant* syndrome), in which she describes the single lifestyle these readers of the magazine and their compatriots have chosen—and their apparent unhappiness.[20] The *Croissant* "victims" deeply regretted having missed out on marriage and child rearing, according to Matsubara, though magazines extolling the freedom and career possibilities of singlehood continued to be popular.

The "independence" movement used the voices and lives of women to encourage singlehood or childfree living. Readers' letters were cited, as in the case of one *Croissant* correspondent who said "When I save up ¥5 million, I am going to divorce him!" Biographies of famous single women such as actresses and writers glamorized the independent life. In three years, one hundred such biographies were featured, including the stories of Ichikawa Fusae, an elderly Diet member, Inugai Tomoko, a social critic, and Kirishima Yoko, a well known feminist writer. Nearly all of these had once been married and some had had children, but all were now living alone. They were all well educated, graduating from elite universities, and all had careers or professions. They had thus, to some degree, pursued at least one of the courses professional experts prescribed, including the raising of children. The young woman emulating them and beginning with their endpoint of singlehood might thus miss the fact that most of these women had earlier conformed to society's expectations before launching their independence.

The magazines also extolled international travel and study as a means to fulfillment for middle-class single working women. Foreign universities received many such women who had already worked for two or three years—by 1987, 35 percent of Japanese women studying overseas were OLs in their mid- to late twenties, most past the "ideal" age for marriage. A foreign degree might give them a post facto reason for not having married, according to Matsubara.

As birthrates fell in the 1990s, women's attitudes reflected their involvement in work, careers, and education as well as a lack of trust in men, a lack of satisfaction in family life, and occasionally, an aversion to children. In 1990, a poll among young working women revealed that 15 percent "didn't like children," and 11 percent said they would marry but not have any children.[21]

In response to backlash created by the call for more children, the editors of women's magazines created new models for family life, attempting to make marriage and childbearing palatable for those young women who might be tempted to stay single. Professionalizing homemaking and child rearing through articles such as "a study of frying pans," or "how to survive in the academic success ladder" (on child rearing in the credential-driven society), or "the use of day nurseries" was not new: they recalled "domestic science" articles in the first wave of women's magazines in the 1920s. At the same time, however, articles such as "how to break an engagement" or "marriage is dangerous for women," or "a childless lifestyle" were very compelling.

By the mid-1990s, Croissant and other magazines had begun to reverse the course of their earlier influence, in part as a response to the public concern with the falling birthrate. Mine, a women's magazine similar to Croissant, published an article in 1994 on the rising age of women having their first babies. This article encourages women to have careers—it offers the comforting suggestion that medical technology supports older mothers but still warns that babies of older mothers may be more at risk for medical problems and congenital disorders. The older mother is, it notes, more satisfied, mature, and secure and thus a better mother in the

end. The article seems to hint that having "late babies" is a Western phenomenon, for the cartoon women depicted in illustrations have light
brown or blonde hair and Caucasian features: Western women are useful
models (sometimes cautionary models) of professional independence.[22]

Croissant magazine has turned 180 degrees away from its earlier support for independence and self-sufficiency and now features articles on
cooking treats for your husband, and on the professionalization of the
housewife role, as in "A housewife is a chef, a psychologist, an educa-
tor, and a flower artist" (April 1995)—aiming now at a readership of
committed young wives, rather than young professional workers. *Croissant*'s original audience, who are now in their thirties and of whom a
significant percentage remain unmarried, seem to contemporary writers
like Matsubara a lost generation. Although the common perception of
the last possible moment for marriage has risen to the age of thirty or
even thirty-one (as in the phrase "New Year's Woman," using December 31 as indicative of the last date possible for marriage), women in
their late twenties, whatever their earlier interests and desires, are thinking of marriage, even as a temporary expedient to assuage advice columns
and expert opinion, and see unmarried women in their midthirties as negative models. While college-graduate working women may delay marriage to their own particular "New Year's" deadline, the national average age at marriage is lower, at 27.7 for women, 30.4 for men.

As we will see in chapter 7, consumer "imperatives"—personal and
social needs to consume goods—may appear to give young women a
frivolous, materialistic, and selfish image in contemporary Japan. It is a
long way from the role definition of women committed to family and the
maintenance of human relationships to the consumer identity of affluent young shoppers. At the same time, young women are serious about
their own futures, planning for the long term, and establishing career
trajectories: in fact, life itself is "a plan," something they can predict and
mold. This seems to older people both impractical and irresponsible—
in the sense that these young people seem to be ignoring their families,
tradition, and the wider community around them—and at the same time
unromantic, leaving no room for development of "dreams" or the force
of love and commitment. Their elders see them as unrealistic, unable to
take into consideration the vicissitudes of life that may throw their plans
into disarray.

The "*Croissant* syndrome" is in fact a historical instance of a framed
clash between ideology and the ordinary real lives of women. Young
women had already begun to delay marriage, even without *Croissant*'s

glorification of singlehood. Eventually, most women accede to social and biological pressures to marry. The young women who have "played" out their twenties as high-spending "*Yenjoy* gals" have money, looks, and youth and may covet their freedom. But after they turn thirty they may hit a life-stage wall and receive hints, subtle or not, to leave work to give place to younger women. Being fired may well lead them to marry, as a "natural" life course option. If (typically) they have found husbands at work, they may be forced by company policy or pressure to change jobs to avoid nepotistic embarrassments. The performances of work and consumerism these young women experience seem far from the commitments they will make to marriage and child rearing. Their relationships with men, most particularly, seem remote from the images of marital relations passed on by their mothers and grandmothers.

SEXUALITY IN FAMILY LIFE

Family life in Japan has rarely been (publicly) depicted as an arena for sexual activity, much less romance in the Western sense. Virginity before marriage may have been a requirement for elite young ladies in prewar society (upper classes having been most influenced by the borrowed Victorian moral codes in the Meiji period),[23] though romantic love in marriage has never been a fashion in literature or ideology.

For Nishimura Kaya, sexual activity does not connote romantic attachment. Or vice versa. Kaya is twenty-six and for two years has been dating a young man she knew in college. She likes him a lot, she says, though he is not someone she'd marry. They are, she adds, like brother and sister and she has no sexual or romantic notions about him, though he's reliable and generous. He may be dating her exclusively, but she says she is seeing other men, one of whom she has sex with, another she calls her "lover" but with whom she is delaying sexual involvement. To the interviewer this seemed contradictory or at least complicated, but she says there is little confusion for her, just not enough time to enjoy their company. There is nothing very compelling for her in these relationships and they were far from the first things she wanted to talk about (the primary topics were jobs, money, and travel); she showed no signs of embarrassment or puritanical avoidance. She said that when she gets married it will be with a "safe" person, not one she might "risk" falling in love with, and she said that if she weren't in love with her husband, it might be all right to take a lover.

The calculations of some young women with regard to their future "security" as wives seem to leave sex out of the formula for a success-ful marriage. Traditionally, the formula for male sexuality indicated sex for procreation in marriage and sex for pleasure outside marriage. Vo-gel notes the relatively low frequency of marital sex in the 1950s and the increase in workplace affairs that, he says, "need not disrupt [a worker's] relationship with his wife."[24] Women in Japan in the 1950s rarely ad-mitted to premarital knowledge of sex or pleasure in sex. In a *More* re-port, published in the late 1980s, women reported both more activity and more pleasure, and the rate of extramarital sexual activity for women—a category not even present in earlier studies—indicates young and middle-aged women reporting such relationships. Of those in *ren'ai* ("love" marriages), 60 percent had had sex before marriage compared to 30 percent of those in *omiai* marriages.[25] The "reporting" issue is not completely resolved; it is likely that women have begun to report more sexual activity than they would have reported in the past, as the image of the prewar chaste good wife has receded and the definition of hus-band-wife relations separate from their roles as parents is still vague and unmarked, a relationship without an emotional or sentimental program.

In chapter 4 the wish of a young mother "to fly" resonates with an earlier use of the notion of the "flying woman." The *tonde iru onna* was a concept borrowed from Erica Jong's *Fear of Flying,* very popular among women in Japan in the 1970s. The phrase came to mean a woman sex-ually liberated and enjoying multiple relationships with men without re-sponsibility or commitment, or, by extension, a woman who makes her own decisions, through life.[26] "Flying"—with either sexual connotations or a more general sense of exploration and adventuring—seems restricted to the years before and after child rearing. Sexual satisfaction is not some-thing to expect from marriage.

Indeed, planning for marriage goes on almost without concern for what kind of relationship to establish with a marriage partner: boyfriends are for fun and romance,[27] and so compatibility and personality are im-portant, but a future spouse means stability, so income and status are more important. Young men complain that their brides have less inter-est in them than in planning the ceremony, clothing, and food for the wedding—and decorating the new apartment.

Whether unmarried young women are seen as scheming careerists, with the unreasonable expectation that life will fall in with the plans they create, or as mindless trend-followers, "grasshoppers" who have no prac-tical plan for life at all, to their elders they are problematic. Feminists decry their lack of interest in serious women's issues, traditionalists say they show no respect for values, idealists wonder if they have any dreams. The image of the *ojoosan*, which until recently represented a young woman of good family, well brought up with an elite education and all the graces, prepared for the responsibilities of the "good wife/wise mother" role, is now displaced by the image of the woman ill-equipped for adult roles and realities, the marriage-avoider, or by the derogatory term *ikazugoka*, referring to the selfishness and immaturity of an unmarried woman between the ages of twenty-five and thirty-five.

REPRODUCING IMMATURITY

Sakagami Yuko, a psychologist and author of *Yukkuri otona ni naranai yoi* (It's just fine not to become an adult), worries about such young women. Sakagami's concern is not the falling birthrate but the dependency that causes young women (and men) to lack responsibilities and the skills to manage them, until they are forced into the world by the demands of work and marriage. Even then, she notes, they have lived so long under the protection of their parents that they are not prepared to manage and must rely on "manuals" for life supplied now by the publishing industry ready to capitalize on the audience of naive *Mi-ha*, or "adult children," in today's jargon.[28]

She says that the "dangerous" time is between college and marriage— when young people may still be living with their parents. These parents are young themselves, still vital and busy, not yet needing their children's care, or having much time to train and prepare them in the life skills they will need. They are the parents who, when their children were in school, felt that much of life training was to be left to teachers and classrooms. They did not trust themselves in this and felt it was the job of the school to prepare children for life.

At least such busy parents do leave young people to fend for themselves—and perhaps to develop independence. At the other extreme is the mother who has nothing better to do with her time than maintain her child's dependency by providing total, enveloping care. Yoshiko is the mother of Ichiro, a twenty-five-year-old worker for Chiba Machine Works. He commutes two hours each way to work. However, he chooses neither to live in company housing nor to find himself a flat nearer to his office. His mother still waits up for him if he is late and prepares his breakfast and supper every day. He has a girlfriend whom he sees on weekends, and she too lives at home and hasn't learned to cook or clean. Yoshiko worries that her son won't be competent enough to live by himself, but she is relieved that he is near at hand: she can iron his suits or nurse him through his hangovers.

Sakagami fears that such young people, going from Mother to married life, will have a rude shock and won't be able to fill their new roles well. Young women will have it better than young men, she says, because even at home daughters have thought of themselves as independent and have at least adventured with friends in Japan and overseas. In contrast, middle-class young men usually go from monitored choices and tasks in the workplace and undemanding hours with workmates at the after-hours bar to the shock of marriages where, perhaps, unlike their fathers, they may have to make their own noodles. Sakagami says the mother-son relationship is eternal, that Japanese women feel the maternal instinct toward all men, keeping males dependent on females throughout their lifetimes, but this may be changing.

Dependency, encouraged at home, developed further in the examination system, and relied on in the workplace, is the concern of commentators. Young women may have a kind of spurious independence, buffered by family and full of freedom rather than demands of maturity, before they become wives and mothers, yet in these new roles they experience their responsibilities as a shock, since they feel helpless in many of their new tasks and pass on their own experiences of childhood to their children. The excuse middle-class women give for the reproduction of dependency in their children, of course, is that they must protect their children while they undergo the harsh and incessant study necessary to their academic advancement. Domestic chores are rarely expected from children, and in such families, children are rarely allowed or encouraged to take on after-school employment of any kind, even babysitting. Many academic high schools actually prohibit such work.

The children who emerge from this environment are often unable to fend for themselves—even girls, less apt than boys to engage in the highest competition for the highest status universities, are unlikely to know how to prepare a meal or do the laundry or vacuum the floor, unless of course their mother works full time and there is no one else to help. But as such tasks are still written into female roles, it is likely that a girl has absorbed at least some of the lore of maintaining a household.

Echoes of the television advertisement for instant noodles of several years back may still be heard: a young boy of about eight sits at a kitchen table, chopsticks at the ready, while a young girl of about the same age, wearing an apron, stirs a pot of noodles, saying, "I'm the making person," to which he replies, "I'm the eating person." While protests against

gender typing force such commercials off the air, there has been little
change in the social environment supporting the role division.

A mixed message and double burden for women has emerged: by law
equally endowed with the potential for high levels of attainment in education and employment, raised by mothers who neither train nor del-
egate tasks to them, and exhorted to be independent socially, they still
confront the fact that domestic and child-rearing tasks are unambigu-
ously theirs, and that combining these with the dubious joys of mainstream full-time employment is virtually impossible.[29] It should be noted
that Yoshiko, the doting mother of Ichiro, is also a full-time professional
employee.

Having a baby creates the largest shock in the lives of young women
today. As we saw earlier, husbands seem able to share domestic chores
only until a baby is born. While young women and middle-aged women
seem still to be availing themselves of pleasures and freedoms, young
mothers in between are a new kind of *hakoiri okusan* (housewife-in-a-
box).[30] Some choose not to have any children at all.

It is scarcely any wonder then that women, in what might be a transitional era, are "choosing" family and career configurations they feel
they can safely accomplish with success—success as measured in economic
security, the realization of their children's academic/social potential, and
their own fulfillment within the parameters of community opinion. In
the 1950s, these goals could be accomplished in a family of three children, in the 1970s, in a family of two children, and now, in the twenty-
first century, it is an uphill battle to achieve success with one—but not
to have children at all ipso facto removes chances for success in two of
the three most crucial measures—success as a mother and approval from
the community.

CHILDBEARING AND POSTWAR HISTORY

What has happened demographically in Japan during the past fifty years
to produce a striking new fall in reproduction, a birthrate shock? The
first demographic transition, the switch from high fertility and high mortality to low fertility and low mortality, began early in the nineteenth
century and carried on into the Meiji era.[31] Even before modernization
had improved health and sanitation and lowered mortality rates, Meiji
families tended to limit their size, investing more in fewer children, at
least in part because education had become a measure and means of life-
chance improvement. But the second demographic transition, in which

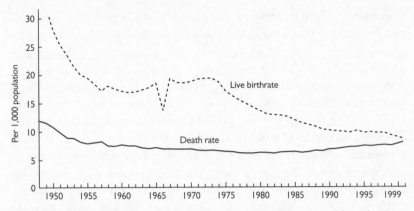

Figure 5. Birth and death rates, 1950–99. From Ministry of Health and Welfare, *Statistical Handbook of Japan* (Tokyo, 2001).

the birthrate dropped to below replacement level, has led to the crisis decried today as Japan's denial of the future.

Modern birthrates held fairly constant in Japan until quite recently—in the 1930s, the average was 4.24 children. Between 1947 and 1949 there was a brief postwar baby boom, then a slight decline, and between 1949 and 1957 there was a drop from 4.54 to 2.04 children per woman. This average remained steady until the 1970s, when the current downward trend began (figure 5). Before 1990 there was no particular outcry: the economy was doing well and family life seemed stable. By then—a year or two into the effects of the burst bubble economy and the recession—the birthrate had dropped to 1.57 children per woman, startling the public and creating the 1.57 *shokku*. This rate has further declined to 1.34 nationally (1.1 in Tokyo) and it is predicted that it will decline nationally to 1.32 by the year 2010. Suddenly reproduction has become a topic for public debate.

Why such a personal matter has become the object of political concern has a long history—but a distinct immediate causal frame. In the Meiji period (1868–1912), as we have seen, political leaders sought to create a new society and incorporate the modernizing, industrializing influences of the West without eroding Japan's fundamental social structure and values. But first they had to identify them. After nearly three hundred years of isolation, what it meant to be Japanese had little rhetorical or ideological resonance as a national construction.

The modern citizen of the Meiji nation-state was a member of a family and community, the center of a set of concentric circles of membership, each of which maintained (and patrolled) the behavior of each member. The first circle, of course, was the family as the lowest level of "official institution," reporting to the bureaucracy and representing the state, its policies, and laws as they governed members of the family. It was this image that guided officials as they created the Meiji Civil Code of 1898, creating a continuous affiliation from child to father to state. And reproduction, especially later in the period of wartime mobilization, became a national rather than a personal and familial concern.

Strong Nation, Strong Army was the slogan guiding pronatalist reproductive policy. During the early years of modernization, the efforts to create a modern army and workforce included a strong antiabortion campaign (by 1880, abortion had become a crime). Earlier, in 1869, the government had sought to limit abortion by making abortifacients illegal, and by controlling midwives through local licensing (and oversight). Once abortion was eradicated, it was said, the babies who were born would make up an army large enough to take Manchuria.[32]

Education, health care, and sanitation were improving too, and the rate of infant mortality declined, allowing for more children to survive, at least among the growing urban middle classes. Among the poor, especially the rural poor, however, the limit on the mouths they could feed did not significantly change, and infanticide did not noticeably decrease though abortions were harder to come by.

The brief era of open information and relative reproductive freedom in the Taishō period (1912–26) accompanied the increasing involvement of middle-class women in higher education, and the entry of large numbers of working-class women into the industrial labor force. Margaret Sanger, the birth control activist, visited Japan in 1922 and though she was barred from distributing birth control devices and from speaking publicly on birth control, feminists and journalists supported her ideas. Birth control clinics were established in the late 1920s and early 1930s.

MORE AND BETTER BABIES

During the 1930s, the call for reproductive patriotism increased and slogans such as *umeyoo, fuyaseyoo!* (give birth and multiply [to strengthen the nation]) linked childbirth to Japan's expansion at home and overseas. Contraceptive goods disappeared and birth control clinics closed. But the government was particular about who could be born. The National Eugenic Act of 1940 allowed for abortions or "eugenic surgery" to prevent births in families with hereditary diseases and mental illnesses.

The "national mission of motherhood" campaign included awards given to families with ten or more children, and anyone engaging in birth control could be labeled a traitor. Activists lobbying against these policies were imprisoned.

Critics have pointed out that the National Eugenic Act of 1940 and its later amendments contradict the stated goals and rationales of official Japan. "Eugenic surgery" is thinly veiled approved abortion, yet official campaigns continued to label abortion and other forms of medical or physical intervention to prevent live births dangerous to women's reproductive health. This contradiction persisted into the postwar years, when a baby boom seemed to threaten the nation with overcrowding. The 1948 Eugenic Protection Act approved abortion, citing the need to prevent births of defective children. Women could now legally obtain abortions for a wide range of reasons, including the health of the mother and financial circumstances that made it difficult to raise a child. When the high-dose hormone-based contraceptive pill first came into use in 1955, Japanese doctors hailed it as an alternative to abortion, which seemed to pose more health risks than the pill. When the birthrate did drop, in the latter half of the 1950s, the family planning effort (including the legalization and distribution of contraceptive drugs and other means of birth control) lost its impetus.[33]

CONTRACEPTION IN POSTWAR JAPAN

In 1968, the Ministry of Health and Welfare prepared a document called "Opinions on the Formulation of a Comprehensive Policy for the Protection of Mother and Child Health." By this time, the concern was not overpopulation but the decrease in the birthrate, and behind this document was a fear that the economic boom of the 1960s would be aborted along with the future labor force. At the same time, women's groups and other concerned activists were attempting to educate women to understand and take control of their bodies and sexuality. The movement to legalize the birth control pill was created.

Chupiren (women's union for liberalization of abortion and the pill), the radical activist group founded by Enoki Misako, advocated the legalization of the pill for contraceptive purposes. This group's strategies and activities were bold and colorful and their "shock tactics" attracted the attention of the media in Japan and overseas. Chupiren used confrontation and shame to raise public awareness of women's position, including visits to the offices of husbands who had abused their wives or neglected to pay alimony to their divorced wives. The shock team would storm in, wearing their signature pink hard-hats, and denounce the errant husband, shaming him in front of his workmates. Other women's groups dissociated themselves from this group, preferring less flamboyant methods.[34]

Abortion continued to be the most frequently used means of birth control, and family planning seemed to be remedial decisions made ex post facto. Public officials cited concerns over women's reproductive health as the rationale for keeping the low-dose (below .05 mg of estrogen) birth control pill off the market for over thirty-five years.[35] The high-dose pill (above .05 mg of estrogen) may legally be used for menstrual irregularity but not as contraception. There is widespread fear that there will be adverse side effects from prolonged usage, even of the low-dose pill, and 63 percent of women who support the liberalization of access to the low-dose pill say that they would not use it themselves. A typical response from a young woman is "Even if it is said to have no side effects, I would still be very much concerned because ultimately I am dealing with my own body." This attitude may change; the low-dose pill is legally available now, as of June 1999. Sexuality has become an aspect of the public performance of identity among young urban men and women (who flaunt their sexual activities), to the disgust of their elders. To some, it is merely a "trend." One woman said, "It's become cool to act according to your animal instincts."[36]

Coleman has shown that Japanese women prefer methods that interfere least with their natural rhythms and avoid methods that may produce side effects or require women to women touch their genitals (as diaphragms do). The intrauterine device is also not popular and some types are banned for health reasons. The idea of taking a pill every day also means to some women that they are consciously defining themselves as sexual beings, which makes them uncomfortable. One woman in a women's health group said, "I don't have sex every day, and I don't need contraception every day either. [But] if I must take a pill every day, I feel my whole life will be revolving around the pill."[37]

Sex education in schools contributes to this hesitation: the curriculum avoids explicit treatment of women's sexuality, and its vagueness promotes uncertainty. Since the late 1980s, however, popular teen magazines have featured very explicit, nonjudgmental, and upbeat articles and manuals on sex, including contraceptives, techniques, and survey research. The young people also learn from experience. The reported rate of teen pregnancy is very low, though the reported rates of sexual activity are high. Young women in their late teens and early twenties are more likely to be using the low-dose birth control pill than before, usually by purchase overseas or by prescription "for menstrual irregularity and acne" according to their mothers. Their birth control choices as married women in the future remain to be seen.

Couples find ways to avoid pregnancy without oral contraceptives. Chief among these methods is the use of the condom. Over 80 percent of couples report using condoms although many of these also use other methods, such as the Ogino rhythm method, or the basal body temperature method.[38] In the 1960s and 1970s, condoms were sold door to door by older women called "skin ladies," who would sell them in bulk quantities to housewives in the privacy of their homes. Condoms have been popular since the first postwar family planning campaigns, when family planning agencies obtained their main funding through the sale of prophylactics.

Many men dislike using condoms and may, particularly after an evening of drinking, neglect to do so. Among women in their late thirties and forties and older, it is still considered somewhat indecent for a woman to be sexually knowledgeable or take initiatives in sex, including responsibility for contraception; hence they may need repeated abortions. This group, however, is fast moving out of its reproductive years.

ABORTION — THE LUNCH-HOUR OPTION

Although Japan ranks as a "poor access" country in availability of contraception (international agencies also confer this rating on one other developed country, Ireland), it offers relatively high access to abortion.[39] For several decades abortion, cheap and safe, has been used when contraceptive measures fail. In 1966, the notorious "fire horse" year in the Chinese calendar, there was a striking drop in births as couples avoided bringing to term a pregnancy that might produce an aggressive, unmarriageable, "fire horse" girl (see figure 5).

In the late 1960s and early 1970s, abortion became so commonplace that women referred to it as a "lunch-hour" activity.[40] Indeed, a first-trimester abortion could be obtained during a work break. In these two decades there are reported cases of women having over twenty abortions, and over 50 percent of women had at least one abortion during their childbearing years. In 1992, the abortion rate went down: about 30 percent of women in the *Mainichi Shimbun*'s family planning survey had experienced abortion, with 10 percent having had three or more abortions. The cost of a first-trimester abortion is low (from $500 to

$1,000), well within the means of the women, mostly married, who seek them.

Abortion has indeed become big business, and doctors who receive much of their income from performing them may not advise their patients to use other forms of birth control. Yet many doctors have joined the pro-contraceptive-choice movement, including Wagatsuma Takashi, an obstetrician who says "Japan is the only country that legalized abortion and approved family planning but does not use the pill. Japan is a unique country. It is almost a crazy country."[41]

Abortion in Japan attracts much less public protest than in the United States. Personal grief, guilt, and physical problems are noted by clinics, and a pro-life movement is small and not influential.[42] Women's health groups organize their protests carefully, as they do not want to deny access to abortion but do want to make its risks known in a context of reproductive choice.[43]

Recently there has been a shift in policy, approving abortions only during the first 22 weeks of pregnancy, down from the limit of 24 weeks earlier legalized. The debate included discussions of the viability of a premature (23-week) fetus but the decision seemed to represent governmental intervention in reproduction consonant with pronatalist sentiments, which surfaced at about the same time.[44] Policy activity related to women's health is governed by large male-dominated agencies such as the Japan Association for Maternal Welfare, where only 10 percent of the membership is female, according to Ashino Yuriko, deputy director of the Family Planning Association of Japan; nongovernmental organizations have little ability to influence policy.[45]

LIMITING BIRTHS, ENABLING WOMEN?

Kozue is married and childless at forty. Her husband and she rode out the blandishments of their parents, who couldn't understand why they didn't want children. Kozue is an illustrator for a children's magazine and baby-sits happily for her sister's small children but never wanted any of her own. Her husband is a university professor and is home several mornings, when they work near each other in the room designated as a study/studio in their condominium.

Why are more young couples choosing not to have children? In official attitude polls 43 percent of respondents say that marriage doesn't have to mean children, an increase since 1992 of 12 points.[46] Various factors support the no-birth or one-child option, though perhaps the most significant reason families have limited their fertility recently is economic; as Hanley and Yamamura have shown, economic factors tied to the high cost of raising "high-quality children" dominate.[47] Having no children at all may enable a lifestyle like Kozue's in a couple-centered marriage. As Ochiai Emiko notes, once "the internal contradictions of a nuclear household with children" as a location of "togetherness" grew irksome, the deliberate construction of the no-child family was feasible.[48] The "companionate" marriage extolled in the 1960s and 1970s as an aspect of *maihoomushugi* seemed possible now only without children, given education's escalating importance to their care and success. A successful child in the conventions of middle-class families takes single-minded involvement on the part of the mother and a substantial investment of money; marital bonding is secondary to this effort.

Limiting births *is* primarily about economics. Couples may have wanted more than one child but they say money factors have kept them from the desired average of 2.18 and much farther from the Ministry of Health and Welfare's goal of 2.64. I believe that the rising value of female children is another factor in the decline of the birthrate—that parents can now realize their goal of raising a "high-quality child" with a girl just as they can with a boy.

This revaluation breaks with the past, when even recently male offspring were necessary to complete a family, to work in the family trade and provide income, to assure the continuity of the lineage, and to ensure the welfare of aged parents. Having a son ensured that a female caretaker, his wife, would be available to his parents.

Still in economic considerations, the difference today has both a negative pull, constraining families to restrict births to the number of children they can afford to educate successfully, and a positive push, enabling girls to succeed academically, professionally, and economically. Some families now consider daughters more responsible in caring for elderly parents, and gender-blind family planning may be on the horizon.

PLAYING THE CONTRADICTIONS

Mariko, whose profile is given above, is fairly distant from these transitional women. Earning a "supplementary" rather than a "living" wage, she has neither economic independence nor domestic autonomy in the household she shares with her husband's parents. Her authorities are her family, or rather, her husband's family. Her husband is expected to per-petuate the family business, and it is likely he will grow into this role and expect his own son to do the same, bringing a daughter-in-law into the household eventually. These conditions themselves may not be "oppres-sive," deliberately constraining women, but they nevertheless contain their options.

Shizue, the second woman described above, may also have some lim-its on her potential—she is divorced, has two children, lives with her parents—but she is a skilled artisan, a professional with a dossier. She has a talent rather than a role. Skill-based identities in Japanese pro-fessions among the middle class are less conventional than role or sta-tus definitions. Technicians are on different employment tracks often from those of generalists, but for women, conventional trajectories and definitions are often irrelevant. What she lacks is a salary to make her self-sufficient. Even so, a self-sufficient independent household would not completely solve her problems, since sharing with her family means there are other adults present to help care for her children, even if the older parents are themselves in need of care. If she lived apart from her par-ents, she says she'd have a harder time because she would have to travel to care for them.

What Shizue also illustrates, in spite of her fairly modern education and employment, is the traditional Confucian crunch: the social, moral, and physical need to care for people at both ends of the life course. At the moment we see her, she is able to manage through a temporary strat-agem: the part-time assistance of her son, whose time and energy will soon be siphoned off in service to his own (and the family's) future wel-fare, as he enters the period of intense study. Then Shizue will have to enlist the support of her younger child or find other means to care for her infirm mother. Part-time nursing care is possible at home, partly funded by her municipality, but her father strongly objects to having a nonfamily member in the house. She is better off, she says, than one of her friends who lives in near poverty because her own family disowned her when she divorced. Shizuko, the unmarried woman in her thirties, and Kozue, the married but childless woman, made choices though not in the thoughtless, selfish sense the pronatalists abhor (while Yanagihara Kazuko's choice was full participation in family *and* production).

These changing experiences of child rearing (or not) reflect longer life spans for women as well. When a woman has thirty or more active years ahead of her after her youngest child has graduated from college, she has to fill her life with objects of attention. By the 1970s midlife participation in work, hobbies, and perhaps extramarital liaisons seemed to indicate a search for a second, post-children, life purpose.

We can see women's lives now as a set of competing roles, complementary or contradictory values, as experiences of juggling and compromise with the lives given to them by media advisors or professional experts—or we can see them as transitional, enabled by education and law to have new roles and options yet not fully emergent in social, economic, and political terms. None of these frames, however, explains and defines Mariko and Shizue, or any other woman who is engaged in choices of family and work, and none acts as a reliable predictor for their and their children's lives in the future. Women's lives have changed in many ways since the 1950s, and yet the changes do not necessarily create diversity in their options. The possibility of choice lies within these options, but family and economics, as well as social and cultural influences, constrain them.

On structural, cultural, and ideological dimensions, it has been hard to separate family issues from women's issues. A woman's structural location is in the home and she operates in the workplace, representing a contradiction that a man's participation in both institutions does not imply. That his work in the corporate sphere is a 100-percent commitment does not diminish his family role. The cultural definitions of a woman's role in the family and at work still seem limiting because of their totalism: being a worker and a mother means being two whole people, in middle-class views.

The social units relevant to a woman or man or child may be smaller now than in the prewar, or even the immediate postwar years, yet the shift in scale does not necessarily enhance the choices of individuals and families—as the American notion of "individuating" would suggest. In fact, this shift works in the other direction. Policymakers have chosen to look at the issues raised by a demographic shift to an "aging" society as the results of women's choices to limit family size and thus the size of the future labor force and, ultimately, the resources available to care for the elderly as well. Their choice to make women's choices the problem only exacerbates the narrowness of roles and resources within the smaller families who must find their own way to cope with conditions unaddressed by social services. The next chapter's story lines converge on the "birth strike," which commentators and policymakers implicate in the impending tragedy of the abandoned elderly.

Twenty-First-Century Blues

Aging in Families

Honma Shigeru is eighty-two; his wife Shizuko is seventy-nine. They are reasonably healthy and live in a small condominium in the building where their eldest son lives. They try to be independent of the younger generation, which means trying not to ask for things explicitly. Their daughter-in-law, however, fills the gap by providing much they do not have to ask for, allowing them to keep their dignity as they unprotestingly accept the evening meal she brings them. They live on Honma-san's pension and savings. Their son worries constantly about what will happen when one of his parents dies, especially if his mother dies first. His father, though strong, seems to be slipping a little: his memory is failing and also his capacity to care for himself in small personal ways. His son dreads the prolonged and intensive care of a physically dependent father, which will fall to his wife, the dutiful daughter-in-law.

If the adults who make up a household are middle-aged, they must now explain the presence or absence of elderly people in their home. This generation of middle-aged people is likely to be supporting adult children as well as considering the future of their own parents. There appears to be no "natural" understanding, no cultural assumptions of lineage, or even of three-generation households. The three-generation household (*sansedai kazoku*) now refers to co-residence and not to an encoded *ie,* the incumbent family stretching backward and forward in time. In lineage-based family codes of the past, the older generation would be in a stewardship position, a ritually superior position, and in control of resources and the young. Now the older generation act as child sitters and home minders or live with their children to be cared for themselves. There is little evocation of elder power and authority in such a household. About 60 percent of people over sixty-five years of age live with their relatives now, but this arrangement results from a later and more ambiguous accommodation rather than continuous co-residence, as a nuclear household (*kakukazoku*) with add-ons. There are now more Japanese over sixty-five than under fifteen, and aging population and declining birthrate alike fuel commentators and policymakers' *shokku* and highlight changes in family and society that compromise older understandings.

The elder Honmas' story is similar to those told by many in the younger generation: the messages in the telling are usually those of burdens on the young, rather than the concerns of the elderly themselves. The narratives of policymakers are strident while the elderly themselves express different thoughts, most of them more positive or at least less pitiful. They emphasize what they want to do in their retirement years and do not dwell on physical or economic dependency. Official interest in the elderly of course is more concerned with costs to the public. Predictions of the rates of bed-ridden elderly and future needs for institutional housing and health-care resources have dominated policy, governmental research, and the news media.

In her novel *Twilight Years,* Ariyoshi Sawako described a family similar to the Honmas, its resources and functions increasingly focused on an elderly father-in-law whose advancing senility becomes the core reality for all members of the household, particularly his daughter-in-law. While Ariyoshi's novel at the end depicted the emotional reward caregiving provided for the "sacrificing" daughter-in-law, readers responded more to the negative aspects of the old man in the household. When this novel was published in 1978, it raised Japanese consciousness about the plight of families and the elderly. Rather than discuss older people's contributions to society or their active involvement with younger people, Japanese social commentators, columnists, television soap opera scriptwriters, and politicians chose instead to emphasize grim projections from economic and demographic data. They developed these projections into cautionary tales of abandonment and neglect. The obvious truth, that more people nurture their elderly relatives than abuse them and that more elderly are self-sufficient than not, did not feature in scripts of aging parents and families' frighteningly un-Confucian choices and behavior. The scripts have an impressive battery of data to support them.

By 1990 in Japan a noticeable public discussion in media and in official pronouncements appeared to cluster around population issues that soon became known as the *jinko mondai*—the population problem. Changes in family patterns and individual behavior were, and are, the root of this concern about the nation's future and the recessionary issues confronting policymakers. While some overpopulated countries may envy Japan its low-birth situation, the smaller ranks of succeeding generations will unsettle all social systems. Alarm at the falling birthrate, the rising rate of the elderly, the diversification and shrinkage of the labor force, and the increase in foreign workers dominates the news and official documents, and the future landscape of abandoned elderly scraping to get by as their grandchildren, indulged and materialistic, ignore them shows up in endless soap-opera material.

These dour predictions have been encapsulated in the sound bite *obasute shakai* (throwing-away-Granny society), a phrase that alludes to the old legend of the virtuous death in agrarian hard times. Among the elderly in this generation, however, the story of the old woman whose filial son carried her to the top of Obasute-yama (throwing-away-Granny mountain) so that she might experience a virtuous death exposed on the mountaintop in midwinter, is a reference to unsatisfactory nursing homes to which some feel an *un*filial son has relegated them.[1] Today, the phrase "throwing away Granny" raises questions about societal interventions in the care of elderly. The choices of private families have been transformed into public, national, concerns. Traditional values are frequently invoked to spur the family into action but may ensure neither the cohesion of families nor the security of resources to care for elderly without some responsibility on the part of the state or local agencies.

THE CROSSOVER

In 1997, a published graph showed two intersecting populations—aged Japanese sixty-five or older, and youths fourteen or younger—the line of increasingly dependent people rising, that of future producers falling (figure 6). This graph made shockingly good television, especially when accompanied by commentaries on unfilial youth. The year 2007 will also be a year of *shokku,* according to Nihon University's Population Research Institute. Then 20 percent of the population will be over sixty-five, having doubled from the 1985 rate. This represents the fastest aging population in the world.[2] And by 2025, another study showed, almost one in two adults will be elderly.[3]

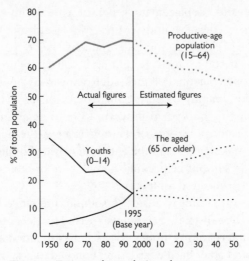

Figure 6. Estimated population changes, 1950–
2050. From *Yomiuri Shimbun,* January 22,
1997.

Japanese leadership in aging is not a source of pride, although it reflects high levels of public health care, social services, and stability. Japan's national health insurance, pensions, workers' compensation, and national nursing-care insurance provide a social security system that appears to be more than adequate. Even though the boom in the elderly population was anticipated, there is a sense of crisis. The crisis focuses both on the experiences of families and on the future shortfall in the tax base supporting national programs as the working population shrinks. For every person over sixty-five years of age in 2050, it is estimated that there will be 1.7 working people—far below the level of 4.4 for every elderly person in 1995. Another way of saying this is that the ratio between the number of working adults ages forty-five to forty-nine and the number of people needing support ages sixty-five to seventy-nine has fallen: this ratio, called the "family support ratio," is predicted to fall from 0.52 now to a low of 0.38 in 2010. In the United States, the ratio is 0.871 and in France, it is 0.592. Japan's ratio will be the world's lowest by 2005.[4] The youthful working population simply will not be able to support the welfare of the retired population.

Blaming the young for the problems of the aged is of course nothing new. As the "reverse pyramid" (*gyaku piramido*)—the phenomenon that turns the population pyramid on its head as the baby boom bulge moves

up to old age and "replacement generations" continue to shrink—
becomes familiar in the news and in Ministry of Health and Welfare white
papers, the ratio of elderly to youthful productive workers and their prog-
eny (if any) has become a focus for critical attention (figure 7). Planning
for old age through personal savings, squirreling away bonuses and pensions, and making family-based care plans are not seen as sufficient responses. Developing a national program to buttress an ideological defense of the responsible unit of Family is now the action plan of
policymakers, making public mobilization of private families explicit. In
the past, almost without help, families took care of their own without
these government-inspired injunctions.

In January 1996, Prime Minister Hashimoto presented his inaugural
address to the Diet. Instead of treating expected matters of state such as
deregulation, international policy, the security relationship with the
United States, and other hard-edged, time-honored topics, the prime minister chose instead to focus on Japan as an aging society, fraught with
domestic problems that now overshadow its economic and diplomatic
international relationships. He cast these problems in terms of future
budgetary allocations needed and the social and cultural changes that
will accompany such a rapid and vast shift in the population.[5] The problems he described were already well known to the reading, watching, and
listening public, but Japanese soberly attended to Hashimoto's concern
as confirmation of what they knew: that Japan had taken a global leadership position as a graying society—said to be aging ten years more rapidly than the United States—and that it would have to find "unique" solutions to its demographic crisis.

Financial risk, emotional stress, and psychological guilt surround the
images of elder care in the future. An ethos of filial piety will no longer
goad the young into taking on the moral (and morally rewarding) commission of care. Care in the future might require a cooperative relationship between individual, family, and state responsibilities but would not
emerge from cultural logic framed as "Japan's uniquely beautiful family traditions." Attempts to engage families in a middle-class version of
responsibility through part-time, restricted home aides and other services would do little more to lighten the burden than the child-care stipends
of $50 a month did to encourage people to have more children. An un-
convincing call to morality, an appeal to sentiment, and a sop to the bottom line are not enough, apparently, for families who must figure it out
for themselves.[6]

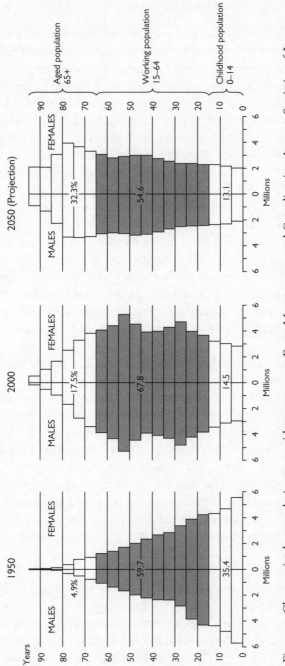

Figure 7. Changes in the population pyramid, 1950–2050. From Management and Coordination Agency, Statistics of Japan (1990); Ministry of Health and Welfare, Estimates of Future Population (June 1991).

FAMILY MEANS GRANDMOTHER

One six-year-old, asked to draw a picture of his family by his first-grade teacher, drew a picture of his grandmother and commented that everyone else was pretty busy but Grandmother was always home. The boy is an only child. His two parents are working and Grandmother is the one he sees most. Mother takes him to school in the mornings but Grandmother meets him there in the afternoons. His family hasn't always lived with her, but when his grandfather died, his father, the eldest son, from the proceeds of selling his parents' rural house, added a wing to his Tokyo suburban house, eliminating a small yard, and Grandmother moved in.

So far they are doing well. Grandmother is a patient, creative woman who has a small loom for her weaving. She is still very fit and strong. Moving meant losing her social networks, however, and so her grandson provides her with his company, and the company also of another grandmother who picks up her grandchild at school. This family exemplifies the reversal of roles from the prewar period. Now, grandmothers are in service to the younger generation, not the opposite. Parents and parents-in-law act as babysitters for 70 percent of working women.

As in this case, help from younger people is often associated with a shift in residence on someone's part. The Honmas live very near a child and therefore are more than symbolically in his care. For others of their generation, the U-turn is a common phenomenon. In this bilaterally arranged household, one son or daughter and spouse and children may return to a reformed three-generation establishment. If the premises are large enough, this would usually be the older couple's house, but equally often the older parents live in the junior couple's home or in housing near them. If this scenario is not possible, a family may divide as in a job-related separation and the caregiving daughter will go to live with her parents and children while her husband remains in their original home.

The rate of elderly living with kin is declining but is still higher than that of other advanced nations, where the highest rate is about 25 percent. Rural co-residence is higher than urban. Very few urban households also have continuous three-generation residence; most have *become* three generations after some years of two-generation living (figure 8). These families have to make novel intergenerational arrangements, and no formula exists in spite of the hopes and implications of public policies.

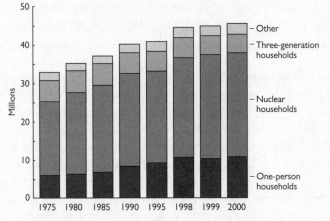
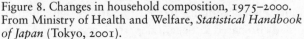

Figure 8. Changes in household composition, 1975–2000.
From Ministry of Health and Welfare, *Statistical Handbook
of Japan* (Tokyo, 2001).

FILIALITY ON NEW YEAR'S DAY

The most important of family holidays in Japan is New Year's—including the days of preparation leading up to it, the assembly of the branches
of the family at the main house, and several days of feasting and family
entertainment. Alternatives to a family New Year's are few. Those foreign visitors caught in Japan over New Year's may have a bleak few days,
seeing no one around. Above all, it is a day to observe age hierarchies
and traditions with ritual meals. And in families reconstituted for the
holidays, it may occasion friction between generations.

At the age of thirty-two, Kitajima Satoko was being put through the
paces of traditional homemaking rather late in life. Her husband's older
brother had been posted overseas with his family and so would not be
hosting the two- to three-day family event this year, leaving it to his
younger brother and his wife to serve those who would assemble at the
ancestral home. The arrangement had been that the elder son would inherit the home, help support his brother's children through college, and
of course take primary responsibility for the care of the aging parents (a
necessary compromise to keep the family's heritage intact, since the 1947
constitution outlawed singular inheritance by the eldest son). When he
left for Germany, he asked his younger brother to help so that he and his
family could go skiing in the Alps instead of serving up ritualized togetherness with his wife's laboriously created and elaborate foods.

Satoko wasn't used to her in-laws' house, to the old-fashioned elec-tric rice maker (without a timer) that forced her to wake early to pre-pare breakfasts, instead of setting the machine to cook while she slept. At home, she'd let her husband and children get their own (usually modified Western) breakfasts. She didn't know the local shopkeepers and didn't have a clue how to prepare all the components of the *jubako,* the beautiful tall lacquered box with layers for the special foods of New Year's. Traditionally the women of the household prepare these foods, including *kuromame* (sweetened black beans), *tsukudani* (salt-sweet pre-served tiny fish and seaweed), *nimono* (boiled and seasoned foods), *kin-ton* (mashed sweet potatoes with chestnuts), preserved kumquats, and other preparations made with soy sauce, sugar, and vinegar that keep for several days so that, in theory, women will be free to enjoy the holi-days without constant cooking. In the city, Satoko would purchase many of these already prepared in elegant department store food halls or in lo-cal specialty shops. In the countryside (now actually suburbia) and gov-erned by the traditions maintained faithfully by her absent elder sister-in-law, Satoko had to cook from scratch.

She found it best to engage her mother-in-law as a mentor, to teach her to make these things. This served two functions; first, her mother-in-law felt respected and second, she did much of the work herself, rather than leave it to such a doubtfully trained city woman. Satoko's husband chafed during this time, having no function whatsoever and being pa-raded through the town by his father, whose own uselessness during hol-iday preparations made him restless and prone to drink even more than the holiday usually called for. Their children were grandparented and in-dulged the first day of the New Year, but after planning the spending of their *otoshidama* (New Year's gift money) at music shops and restricted to a neighborhood they hardly knew, they were restless too.

The visible elements of the *ie,* the household currently manifesting the power and traditions of the patriline, are strong. For a few days at New Year's it is easy to ignore the elements that do not reflect patriarchy and filiality and imagine that Confucian morality and reverence for age are alive and well. Knowing they will return to their customary city life, younger generations of relatives savor foods and rituals that reinforce the understandings of continuity, the cohesion and self-sufficiency of the household, giving careful but selective attention to contradictory realities.

The image of Japan as paradise for the elderly, where "old age is recog-nized . . . as a source of prestige and honor," has little weight today.[7] Eu-phemisms such as "silver power" do not bridge the gap between ideals of Confucian filial piety and circumstances of the elderly's place and care. One effect of targeting the actions or inactions of the younger generation is to deny the elderly themselves a role in events or reduce them to recipient status, dependent and voiceless, to exacerbate rather than minimize the effects of the "Confucian gap."

The elderly are a strong and growing consumer market. The Honmas, whose story is outlined briefly above, are serious about their independence, active in their circle of friends, not sitting and waiting for handouts and meals, and not passive in their responses to their children. But quotes from them and their age-mates rarely show up in the popular media. Why they do not, and how the story of elderly victims and discarded family traditions has coopted Japan's future, shape this chapter.

GETTING VIRTUE OR JUST GETTING OLDER?

Deference and respect for the elderly in Japan were formalized in the sixteenth century. Under Tokugawa Hideyoshi a council of state of "the five great aged" was created.[8] The concept of national governance by the *genro,* or "elder statesmen," continued through the nineteenth century and well into the twentieth and reflected the association of age with increased virtue and authority.

Those over sixty-one years of age expected to retire from economic production or positions of mundane practical management into positions of retired privilege and titular authority, if not power, although most able-bodied elderly continued to contribute their labor to the activities of their extended family households.[9] An elderly mother-in-law would hand the rice paddle to the eldest son's wife and, with this act, transfer at least official domestic management to the younger woman, continuing to work in the household as long as she could; her husband might monitor local affairs. As they disengaged from family and community obligations, there would be more "freedom." In Ruth Benedict's charting of "freedom" and "responsibility" over a traditional Japanese life course, she noted that at two points in the life cycle the greatest freedom correlates with the lowest responsibility and that these fall at the beginning and at the end of life.[10] The shift in the elder years reflects an agrarian correspondence of physical capacity and productivity as well as an association between age and higher levels of spirituality, especially in Buddhist culture. After responsibility for productive labor and household management— material things—comes attention to ancestors and to the gods through religious ritual and practice.

The exchange for greater "freedom" in Benedict's chart is complicated by differences of occupation or class. Freedom from household responsibility might also mean freedom in self-expression—at least for some elderly. In the past, especially where neither samurai nor middle-class norms prevailed, freedom of self-expression was traditionally more acceptable in the elderly who have had "special privileges in deportment," including the use of obscenities and sexual jokes and performance of lewd dances by older women at village gatherings.[11] In *The Women of Suye Mura,* Robert Smith and Ella Wiswell present portraits of women in a farming village in the late 1930s that reveal middle-aged and elderly women's capacity for public display of feelings, for sexual expression, and for seemingly unimpeded management of gossip, quite at odds with received views of oppressed elite women hidden in their houses.[12]

Social class distinctions explain the differences in behavior between prewar rural women and their upper-class counterparts. The general view of postwar society is that middle-class norms (involving the good *okusan* who observes the proprieties) have permeated family life. Christena Turner points out that while some middle-class behavior may indeed trickle down, older working-class women look rather similar to the 1930s Suye Mura women, at least in their uses of humor and defiant behavior as resistance.[13]

RETIREMENT AT TURBO SPEED

Disengagement from duties today may not mean isolation or separation from other people, and it happens years before "age" represents debility. The "young" old are retired but physically able to pursue jobs and other regular activities. Many people who retired with full health and energy find that this period allows them to demonstrate a self they had not known or had deferred to more immediate imperatives of work and relationships. For some elderly today, this is a period of engagement in a new *ikigai*—the core activities that give life meaning.[14]

The average age at retirement continues to rise. In the 1970s, most large organizations had rather early retirement ages by American standards. At fifty-two, a worker could begin to see retirement as a near possibility, for that was the age earlier set for retirement in the 1920s, when in fact the life expectancy was about the same as the age for quitting work. In a seniority-based promotion and wage system, companies might well retire their older and more expensive workers and hire replacements from cheaper youth. As the population of youth continues to shrink, however, and as older workers are healthier and more productive than in the past, companies are more likely to keep older workers on the job, often until the age of sixty, when governmental pensions begin.

The average retirement package for a male, college-educated worker was $229,000 in 1996. Most company pensions are lump-sum, single-payment allotments, originally designed to help retiring employees purchase their own homes or take care of debts for children's tuitions and weddings. One model of disbursement of retirement money rewards skill and productivity with "points" at each promotion level. These points are added up at retirement and used as indicators for the size of a retirement package. Another allows employees to choose between the traditional lump sum at retirement or a "full-salary" plan in which the amount doled out each month equals their monthly salary at a standard retirement age (the second option disburses money withheld prior to retirement but without accrued interest). Now that more younger employees say they prefer the option of changing jobs, companies are interested in attracting and keeping them to retirement age, but on terms that imply both choice and flexibility, buzzwords in the vocabulary of new recruits.

Working after an early retirement from the first job is now very common. Most people who work at postretirement jobs earn very little, three quarters of them earning less than a taxable income; some even manage to find a second postretirement job. But these jobs are hard to get, and senior "job banks" have many applicants. Individuals who can forgo additional income instead choose volunteer activities or hobby groups, such as gateball or women's choruses. The labor force shortages predicted by the shrinking birthrate have not yet had an impact on the availability of jobs for the elderly, nor have they forced consideration of across-the-board shifts upward in the retirement age.

In Japan—which leads other nations in life expectancy (figure 9)—there is now a period of more than twenty years between retirement and death for most people. And for many this is an expensive time of life, especially for those who married late and had children whose financial needs peaked just at their parents' retirement. Often the desire to purchase a single-family home with the pension as down payment must yield to the needs of children. But most middle-class elderly find at least some positive aspects of life in retirement.

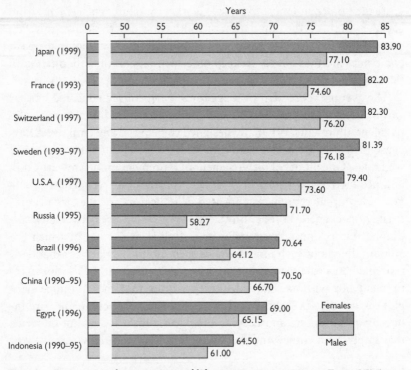

Years

0	50	55	60	65	70	75	80	85

Japan (1999) — 83.90 / 77.10

France (1993) — 82.20 / 74.60

Switzerland (1997) — 82.30 / 76.20

Sweden (1993–97) — 81.39 / 76.18

U.S.A. (1997) — 79.40 / 73.60

Russia (1995) — 71.70 / 58.27

Brazil (1996) — 70.64 / 64.12

China (1990–95) — 70.50 / 66.70

Egypt (1996) — 69.00 / 65.15   Females

Indonesia (1990–95) — 64.50 / 61.00   Males

Figure 9. International comparison of life expectancy, 1990–99. From Ministry of Health and Welfare, *Statistical Handbook of Japan* (Tokyo, 2001).

"NOW, IT'S LIKE HEAVEN"

For those older people who are independent both financially and physically and who live with a spouse, indeed, *Ima wa gokuraku da wa*. The woman who thus exulted in her life with her husband after retirement was contrasting their life with that of her parents and said that she and her husband are so much "younger" now than her parents were at the same age. With machines to do everything for them, she says, their relationship has a new freedom and more equality. In the "old days," she explained, men didn't carry anything heavier than chopsticks inside the house, but now her husband is a real *ashi-kun* (leg man) who runs errands and does chores for her. In the past even in her *own* marriage, a housewife was *okusan* (inside person) or *okura daijin* (minister of finance), managing the household, but now she's the *gaimu daijin* (minister of foreign affairs)—going out with friends, traveling, running the neighborhood committee. Her husband cooks the evening meal and even takes cooking lessons; the old days when men weren't allowed in the kitchen are over.

This new model of the retired life has been underscored by the media and consumer industries. Magazines for mature people emphasize shared activities such as cooking or other hobbies, and networks of sports and activity clubs all over Japan engage older people beyond their homes, neighborhoods, and regions. Consumer goods specific to the interests of these groups are marketed in their periodicals, such as travel magazines designed to appeal to the older traveler.

TARGETING THE ELDERLY

The elderly are a huge and growing market. As producers themselves they fueled the postwar economy and watched Japan shift from an emphasis on manufacturing and production to consumption. There are twenty-one million now over sixty-five and the average household savings of these people amount to $207,000. Those who are healthy and active have a wide menu of products to consider: upscale leisure equipment; special Japan Rail and airline rates; tour packages including medical checkups en route. Educational tourism now being marketed takes retired people farther afield than previous "safe" adventures to Hawaii and other well-trodden sites of packaged tourism for Japanese groups in the 1970s and 1980s. For older tourists, the cachet of "lifelong learning" legitimizes these adventures, and travel can be seen less as self-indulgence, more as an acceptable life enhancement.[15] And the adventurous cast of educational or hobby-focused tourism draws on group members' specific interests. It is also less expensive than the luxurious tours of the bubble years. Thus it fits several converging realities: it conforms to the straitened budgetary demands of older tourists, brings participants a bonus of knowledge, and meets the new demands of more experienced travelers who know what they want, beyond the typical tourist sights.[16]

Takeda Akio and Sumiko are a couple who took one of the small, well researched educational tours of northern Italy designed for retired food professionals, journalists, and others wanting depth and new skills in Italian language and cuisine as well as deeper involvement in the local communities they visit. Some of these experiences include visits in Italian homes and consultations with local chefs. The ten or twelve participants in each group prepare with reading materials and lectures, and they bring home a wealth of and lore about Italy and very specialized souvenirs that transcend older concepts of the correct *omiyage:* bottles of balsamic vinegar and packets of dried porcini mushrooms. Another tour service offers weeklong (or longer) home stays with Italian families in Siena, with short language and cooking courses added. Older men and women also engage in *agriturismo* in Italy, and ecotourism or ethnotourism all over the world. One group of older women engaged a guide to take them to India for cooking lessons and a stay in an ashram. In fact, these forms of tourism for elderly are versions of what is called "experience tourism," from which life-changing personal transformations may result.[17]

Activities closer to home include senior center activities or the popular gateball (croquet) but, according to Masataka Kuraoka, a local council head in his community, these are not the most valuable to the elderly. What they actually favor, he says, whether they live in age-segregated housing or in their families, are activities with younger people: "the highest quality activities are those that involve spending time intergenerationally."[18]

Elderly consumers are targets for health-care products and services. With greater awareness of health-preserving products, and with more chronic ailments, the elderly are a growing market for medicines, both for traditional "Chinese" herbal remedies and modern allopathic prescriptions, vitamins, and palliatives. Japanese versions of American "new age" spas, with massage, aromatherapy, herbal wraps, and other treatments are popular too, as are exercise classes and health clubs for older members. There are special health food menus and food preparations delivered to the homes of elderly. Among the many new consumer products created for them are health and comfort items such as the Toto company's diagnostic toilet (offering analysis of bodily output as a printout from the toilet's computer or as a direct transmission to a doctor's laboratory).

For those with more serious and restrictive illnesses or disabilities, the development of new technologies has produced goods aimed at expanding the possibilities of care with less burden on family caregivers. One of the solutions offered by high technology in care for the bedridden elderly is a newly developed "sensitive" robot able to respond to at least some of the physical needs of a chronically infirm patient. There is scarcely an area of the lives of elderly not targeted for marketing and new products (such as scissors with soft malleable handles to conform to and enable arthritic fingers). While older people in the past were reluctant to spend their money on themselves, the "new elderly" exhibit no such restraint.

20/20 VISION AND GENERATION

According to official Japan, the year 2020—like 1997, when the numbers of people over sixty-five and fifteen or under intersected, and like 2007, when a fifth of the population will be over sixty-five—will be a year of "age *shokku*." It anticipates that in 2020 more than a quarter of the population will be over sixty-five. The quality of their lives receives less attention than the problems their numbers will cause for social service agencies and families tending to their needs.

Consumer industries and advertisers see this group as an active spending audience for goods, not as burdens and victims. The elderly are market segments, by generations or microgenerations within age cohorts or by historical experience as personality types. And indeed, older people use memory and shared experience to identify themselves, preeminently by the experience of war. What will generations of elderly in the future consider as shaping experiences for their lives? Can there be a postwar without the war?

Today's seventy-year-olds were children when the war began and think of themselves as a wartime generation, while their parents were the prewar generation and their children the postwar generation. Prewar groups seem to younger generations "feudalistic" or "traditional"; to postwar generations (now plural), wartime groups appear to retain effects of mobilization for victory; and their elders see these "democratic" postwar generations as deficient in experiences of character-building hardship and deprivation. Of course, these groups contain people of a range of ages and experience that defies categorization. For example, one older gentleman now in a nursing home is proud of his service in the Japanese colonial bureaucracy in Manchuria and showed his scrapbooks and photographs of his life there in the early 1940s. Another, a pacifist artist, Maruki Iri, who died in 1990, was born in the same year as the late Emperor Hirohito and swore that he would outlive the wartime emperor.[19]

Just as "wartime" cannot describe all the experiences of one era, so too the following outline of generational variation cannot represent all the types a period might produce. Advertisers and marketing experts engage in such exercises to consolidate the audiences for products and services, hoping to "massify" consumption or predict the needs of future consumers. Extrapolating from marketing categories, we can make rough sketches of each of the soon-to-be four postwar cohorts to predict the caregiving needs of elderly consumers.

GENERATIONS OF THE FUTURE

I identify four generations by the critical historical environment of their
young adulthood: for the *kyujinrui* (old breed), economic reconstruction,
for PW_1 the takeoff, for PW_2 the bubble, and for PW_3 the birth strike.

	Age in 2000	Age in 2020
Kyujinrui (b. about 1925)	75	95
PW_1 (b. about 1945)	55	75
PW_2 (b. about 1970)	30	50
PW_3 (b. about 1998)	2	22

Taking these generations as our frame, and seeing how each might be
understood in terms of social and economic change, we can project who
they might be in 2020, with suitable tuning for distinctions in class, gender, and region.

Such charting reminds us that there is no one "older generation" and
that understandings of who older people are will have to change with
time and will have to diversify to include a range of differences. The
elderly will live in a variety of arrangements indirectly or directly supported by their own families, or by social services funded through tax-
ation and public allocations. The families who support them will be various as well, and the relationship between the younger generations and
the elder will depend on many factors, including this one of historical
experience.

Those raised in wartime who came of age after the war and began
their families in the late 1940s and early 1950s, the period of reconstruction, have been called the *kyujinrui,* or "old breed," those dedicated
workers who laid the groundwork for the postwar economic boom of
the 1960s.[20] Their children, baby boomers born early in this period of
rapid growth, are PW_1 (1st postwar generation), a "takeoff" generation.
Encouraged by their sacrificing parents to stay in school longer and accumulate social capital in academic credentials, members of the takeoff
generation grew up in a climate of bureaucratic employment and gal-
loping urbanization. These baby boomers had their children in the early
1970s. As the costs of raising successful children rose, urban housing became scarce and expensive; as a result, nuclear households were more
numerous and had to forgo the experience of a three-generation household. Members of the takeoff generation also knew the belt-tightening

of the energy crises of the 1970s, but compared to what their parents went through, these scares seemed insignificant.

Their children are PW_2 (2d postwar generation), a "bubble" generation, raised in the affluent 1980s but not necessarily experiencing wealth themselves. Urban members of the bubble generation did not hear stories of the extreme hardship and scarcity known to their grandparents and indeed knew their grandparents mostly as people who would fill four of their "six pockets" at New Year's and generally indulge them.[21] Their parents, one generation closer to the war and its aftermath, did not convey messages of deprivation and struggle to their young.

Each postwar generation pushed the age of marriage and childbearing later and later. In 1960 the average age at marriage for women was 24.96, in 1995 it was 27.17, and in Tokyo in 1998 it was 28.2. The bubble generation born in the early 1970s has only just now begun to marry and has delayed childbearing as well. Their rate of childbearing is the focus for most concern and makes the youngest group, PW_3 (3d postwar generation), a "birth strike" generation, born to the current generation of parents who are said to reject childbearing. It is the most appropriate epithet for these children, though I argue above that their parents are delaying marriage rather than childbearing. The total number of their children is said to be insufficient, as we have seen, to maintain national economic and social strength. The late-twentieth-century recession offers bubble-generation couples the same contrapuntal juxtaposition of optimism and crisis their parents knew, but they are reacting with more cautious planning for the future. In 2020 then, who will be the families and what, in particular, will be the social, economic and historical frame for that generation of elderly?

What is expected of care and support will vary by the experience and norms of each generation's upbringing. Those now in their seventies cared for their parents and would expect similar care from their children; those in their fifties nearing retirement age themselves are in a more ambiguous cultural setting and were probably raised with an "incompletely filial" set of values, though of course they are old enough to see their own future dependency looming as they struggle to care for their parents.

Our imaginary four-generation family of the year 2020 contains a nonagenarian who is in the care, presumably, of at least one child and grandchild. Such a person might be in a nursing home, depending on his or her physical condition and the available resources at home. Nursing home fees will have skyrocketed and state subsidies will, it is now feared, be very inadequate. Trends now proposed to cut back pensions and to delay payout to age sixty-five will mean that families will be saving more, spending less, for the care of two generations of elderly, the ninety-five-year-old and the seventy-five-year-old. The bubble generation in this family probably had two children when the parents were in their early thirties, the takeoff family had two or maybe three in their midtwenties, and the *kyujinrui* had their first children in their early twenties.

Children in the birth strike generation will be in school or at work and will not even be contemplating marriage yet. By 2020 their income will be needed to supplement their parents' income (both parents would be still working at least one job each). The ninety-five-year-old, if he or she is in a family home, will need occasional intensive care; visiting nurses, home bathing services, and respite care teams might come into play. There will be a very large market for such home-based services, as well as for medicines and "comfort" equipment. How well do these imagined scenarios play out in a real family?

MANAGING WITHOUT A MAP

The Honma family described above is doing fairly well at the moment. Their situation of semi-independence between the two households in the same building is fragile, however, and if Shizuko becomes seriously ill or dies before her more forgetful husband does, clearly the situation will change. There is only the family to cope with the problems that dependency produces, but in their case the family has resources and personnel available to "manage" the needed care (though not as naturally as in a three-generation household—now rare—where older family members have lived continuously and where care for them progresses easily, rather than as a response to crisis).

"Hybrid" living arrangements are often part of the realities of older people.[22] In Maeda Kinuko's family, also reasonably well off, family members share the care of the older generation and act as visiting nurses; so far at least, their arrangements work well. Kinuko is a career woman in her fifties whose parents now enjoy reasonable health and mobility. Her siblings and she set up a system of rotating care with no precedents in the *ie* model but with a sense of responsibility that transcends ideology. Her family had some land that had been broken up and sold during the postwar land reform and all five children received some of the proceeds. They all own homes in various parts of Japan. When the youngest left to work and marry elsewhere, the children held a family conference with their parents at which it was decided that each child would spend a year in a fixed rotation (beginning with the one who left home first, on down to the newlywed) living at the parents' home in Osaka, sharing the care equally.

When each child's own children were very young, this was not a serious dislocation as the parents doted on the grandchildren, taking care of them and requiring very little extra care themselves. Moving the whole household was less likely than moving the daughter or daughter-in-law and her children, of course. When the children were of school age, a family could not uproot them for a year, as staying on track meant staying in the same school, so an interim system was put in place—a "surrogate" couple were hired as housekeepers and the "responsible" child paid frequent visits to be sure that all was well.

Now Grandfather is the survivor in his generation, and the children themselves are near retirement age. The "modern and democratic" (as Kinuko wryly calls it) system put in place in the 1980s has yielded to a more practical decision to have the second child, a son, divide the proceeds from selling his urban condominium between the other siblings as compensation and retire to his parents' home as heir. The original program (a kind of serial U-turn plan) put parents' comfort above children's convenience and yet was not based on filial self-sacrifice and devotion alone: it was, however, dependent on the fact that this family could afford to maintain the ancestral home. Kinuko could manage this arrangement in any case only because her income (and that of her husband) covered her share of maintenance and her frequent trips to Osaka.

Other less well-off families—with similar desires to equalize the care—practice *taraimawashi,* in which the elderly couple move between the families of their children in turn. This is awkward and usually uncomfortable and in any case cannot be managed if parents become disabled or physically dependent. In one such family, the circulating stopped when a parent needed a wheelchair: only one of the homes of the children could be adapted to such a device. But reliance on institutional care outrages traditional sensibilities: families who cannot manage elder care that is value-approved will not talk about it and feel great shame if they have to use institutional nursing care.

LIFE EXPECTANCY—A MIXED BOON

Japan's leadership in the rate of elderly in the population also represents leadership in longevity. The life expectancy for men and women in Japan keeps rising. In 1993, it was 82.51 years for women, 76.25 for men, while in 2001 it was 83.99 for women, 77.10 for men. Compared to the levels of 1947 (54 for women; 50 for men) this represents a striking advance in social and health conditions. However, the gap between males and females has increased, not decreased, from 3.9 years in 1947 to 6.24 in 2000.[23] The higher the age group, the more likely it is to be heavily female, and the more likely to be relatively poor and dependent.

What is of greatest concern is that the number of people needing the most care will continue to increase as the number of those who contribute to their care, directly or indirectly, will continue to shrink, eroding the resource base. Meanwhile the cost of health care and other social services will quadruple by the midpoint of the next century.[24] The cost of social welfare for elderly is high and the institutional provisions for them so far have not met the demand—burdened as that demand is by values and precedents.

CAN A REVERSED PYRAMID STAND?

The shrinking birthrate, the rising rate of elderly, and the eroding social and economic base of Japan are in fact separate but converging problems. Public discourse in Japan lumps them together as the "family problem." In media and official formulations, "family" has meant "women" as the source of these problems and ultimately, and only if they cooperate, as the solution. There is a tendency to blame women for not having more children, putting both the labor force and the elderly at risk. Families are seen as abdicating from responsibility for their dependent elderly and as creating antisocial, selfish "only" children who will, it is feared, deny their parents in the next century. The so-called Asian family welfare model, relying on kin for caregiving, is still seen by some as the only answer. Is this really the only way to meet the needs of families and individuals, and does this response reflect real experiences and data?

In the case of the rising rate of the elderly, the "reverse pyramid" in the population structure will mean more reliance on traditional family care as well as a need for more institutional services. The sheer facts of smaller families, fewer at-home housewives, and more retired people will necessitate governmental intervention, but as we have seen, the funding of these services will still place a burden on family and society. Especially for the care of the oldest elderly, the most rapidly growing segment, who tend to be bedridden (*netakiri*) more than those of other age groups, extra-familial care systems will be needed. Even now, because of better health care, paradoxically, greater longevity has increased the rate of bedridden elderly; the rate of those afflicted with senile dementia in Japan is three times that of the United States.[25]

If nursing homes are still seen as latter-day throwing-away-Granny-mountains where the old are left to die, why do so many older people say that they would rather live there with other elderly than with their children? The popularity of graded care nursing facilities, with progressive assistance provided according to the independence of residents, has produced long wait lists for the good facilities. Some informally arranged care is available to fill the need for places where older people can comfortably convene. A 24-hour bathhouse in Nagoya acts as an informal hostel for the community's elderly, who may extend their overnight stay indefinitely, in some cases using the bathhouse for years as their unofficial primary residence. This kind of place has very good facilities, though it has no on-site health care beyond the mineral baths. It is very popular among elderly who feel useless at home and who become voluntary "residents," highly engaged in the social life this ad hoc arrangement affords.[26]

Hospitals are used as residences as well. Since 1973, when health care was made free for the elderly and covered almost all hospital, clinic, physician, and other costs, there has been much more use of hospitals and clinics, for long-term bed care—even for those not sick. There are about 700,000 hospitalized elderly, and most of these are apparently what is called *shakaiteki nyuuin,* or "social admissions." The irony of well care in hospitals is caught in a current joke, in which a group of elderly are chatting in a hospital lounge when they notice that one of their number is absent from a gathering and fear that he might be ill.

Such communities of elderly would decrease the isolation some experience and would minimize the frictions created in the reversal of dependency roles at home. Japan's suicide rate among the elderly is said to be among the highest in the world, especially among women over seventy-five. It is estimated that family problems account for three-quarters of these cases.[27]

Those who say they will rely on children in their old age are a shrinking segment of the age group. Those who do are bilateral in their preferences, considering daughters as good (or better) in this role than sons and definitely better than relying on a resentful daughter-in-law. Among older elderly, however, a reliance on sons is more common—74.6 percent say they expect care from their sons, 6.4 percent say they expect it from their daughters. An increasing percentage, up to 35 percent of those over sixty-five, say that they hope to be independent. Some elderly now wait until they are seriously physically dependent or suffer a crisis of some kind, until they have an accident, break a hip, or suffer from serious memory loss before they move in with their children. Many say that they do not want to be dependent until they absolutely must—so the move to a son or daughter's home represents an unpleasant acknowledgment of physical dependency. Economic assistance may also decrease as the savings of older people today exceed the disposable income of the pressed junior generation. In the 1960s, 30 percent of elderly relied on children for all support; in the 1980s, 16 percent need their children's economic support.[28]

Throughout the 1980s, officials had applauded the private sector—including the most private of sectors, the family—"as society's hidden asset" in a "Japanese-style" welfare society.[29] Family care has never been the only recourse, but the current preference for family care among officials relates in part to the changing economic situation and in part to the failure of several private sector programs. Some experiments, such as the Silver Columbia Project in which elderly were to be "offshored" to attractive retirement communities in oceanside locations in Argentina or the Gold Coast of Australia, were aborted because of bad press and public opinion referring to them as a kind of private export of Japan's elderly overseas. That they were private initiatives did not reduce the damage to the national image they were said to have caused.

In fact, private retirement arrangements are becoming more popular. Costs vary. Some appear very expensive, charging for example $385,000 for "lifelong stay" plus $1,300 per month for maintenance. For this, residents receive meals, 24-hour nursing care, hotel-like facilities, sports, and cultural facilities.[30] The idea of choice in lifestyle for the elderly may be only for those with means, and tenants in retirement homes like this amount to fewer than 1 percent of the elderly population.

More likely for most people who cannot afford this is family care, or less luxurious nursing homes. The Golden Plan, in place since 1990, in keeping with official desire to keep care based in families, provides for more nursing home capacity but emphasizes support for family caregivers. The Golden Plan would provide respite care, short-term nursing at home, visiting health aides, and meals on wheels. It invokes the Asian model of welfare supplied by the family and cites law proposals in Singapore, enforcing care of parents who may sue their children for support. The New Golden Plan of 1996 rehabilitated the Golden Plan, bowing to reality a little by raising the level of extrafamilial supports and transferring responsibility for at least some aspects of care outside the household.[31] The original impetus behind the plan has continued however in policy documents using language such as "private sector vitality," "the Vigorous Private Welfare Society," and "self-help" among families.

Where families cannot manage, voluntarism is encouraged. Middle-aged women particularly join volunteer groups to supply meals, visit the elderly, clean, shop, and do laundry for them. Local organizations make creative arrangements to engage people in community care. In one area of Tokyo, Setagaya-ku, volunteers caring for elderly receive "banked" hours for the hours they now put in, against their own future need for care. Local municipalities also encourage donations of time or money toward care of local elderly elsewhere. Some elderly people feel reluctant to receive the free services provided by people in their own communities, and families using these services sometimes ask home aides to park their cars away from their houses to avoid "shame."

While some services such as home aid, cleaning, and feeding are subsidized by governmental agencies, private sector institutions are urged to fill the gap. In one program seniors pay monthly fees to a governmental agency that will reimburse care providers. The rest is covered by co-payment between seniors and governmental funds. One service already in place is "care-driving," a senior taxi service for elders who need both some home care, such as cleaning, and a drive to a hot springs. One entrepreneur runs a training service for home helpers, coaching them to use polite language or casual language according to clients' preferences, to memorize the popular songs of a half century ago, and to change adult diapers.[32]

WHO WILL PAY FOR THE ELDERLY?

Payouts of social security funds may deplete the pension reserves before the crisis year of 2020. If the social welfare burden is three quarters of the total national income, as predicted, then taxpayers, a shrinking percentage of the population, will take on a greater share of it. It may be necessary to squeeze the elderly themselves and force greater self-reliance. The bubble generation—the baby boomers' children—who now save less than their elders will have to scrap their lifestyle of consumption.

The national economy thrives, and resources are available for social services when savings rates are high. But in the year 2020 there will be a double whammy to the economy as elderly begin to pay out their savings and the contribution of the much smaller working population shrinks. Social security spending in 1993 was 16 percent of the national income and 12 percent of the gross domestic product (GDP). In 2025, social expenditures are projected to be 27 percent of the GDP.[33] To maintain the resource base for these expenses, it will be necessary to dun workers 61 percent of their incomes for tax and social security in 2025 (the rate is now 37 percent), and employees will have to put aside 35 percent of salaries toward their pensions as opposed to 12.4 percent in 1989.[34]

More people will work after retirement to make ends meet, especially as the age when pension payouts begin to rise from sixty to sixty-five. And more of them may live with children than currently would like to, although in similar conditions in America and western European countries, the rate of elderly living with children has fallen.

MANAGING THE MESSAGE

Unlike childbearing, aging does not have to be marketed: it happens to everyone—but it too has a media profile. As the baby boom generation moves up the population pyramid and begins to experience some of the difficulties of aging, the image of the elderly appears in the mirror. The description of Japan as an "aging society" has given way to the phrase "long-life society," which shifts the meaning of the elderly from a burden on society to a sense of productivity, health, and independence. One notable "friendly" image is that of the famous superstar centenarian twins, Gin-chan and Kin-chan, who in the early 1990s seemed to be on nearly every quiz, variety, and talk show—they are a good example of the Japanese marketing of cuteness—decked out in cute childish colors, hats, and flowers in their hair, they are always cheerful, giggling, rather like dolls. In fact, they are like Japanese pop stars or cartoon characters in that a line of "signature" products has been marketed with their images on them.

Educators have begun to create "elder awareness" in school classrooms to make sure children with no home experience of older people see age as normal, human, and integrated in their lives. Visits to nursing homes (like visits to day-care centers) are part of "community service" and make the elderly (like babies) a "friendly" concept to young students. The cooperation between the Ministry of Education and the Ministry of Health and Welfare, officials hope, will support three-generation family care as "our hidden asset of social welfare."

There are some indications that official pronouncements touting this "asset" are soon to stop. While families do and must care for their own members, popular understandings are not based on "family values" or adherence to a model of behavior encoded as the *ie*. Japanese papers run headlines about the erosion of filial piety, the physical and emotional abuse of the elderly by adult children at the ends of their ropes. Editorials say that prosperity has weakened family morality, as only 23 percent of Japanese young people say they will care for their parents no matter what, compared to 63 percent in the United States, a surprising piece of comparative data for those who believe that America is the country sending its elderly to isolation, penury, and lonely death. In fact, there is said to be more intergenerational conflict in Japan than in America. It is interesting that images and realities on both sides of the Pacific are so far apart and that our stereotypes of ourselves and each other are so wide of the mark.[35]

There has never been a singular experience of aging in Japan, or of the relationship between generations. In the past, tales of loving care by sacrificing younger generations or stories of "filial" abandonment overlooked the fact that elderly people are not always dependent. More recently, accounts of the heightened sociability, independence, and spirituality of the aged neglect the many who must rely on kin or society. All of these stories are perfectly Japanese. But complicated and diverse ways of aging don't make an ideology of the perfect Japanese family. The common account of Japan as a good place to be old, where the elderly are respected and cared for, vies with newer tales of the family as a place where national fiat and economic need force the nurturance of older relatives who are at high risk for abuse there as well. In 2020, when those over sixty-five will be a quarter of the population, there will be no singular prix-fixe model of care that works. The already existing diversity of options will then represent an à la carte menu from which individuals and families will order what they can afford to provide—for many, a meager repast.

PART THREE

Consuming as Survival

Marketing
the Bite-Size Family

Consuming Images, Supporting Realities

A young woman leans against a stone pillar; she faces a temple surrounded in mist. It is early morning and an old couple are slowly walking on a path toward the temple. In the young woman's hand we notice a *furoshiki*-wrapped box. The caption reads, "It's been a long time; won't you go home?"

Travel poster, Tokyo, July 1997

The essence of nostalgia is in the creation of personalized, perfect images of the past, locating this wholeness in a particular place and time. Nostalgia invades the present too: brooding over contemporary experience and conditions—over deviations seen or made from the perfect model—can inflect attempts to fix the present. In Japan, imagined families are more than sentimental references to the past; they are also potent means of holding the present accountable.

The young woman holding a package wrapped in an old-fashioned patterned cloth, we imagine, has gone "home" to her grandparents in the country and holds a traditional present in her hand. But the ad does not show her running up to them or engaging with them in any way. Instead, it shows her motionless as she watches the couple—yearning and guilty?—hoping to return to the lost family, unable to merge her reality with her fantasy.

In America or Japan, "going home" to the imagined family can only be a fantasy. Management of the present conditions of families evokes the fantasized past, even if it never existed for most people. In America, popular depictions of the nineteenth-century household show a large and harmonious establishment in which everyone dutifully upheld the ways and order of the home. Children received the skills needed for their liveli-hood and the values of an American "way of life" that brought the fam-ily together for Thanksgiving dinner.[1] In Japan, the rural extended fam-ily implies togetherness too, but in service to a wider society than the dining table. It implicates its individual members in the greater organic unity of the state. As a tool for what Sheldon Garon calls "moral sua-sion," its very vagueness makes it a potent and malleable image.[2]

Demographic verification of nineteenth-century households was never the issue. Most American grandparents died before their grandchildren got to know them; most children had limited access to their parents; many couples were separated by early death; and households held varied and unpredictable assortments of individuals, many unrelated by blood. Change and uncertainty characterized the life course of families more than stability and security.[3] Moreover, ideologies of self-improvement, independence, and success contradicted images of family loyalty and in-tergenerational continuity. Success appeared to mean rupture: leaving home to go West or actively breaking away. And yet, evocations of the large, tight-knit, self-sufficient, orderly family are part of an American ideology of family that drives at least the rhetoric of policy, for issues ranging from welfare to school prayer to responsibility for dependent elderly and children. Our past perfection is full of internal contradictions.[4]

Who can or could approximate the Japanese family's golden-age model? As we have seen, only the elites and the wealthy lived up to the Meiji code's 1898 standards. The "consumer democracy" today creates identities for individuals, as well as households, but household roles of-ten resemble ill-fitting clothing, and attempts to reoutfit families have not been completely successful: even middle-class families caught up in consumer trends do not find that the one-size-fits-all version of family suits them.

After the devastation of war, Japanese leaders did not repair to the prewar past (as American politicians and ideology-spinners did) but in-voked policy and rhetoric to discredit the nineteenth- and early-twentieth-century family models as patriarchal, nationalistic, and "feudalistic." In the boom years since the 1970s, several fashions in family, far from tra-ditional, have emerged as objects of yearning. These lifestyles are part of the close interaction between consumer industries, their intermediaries in advertising and marketing, and the consumers who pick up concepts of what their family should be. The young married couples who see the decision to buy a living room carpet to cover the tatami and "go with" their furnishings as a lifestyle choice act "subversively," not only in covering the traditional tatami matting but even in making a couple-based choice of their own. The middle-aged woman who hires a plumber to install a dishwashing machine larger than the little portable sink-top versions adds to her family time (she can actually get her husband to load this one) as she ignores postwar conventions of the division of labor in the home. The elderly husband and wife who pay an agency to send a young man to visit them and run errands for them, "standing in" for their son who is in Europe, please themselves but most definitely defy understandings that such help should not be paid for *or* needed.

The organic feeling of family most Japanese express does not come close to the postwar middle-class ideal. You do not need a continuously cohabiting extended family to feel like family, nor do you need the full surround of suburban nuclear intimacy. Family is more than the sum of its model's parts. Much of the shortfall, the difference between reality and ideological model, now can be laid at the feet of the consumer marketers, who have organized their audiences around fantasies and dreams. Family, they say, is the site for enacting these dreams of consumption.

Families in Japan have institutional and economic reference points, whereas in America what Robert Bellah has called a "therapeutic discourse" characterizes families by emotional tone.[5] In American textbooks, the family appears as a collection of pathologies, in a table of contents organized typically around problem areas in the family, issues of divisiveness and personal disengagement, or clinical pathologies traced to family dysfunction. In Japan, too, families are atomized—as the products, and objects, of market segmentation rather than as the clients of therapy. Closer to the realities of people's lives are new units to carry out family functions and serve where families left off.

These obviously counternostalgic forces—media constructions of, and commercial support for, new families—thrive alongside equally strong pressures in the same institutions to organize family life around the more conservative, homogenizing priorities of economic and national security. Families dutifully engage in economic productivity and high-level consumption and the care of dependents, as the media encourage them to do. The basic role definitions, expectations, and functions of the family are not disappearing. But at the same time, new "unorthodox" consumer institutions and spaces have risen up to relocate and manage them. We look at some of these necessary adjuncts to family life: full-service convenience stores acting as caterer, concierge, and comfort station, the department store, the bar, and even the vending machine.

Consumption, one of a family's several tasks in service to national goals, may also be an arena for subversion of those goals. The goods and services they purchase are available because they are needed to help ordinary families make do; they do not defend the "beautiful family traditions" policymakers hope to protect.

AT THE FAMILY TABLE

Holidays, as we saw in chapter 6, frame families' shared ritual time. The New Year's holiday is the preeminent family gathering in Japan, a *national* family event. Before the Meiji and Taishō periods, New Year's was not so organized in time and expectations and families were not so uniformly dedicated to a several-day celebration. Standards for cleanliness in the purification of a house before January 1 and for the food preparations for at least three days of entertaining were codified and sent forth through media and advertising, and images of a happy family gathered around a "family" table were new in the twentieth century.

Family-style eating is a product of Westernizing fashions popular at the turn of the century. As Kumakura Isao has noted, the transitions in dining practice reflect changes in family life.[6] Before the end of the Meiji period people were served on individual trays on legs set in front of each diner. Larger tables were introduced: first low tables, then Western-style tables with chairs. Jordan Sand discusses the role of social reformers in the nineteenth century who advocated the introduction of family dining tables to promote a "family circle": one such activist said, "A family meeting is held at mealtime. In light of this, meals absolutely must be taken at the same time and at the same dining table. . . . I mean one large surface, whether round or square."[7] The family circle even began to include women, who in magazine ads by the 1920s appear sitting *with* the family (her husband, his parents, and the children) instead of cooking and serving. Reality may be a little different, especially at events where there are nonfamily guests and the women who prepare the food would be serving through most of the meal.

Other nationally celebrated holidays may emphasize buying more than commensality. Coming of Age Day (the second Monday of January), Girls' Day (March 3), Children's Day (May 5), Respect for the Elderly Day (September 15), and Shichigosan (November 15, when children ages

7, 5, and 3 are presented at shrines for blessing), became part of the holiday calendar only in the twentieth century. Each of these days has its "family marketing" aspect: Coming of Age Day requires that families kit out their twenty-year-olds in fashionable kimono or other dress and fete their new adulthood at temples, shrines, and fancy restaurants. While the new adults themselves may spend the later part of the evening at discos and love hotels in various celebrations with their peers, the "family" aspect of the holiday dominates marketing of clothing and dining facilities, and the responsibility for funding it remains with parents.

Girls' and Children's Days also involve a family investment. Families who have no inherited set of *ohinasama* dolls for display on March 3 buy them at great expense; if they have a boy, the display of miniature traditional armor may be required on May 5, or the purchase of stereo equipment and video games. Woe to families without children, who have no offspring with whom to celebrate. Articles on how to hold Girls' and Children's Day parties in women's magazines increase the performance requirements for mothers and offer challenges to make or buy the perfect cakes, jellied sweets, and other festive foods. What is promised in exchange for this effort are happy children made even happier by mothers who have the time, dedication, and skill to create celebrations of family. And of course mothers are the ones whose investments are validated by their offspring's gratitude. Shichigosan has the same implication; on November 15 you parade your expensively attired children (often with grandparents in attendance) in the crowds at temples and shrines. A family with more than one child at such an event, perhaps a son of seven and a daughter of five, makes a good showing in these days of the one-child family.[8]

The day invented to boost filial piety, Respect for the Elderly Day, has received much editorial attention. Since 1990, when the 1.57 *shokku* drew attention to the crisis of an aging workforce and declining births, commentators have used September 15 as a day of remembrance when "respect" has a new connotation. Filial piety now means protecting the state of the nation through caring for dependent family members. Schools may have assemblies and invite old people to school for celebrations, or elementary school students may visit nursing homes as evidence of attention to institutionalized elders who are clearly not receiving full-time family-based care.

Even without holidays to mark on a calendar, families engage in consumption that identifies family as a location for goods and activities. The holidays just described are national, created by governmental decree, and they promote and celebrate families through attention to ideal models of individuals in their family roles and in their own life trajectories. Non-holiday, ordinary family consumption may better reveal the practical adjustments people make between images and realities.

SELLING FAMILIES OVER THE DECADES

Japanese consumer industries began to engage in image making in the 1920s, when mercantilism created clienteles for Western-influenced goods and when shopping itself became an activity for families. This was a diversion encompassing both play and purchase, as leisure activity and economic activity became interchangeable. The establishment of transportation networks and print media reaching a broad and national audience made consumption patterns more universal and the goods marketed part of a national "standard package" and desired lifestyle.[9]

Japanese marketers have created "generations" of family images similar to the mobilizing images touted by their American counterparts. The 1960s family in Japan mirrored the postwar family in America, a suburban husband and wife in their own home, each with gender-specific tasks. But in Japan, the "professional housewife" managed the home while her salaryman husband committed himself to corporate success. Happy families in America were designed in advertising in terms of the new idea, "togetherness"; in Japan they were depicted in terms of role fulfillment.

In the 1960s and 1970s, American tendencies to permit unisex performance of domestic and child-rearing functions did not spread to Japan, as the demands of the Japanese occupational and educational systems continued to promote a gender-driven separation of roles. Able to supply the income to support consumption, men were earners, and women as mothers were home coaches, organizers, and supporters of children's success. Marketing goods and services to this family meant a focus on women in her newly "professionalized" role in the home.

By the 1980s, however, Mother was not always there in the home and the incidence of *kagiko,* or "latch-key children" began to create concern among educators and child development specialists. Mother's absence, whether for tennis lessons or for income-producing work, was seen as a problem, and when a child of a working mother had problems in school, teachers would cite her absence as the source of his academic or social malaise. The school and workplace as arbiters of family roles yielded to media and women's magazines; television and news media both amplified and subverted norms and attitudes anchoring women to family roles.[10]

At the same time, the rising youth population had to be served. Young working women were extending their period of work life before marriage, previously only from two to five years (depending on whether the woman had graduated from high school or from a two- or four-year college) to ten years or more, and many women were waiting until their mid- or late twenties to marry.

Young women consumers are indeed vulnerable to the blandishments of advertising and marketing, targeted for their disposable income as "parasite singles." Fads in clothing, beauty treatments, and entertainment are picked up and dropped by women in their twenties at a rapid clip. Appearance-enhancing items and fads include fat-reducing soap from China, skin-lightening (and recently, -darkening) creams, diet formulae, and slimming teas. Six months is the typical shelf life of a consumable trend: some may be more durable as the period of young adult "freedom" itself stretches out.

Commentators characterize the short-term fads among young women as frivolous and selfish, and the women themselves as amoral in the pursuit of trends. One example cited is the rental of safe deposit boxes by young women who stow away love letters and memorabilia from past relationships to keep them away from the prying eyes of new beaux or husbands. The rentals are not cheap, and having a box "with a past" is a status symbol among young office ladies, which commentators take as further evidence that women accumulate men in an amoral quest, just as they accumulate designer goods. Young women say that it is just "for fun."

In the 1980s, fun was supposed to continue into marriage. Advertising aimed at youthful families emphasized couples rather than parenting, and the young couple was seen to have an idyllic—even romantic— shared home life. By the end of the decade, lifestyle had become a marketing notion. The apartments of young married couples became the locus of decorator energy and "trendiness." Ironically, marketers engaged the "self-expression" and "choice" of the young housewife as she made the appropriate purchases.

In the postboom era of the last dozen years, advertising is undaunted by economic downturns, and "recessionary" trends too are vigorously marketed. The most flagrant trends of bubble-era luxury spending, such as gold-leaf-flecked coffee in Limoges cups and multiple sets of Louis Vuitton luggage, may have abated, but shopping is still the preferred leisure time activity.

The images of family in advertising now promote a "return to family" in images of grandparents reading to children or taking them on nature walks. Deliberately old-fashioned sepia-toned shots of homes in Taishō-era style and fashion create a mood of nostalgia for gracious, warm family life. In fact, as we will see, the young urban families of to-day rarely see such rural or old-fashioned scenes in real life. They may indulge in a detail or two such as the "intellectual" wire eyeglass frames some young men sport along with the center-parted, gelled-back hair-style of the Taishō 1920s. Even foreign products may be marketed in this way in Japan, showing Western families sitting around a breakfast table, or a young rustic American boy, looking like Tom Sawyer, presenting a loaf of fresh-baked bread to his mother.[11]

Advertising on television may sometimes "sell" a more traditional view of family than does the programming it supports.[12] A "trendy drama" may present the lifestyle of a young female office worker, involved in love affairs but independent, self-supporting, and uninterested in mar-riage. Then in midaction comes an advertisement for a kitchen product, a wedding hall, or a family-focused theme park. *Tokyo Love Story* was one such "trendy drama" of the early 1990s. The lead character, Rika, is the epitome of trendiness: she loves her job, has an active social and sex-ual life and great clothes. She is still in her twenties, the very image of the prosperous independent female consumer. She, and the audience who yearn to be like her, are the targets for the advertisers, who hope to mar-ket both their current free-wheeling spending and their later "nesting" consumerism.

Since more traditional programs such as samurai or family dramas in rural settings are less attractive to the young female audiences whose pur-chasing power is in turn attractive to advertisers, television stations are now dropping these shows aimed at older viewers. Still popular, however, among middle-aged audiences are family soap operas in which women are oppressed by fathers-in-law, engage in feuds with mothers-in-law, or strike out on their own against all odds. These are not the virtuous abused women of the past, suffering in silence, sharing their angst with no one but the viewer. Instead they fight back, deal with the problem at hand, and move on. A happy ending is not required.[13] Comics also appeal to the audiences of the television dramas and they too churn out stories ap-pealing to readers seeking idols, models, and lifestyles, though of course in a mode further from reality. *Shojo manga,* cartoon magazines for young women, feature love comedies, dream visions, historical fantasies, or episodes of sometimes violent and abusive sexuality. As lifestyle arbiters, they may provide more escape than modeling, for all ages.

MEDIA AND THE BITE-SIZE FAMILY

In 1993, on the first no-school Saturday, the karaoke industry designated a "family karaoke day." Karaoke, or singing to a recorded background orchestra, has become a national, even global industry.[14] Most consumers of karaoke are young workers of both sexes, or middle-aged male businessmen. The expansion of the market to families reflects the "leisure boom" of the 1980s, brought home in the 1990s. Family-based leisure, symbolized now in the precious free time of children as much as in the hours snatched by adults from their work commitments, is a governmental priority. Both the emotional health of children and the needs of adults for respite time are seen to be served by families playing together, acting as a unit of leisure consumption. The karaoke industry rushed in to organize free time and assemble the family through purchase of home equipment similar to the technology young people use to entertain each other at rented karaoke boxes, or their fathers struggle to use during compulsory after-hours bar hopping with workmates and clients. Through creation of Family Karaoke Day the industry hoped to bring together what it had torn asunder, an organic (and purchasing) group singing around the *kotatsu*, the living area's small central table that is the heart of a home.

Explanatory models frame the American family as a collection of individuals, even as it operates, perforce, as a cooperating unit. By contrast, they characterize the contemporary Japanese family as a more organic whole that, in practical terms, behaves as a cohabiting set of "consumption units." In both societies, the prevailing explanatory models, whether psychological or socioeconomic, reduce the family. Neither framework provides what policymakers understand to be the present and future need for support and self-sufficiency; neither makes families reliably independent of the need for a deep investment of public attention and resources.

Official policy hardly needs to guide Japanese families or determine the household's shape and activities. Market forces of all kinds handily manage this job and seem to be in harmony with at least some of the economic goals set for family consumer behavior, if not the goals for family self-help in welfare functions. The segmentation of the family into small units—mother and child, father, less often a grandparent—has accompanied the microsegmentation of the consumer and media markets.

Identifying people by their capacity to buy is not a new phenomenon.

However, the force of such identification was perhaps never stronger than in Japan at the end of the twentieth century. The volume of consumption peaked in the 1980s but remained strong. Habits of spending acquired in the boom years were adjusted in kind but not profoundly changed as an activity and what Wakao Fujioka has called the "micro-masses" (as opposed to large-scale homogeneous markets) continue to guide production and advertising of consumer goods.[15] Families contain representatives of several such "micro-masses" divided by age, gender, and style: for example, a grandfather may engage in a hobby of bug collecting, putting himself on every list targeting naturalists or outdoors lovers; a teenage son may be a hip-hop fan and cruise the gear shops of Shibuya in Tokyo for beeswax to mold his nascent dreadlocks—and both may be approached through the Internet or directly by sellers of related products. A younger child may have been enrolled as a toddler in an infant shopping club and may, attended by her cooperative mother, cash in club discount coupons at her "home" department store.[16]

In Japan, the microsegments or units are not however just "consumer animals," passive recipients, or victims of the blandishments of the marketers. Japanese consumers are activists—and the market is not insensitive to its audiences. In fact, "audience" is the operative concept: marketing in Japan is script-writing, and we might easily characterize consumer activity as the participation of the audience in the theater of consumption. Individuals engage in the performance by taking on the roles scripted by marketers. Buying is part of a process of learning a part, in a theater where consumers are actors who make their own demands on the system and attempt to fill their roles as they perceive them. And, as Victor Turner notes, participants are conscious that it is a script they are learning: they may be persuaded to engage, but they are not blind to the art of persuasion itself.[17]

Lifestyle marketing is calibrated so as not to create too large a gap between dreams and reality: this is in part managed by the proliferation of magazines aimed at specific readerships. A personal hook to the reader must exist for a magazine to succeed in its niche; editors, especially those of magazines catering to teenagers, understand just how far they can go to stimulate yearnings without also triggering frustration.[18] A person should be able to alchemize the base-metal drudgery of daily life by means of fantasies—shopping within her budget—but not need to break the bank or the social contract of work and family.

And if the preoccupations of the consumer happen to fulfill the demands of his or her role in society rather than flee from it, so much the better. For what George deVos calls "role narcissism" continues to guide the lives of many Japanese men and women. The corporate warrior image may be parodied, or mocked—as in the recent television advertisement for an energy tonic showing dozens of dark-suited ultra-serious-looking salarymen marching militantly to the strident, purposeful chant (in English) of "Japanese businessman!"—but it still evokes the ambitions of many on the salary ladder. The housewife image too has been diminished by the competing image of the career woman, but the demands of the *ryosai kembo* role of good wife/wise mother remain challenging. Even the description of her job as "three meals and a nap" or the denigration of her concern for her children's educational success as the "*kyō-iku mama* syndrome" does nothing to reduce the expectations for high-level role performance. Daytime television, the magazine industry, and all products and services focused on the home and children depend on the woman taking her job as a job, very seriously.

Magazines targeting women tend to be exhortative and role-defining, from those for young teens, teaching them how to be both trendy and "good," to those for the OLs at the most intense consumer stage of life, or ones for prospective brides busily dreaming and spending. Housewives are not exempt, as their magazines direct them to create a kind of "self-expressive conformity" to the standards of good womanhood. In addition, housewives now must show their skills in economizing while they spend. Many now are learning economies their mothers had practiced or using lower rather than higher technologies (such as fans rather than air conditioners) and shopping at discount stores, which did not exist in their mothers' youth.

They must keep spending, of course, to keep consumption up, and a recent temporary income tax cut of $558 per household was created in 1998 to encourage spending. Poll results revealed that half of all families planned to save rather than spend their rebate.[19] Since most housewives are still in charge of family funds, including their husbands' salaries, they must both spend and save (balancing needed indulgences for husbands and children against luxuries for themselves). In spite of such evidence of retreat from rampant consumerism, however, the Economic Planning Agency reported in March 1999 that "demand for . . . consumer goods has stopped declining," and that consumers who had been waiting to replace certain durable goods like washing machines were beginning to do so; couples who had been saving for weddings were beginning to marry; and corporations waiting to renew computers and other technology were investing in new hardware.[20]

Finally, life stage as well as lifestyle determines participation by consumers and marketing of products and roles by media and consumer industries. Because of the persistence of age grading in Japanese society, people tend to adjust personal style and consumption activities much more by age than do Americans. Industries such as cosmetics and clothing companies reflect this in their segmentation of product lines by age group. Young unmarried women wear very different styles and colors than do older married women, and the clientele observed in clothing stores reflects age and role segregation in clothing. Magazines organized by age and gender amplify this stratification. The "massification" of the market does permit and indeed demand subsegments: the largest possible audience for the smallest number of products permits efficiency and economies of scale, but diversification permits the development of new goods and products that attract more people. The Japanese consumer markets are exceptionally good at both.

The markets owe their huge impact both to the family's smaller size and to its more limited ability to serve and influence its members. As we have seen, women are still in thrall to models of "good wife/wise mother" that now seem to operate only to compel their consumer behavior, rather than their images of themselves or their behavior in families. Families' use of a variety of consumer institutions reflects new functions and roles that may not fully exhibit images of maternal role dedication but do not discard the values and expectations of society. At the same time, their use of these consumer institutions permits a new flexibility, even subtle subversion, of the principles of consumer production and locations of family.

Not all families, rural or urban, can live the consumer dream in any case. Even in the 1980s, when "affluence" was said to characterize Japanese society, the gap between the more and less affluent was visible. The boom years created an image of Japanese consumerism not available to every household. Young people who could not afford to be "consumers in training" felt "bullied" or cheated by society.[21] For adults too, the joys of wealth seemed spurious; middle-class families realized they could indeed get everything they wanted except the time or space in their lives to enjoy the goods. The high savings rates of the first postwar decades could not keep up with the price of land; buying a single-family home became impossible for many who had saved all their working lives for this opportunity. The drop in land values after the bubble economy burst still left the cost of housing beyond the reach of most households. The average condominium purchased in 1997 cost $260,000, or 5.2 times the average annual salary of consumers.

The smaller family—essential to the promising middle-class lifestyle— is the source as well as the product of fractionalizing forces in the market. As a portent of future declines in purchasing, the family's shrinking birthrate is also the object of public concern. Fewer people, an aging society, and more intense marketing sum up recessionary consumerism in Japan. Products encourage and support the centrifugal nature of membership in the household: the home provides fewer of the individuals' needs as surrogates rush in to fill the gap. At the same time, as noted above, role perfectionism maintains expectations for high quality. People are willing to spend for the "taste of home"—even if they spend little time there.

WHO NEEDS A WIFE, A DAUGHTER-IN-LAW, OR EVEN A REFRIGERATOR?

It was already "bug-hot" (*mushi-atsui*) at 7:00 A.M. when a new shop opened its doors in Naha, Okinawa, in July 1997. The shop was quickly jammed. This was the latest outpost of one of the largest chains of *konbini,* convenience stores, in Japan, its first in Okinawa and thus a major moment in its marketing history. The rival chain had already arrived in the prefectural capital, so this new shop represented a challenge to its competitor and to the mom-and-pop shops nearby as well as a testament to the capacity (seemingly bottomless) any Japanese neighborhood has for "convenience." Well before the hour, huge floral displays and congratulatory wreaths decorated the store front and a huge crowd of middle- and high-school students and officials in dark suits and ties waited, already sweating in the tropical heat. The ribbon-cutting ceremony went off smoothly and the hordes rushed inside to shop.

Over a day, a *konbini* witnesses all age groups and occupations and serves all families. Many young customers have never lived without them and others find it hard to remember what life was like without them. The manager of this shop is a man in his forties, but the staff are usually teenagers and many of the clients are too, before and after school hours. Its services and functions are wider than the general store's, where everybody knew your name, your family. And the shop's computer, hard-wired to the home office, lists at least your approximate age, sex, and occupation, if not your name, in the information gathering all *konbini* perform. As they ring up purchases, clerks input data on each customer to inform management of sales trends and needs and to keep the "just-in-time" delivery schedule providing goods as needed, obviating the need for storage space in the tiny shops.

There are approximately fifty thousand convenience stores—most are open 24 hours—in Japan today. From an American perspective, these shops push the notion of "convenience" beyond our wildest ideas of basic needs: they provide fresh (high-quality, not fast-food) packaged meals, every notion and need of a household from laundry detergent to whiskey, ties, underwear, and cameras, school and office supplies, a drop-off point for parcel delivery services, a bill payment site for utilities and other regular services, gift and floral ordering service, copy and fax facilities, and more. Travelers going to the mountains or the airport can send their skis and luggage ahead from a *konbini* and travel to their destinations confident and unhampered by burdens. Trucks bring produce and prepared foods several times a day, ensuring freshness (and sometimes irritating neighbors with noise and exhaust).

Socializing and lingering, which used to promote neighborhood cohesion through the medium of gossip and information exchange, no longer center on the shopkeeper. The less productive small family-run shop is yielding ground to discount houses and convenience stores, the first for price, the second for its predictable stock and around-the-clock availability. The function served in mom-and-pop shops as neighborhood gossip centers cannot be maintained in *konbini*. But there is human contact here, in spite of the computerization, and one manager said he knows most of his regular customers. Young people hang out here after school, and friends know where to find each other. But it is also all right to linger alone and stand leafing through comics and magazines at the magazine racks. Young people especially scan the monthly or weekly magazines for fashion, trends, and motorcycle maintenance. No one complains and in fact, it is said that magazine racks are positioned in front of the windows so that the standing readers face the road, serving as deterrents to potential robbers.[22]

After the morning rush of workers and students, the *konbini* receive housewives from the neighborhood who increasingly use these stores as regular shopping destinations—not replacing, but supplementing, their daily grocery and other shopping. By midday elderly people also stop in. The convenience store's plastic-wrapped individual portions of traditional Japanese meals (many small dishes of different foods, including pickles, seaweed, salted or grilled fish, prepared vegetables, and other foods) allow people who live alone or in couples the variety of a traditional meal without accumulated leftovers that will spoil. Elderly find this acceptable as an alternative either to cooking for themselves or changing their diets to a "Western"-style sandwich/salad or "instant" one-pot food. Even cooked rice is available at a *konbini,* ready to microwave (you can even microwave it at the shop itself). In extremis, there is always the ever simmering pot of *oden* or the hot *manjuu* case for a traditional snack of fish paste dumplings or steamed pork buns—and these are always available.

Elderly residents of the neighborhood find the *konbini* useful not just for food but for services. They pay their utility bills there and find prethreaded needles, easy to open toiletries, and other comforts. The rising numbers of the elderly have not been ignored by manufacturers of such products who may use convenience stores as their main outlet. The "just in time" delivery of fresh goods in small packets pleases older consumers who do not want to carry or store items in bulk or quantity but who still want the foods they would make for themselves if they could.

Women who work, part or full time, appreciate *konbini* but may feel apologetic about using them. In the recent past, before the burgeoning of convenience stores, multiservice department stores near train terminals served the function of take-out kitchens for busy women. In the 1970s, as women entered the workforce in unprecedented numbers, working either full time or "mothers' hours" (during their children's school time) and maintaining the household, these 200-percenters often became *tenuki okusan,* or "no-hands" housewives. No-hands, because they assembled meals from delicatessen foods bought at department store food halls close to their train stop on the way home from work. They might refer to themselves this way in guilty jest, rather like the woman who confesses in a self-caricaturing way to being a *kyoiku mama.* No one, no matter how supported by society in a "virtuous" role, is exempt from self-punishment.

DEPAATO—THE BUSY HOUSEWIFE'S DESTINATION

The function now served by convenience stores was once the exclusive domain of the *depaato* or department store.[23] These general merchandise stores, evolved from the smaller shops of Tokugawa-era merchants, became consumer, culture, and entertainment hubs of urban life in Japan from the 1920s on. Department store visits became a leisure as well as a consumer activity, and young people and women became their chief clients. In Japan's first consumer era, the rapid development of commercial activity was intensified by mass transport, and urban department stores were often located at major train/bus/subway nodes.[24]

As the middle class grew, especially in the postwar years, department stores served families' needs for goods and services. And again, by the mid-1970s, the department stores served both skyrocketing consumption needs and desires with one-stop shopping for time-saving appliances and housewares, clothing and services for children from infancy through high school, even adult education courses in topics ranging from cooking and home economics to literature, art, and international relations.

But the basement and sub-basements (up to three subterranean levels for alimentary goods in some shops) contain the *depaato*'s paramount service for working women. There they find an extensive, high-quality selection of foods, from expensive French wines to huge selections of more humble pickles. Department stores are also the main source for gift foods—corporate or personal—and the wrapping paper of a good store adds calculable cachet to a gift melon or boxed set of cooking oils. These food hall provisions do not come cheap: prices are higher than those of local supermarkets and grocers. But the performance requirements for the good housewife were (and are) equally high and the cost of premium goods is acceptable in terms of the demands on the woman to provide her family with quality as well as sustenance. In a 1992 survey, 57 percent of housewives said they had bought prepared foods such as fried chicken and grilled fish, and 50 percent had bought whole prepared meals.[25]

Even though the family meal rarely takes place now (on average once or maybe twice a week, among the families I interviewed), food quality and presentation are still a focus of marketing attention. Like Kitajima Satoko in chapter 6, more women prefer to spend the extra money for prepared foods than to make these foods themselves: they lack both time and confidence in their own ability. And certain provisions become indicators of attention to cultural imperatives.

STARTING THE DAY

More than any other meal in modern lives, breakfast is fraught with personal and cultural meaning. British tourists take their rashers of bacon or gammon ham and British butter on holiday in Spain so as to preserve the comfort and certitude of home away from home; Americans need their coffee first thing; and Japanese—especially older males—want rice, pickles, seaweed, grilled fish or egg, miso soup, and green tea to prepare them for their day to come. Hotels in Waikiki, New York, and even Dallas have learned this, and many provide a Japanese option to start the day.

Toast, coffee, and eggs have made inroads on the traditional Japanese breakfast. Children rushing to school, husbands grabbing a *mooningu setto* at a nearby coffee shop, women busily preparing box lunches—few actually sit down to a family meal at this hour in any case. And when they do, it may be a hybrid meal, including rice, small cocktail sausages, eggs, shredded cabbage with salad dressing, rice, and pickles. Invariably, however, where there is rice for breakfast, there is miso soup. This soup is the basic element of Japanese family cooking: a fish-and-seaweed-broth with miso (fermented soybean paste), tofu, and seaweed—with mushrooms or other additions.[26]

All this takes time to prepare, even if you use packets of instant broth and have programmed the automatic rice maker to let you sleep longer. And it is unlikely to be a cooperatively prepared meal: fewer men help in the morning than at any other time in the day, and children are encouraged to finish homework, pack their satchels, and eat, rather than help, at this hour.

If there is an elderly relative in the house, then the breakfast meal he or she eats is almost always Japanese. In three-generational homes where the daughter-in-law works in an office or factory, grandmothers are most likely the breakfast chefs encouraging a more traditional meal, and they may well grumble at the grandchildren who want toast and cereal instead. Even for the conservative breakfast eater, however, the convenience store will have tiny packets of pickles and seaweed and salted grilled fish freshly prepared and shrink-wrapped: the old values are not lost but supported and maintained in the face of new schedules and family conformations.

A working mother still has to keep up with the family and anticipate others' needs. She will make breakfast for her husband and another for her children and perhaps grab a piece of toast herself. She will prepare a box lunch for her children (and sometimes for her husband). As we will see, the standard elements of both meals exceed an American repertory of cereal, juice, and coffee or sandwich, apple, and carrot sticks.[27]

Nutrition is an aspect of maternal performance requirements. Because more meals are taken apart than together as a family, a housewife has to make up for the lack of nutrition in the "fast foods" or incomplete meals her children and husband eat outside the home. Schools exhort mothers to provide "something from the ocean; something from the mountains" in every lunch made at home, poetic shorthand for a balanced meal of grains, vegetables, and fish or sea produce. The American cereal company's concern with starting the day right with a healthy breakfast does not come close to the dismay some in Japan express about the lack of a good (Japanese) breakfast: it is perhaps as much about Japanese identity, equated with health and purity, as it is about nutrients. It is also role performance because it takes so much time to prepare, making mothers rise well before the others in her household to make this emblematic meal.[28] And even so, many people eat breakfast away from home and thus replace familial commensality with isolation as a ritual but not traditional practice.

THE COFFEE SHOP—*MOONINGU SETTO* FOR ONE

Coffee shops in Japan are multifunctional: where would people be without these havens of quiet and service? Coffee shops have been popular in Japan since the 1920s and serve many different clienteles. They range from a standard format of small tables, a coffee and food preparation station, a magazine, comic book, and newspaper rack, and a cash register near the door or bar to very luxurious decor in a multilevel establishment and elaborate menus of snack foods, pastries, and ice cream. They may demonstrate themes or personae characterizing performance and style such as Viennese Empire, Greenwich Village, even Hidden Christian, evoking the past when Christianity was proscribed, decorated with statues of the Virgin Mary disguised as Buddhas. Whatever the style, they are important in most urban people's lives as oases of peace and predictability or, as mentioned above, as an alternative to the noise and tumult of breakfast in the bosom of the family, the morning equivalent of the bar-as-refuge.

It is in this function that the coffee shop excels. The classic "morning set" at a typical coffee shop provides variations on the following: a cup of very hot "blend" coffee (a strong dark brew, contrasted with "American" coffee, very weak) or black tea, a plate with two slices of thick white toast (often an inch thick), buttered, a small salad of light coleslaw or lettuce, a single wedge of tomato with a thin slice peeled back decoratively like a wing, and a hard-boiled egg, in the shell. The morning set may vary, adding eggs any style, bacon, or even, in some more elegant districts, croissants. It is not an "American" breakfast but a Japanized, ritualized collection of elements drawn from Western meals. The morning set is served only until 10 or 11 in the morning and is usually a bargain: the coffee taken alone usually costs about ¥400 or ¥500 (around $3.50 to $4.00) while a morning set including coffee may be only ¥500 or ¥600.

The meal is more than cheap. It is predictable, safe, reliable, as breakfast should be, with no adventurous shocks. And unlike the family breakfast, it is quiet. Men often repair to a coffee shop on the way to work (so do women) and read the paper or a comic book from the rack. Later in the day, the coffee shop also serves those who take a break from work or meet with colleagues or clients away from the less private, open-format offices typical of Japanese corporate and bureaucratic life. The steep price of a cup of coffee also includes the "rental" of space and time away from the intensity of urban life, and the proprietors never encourage people to move on.

By the end of the day, depending on the neighborhood, you may find young couples, working women with their friends, or college students occupying those seats. For some a particular coffee shop becomes an alternative "home" or "salon," where friends are sure to find them and where they conduct the business or affairs that fall somewhere between familial and professional: one young woman will use her table to work on her résumé; another to address New Year's cards; a middle-aged man sits with his former high school classmates planning a reunion. Because people outside the family are only rarely entertained in the home, the coffee shop (or a bar) is a viable alternative. It may also be a place for respite time from the intensity of the personal spaces of home: here you share public space with others, but others you do not know. For young people in particular, this kind of anonymous place allows them to go on living in the small family household.[29]

HOMES AWAY FROM HOME, AND THEIR USES

Bars show up near the top of any list of family services. Indeed, while attendance at a bar may seem unlikely to support family life, a bar's function in extending family roles and space has been seen as significant in contemporary urban life.[30] It is more a male than a female haven, and although dating couples and young unmarried women with their female friends may frequent bars, few younger housewives appear, and then with friends or husbands.

Bars are like coffee shops—spaces apart from home or office, zones of freedom and relaxation. But where coffee shops are places to be alone with a book and a cup of coffee, bars are above all social locations and

almost no one goes to drink alone. Drinking at home is usually not a social event; men drinking at home usually do so while watching a base-
ball game or sumo match on television.

As Anne Allison has demonstrated, bars are often places where business colleagues and workmates gather to bond through an attenuated
sexual discourse directed more at male relationships than at "scoring"
with bar hostesses: the latter are a medium for a kind of "homosocial-
ity," men relating to other men through verbal displays, rather than as
direct objects of attention.[31] The role of the bar is to facilitate bonds between men, then, and to provide a milieu for entertainment that is not
available at work or home. Bars are also places where respite time, such
as is also available at coffee houses, may offset the tensions or intensity
of the home.

ALL ELSE FAILING, VENDING MACHINES AT YOUR SERVICE

Ubiquitous in Japan are the vending machines (*jido hanbaiki*) that pur-
vey a wide variety of commodities. These, like the convenience store, make
provisioning basic necessities easy. Cigarettes, canned coffee, soda, and
juice are the most common items sold in these machines, which are "open"
all hours. In addition, you can buy magazines (including pornographic
comics), snacks, liquor, wine and beer, toiletries, telephone debit cards,
fresh flowers—there is little you cannot obtain by dropping coins in a slot.

The drink machines are everywhere: the coffee and tea cans as noted
by blue and red indicators are cold in summer, hot in cooler weather.
Juice, soda, and the now popular varieties of designer water in bottles
and cans are sold in machines on every train and subway platform. At-
tracting young buyers, some drink machines have flashing lights, recorded
music, and a built-in game of chance in which you might win a free can
if your numbers come up right. There is virtually no place without such
machines, from temple courtyards to railroad stations to quiet corners
of rural neighborhoods.

Although some activist groups have curtailed sales of liquor from
machines after 11 P.M. or whenever the liquor shops adjacent to the machines close, hoping to stop juvenile drinking, neither their efforts nor
the movement to stop the sale of pornographic material in vending machines have had much impact.[32] The vending machine industries, and
the distribution of liquor and publications to them, are said to be main-
stays of the "legitimate" operations of organized crime and, as such,
difficult to control.

SHORING UP THE INSIDE WORLD

By convention, the home does not offer a zone of hospitality or a site where prepared foods are handily available to serve acquaintances or strangers. Men and women meet colleagues, friends, and even family for meals and events in places away from their living quarters, using the conventional argument that their home is too small and crowded for the entertainment of nonfamily members. In fact, the word for home, *uchi,* is synonymous with "inside" and family; it connotes an interior protected from outside nonintimates. Yet this shoring up of inside space is a recent, postwar phenomenon, setting the home's informality and downtime comfort apart from the more formal settings and responsibilities of school and workplace. Men bring colleagues home only very rarely; children only occasionally bring friends home for meals or for play.

Women entertain very intimate school friends and neighbors at home but for more celebratory or formal occasions meet them at restaurants, or pastry or coffee shops. For women, the display of their performance as housewives that their friends' visits would imply is a deterrent: most would prefer not to be exposed to the competitive scrutiny of others.

Occasionally, especially in rural areas, older neighborhoods, or in families with elderly at home, visitors may drop by without warning, but this happens less frequently than in the past. People explain the change as owing to people's busy lifestyles as well as to the use of telephones and other communications media: now one calls ahead, and a visit without prior arrangement is a real surprise. Young people, completely "connected" to each other via their cell phones with e-mail access, meet via such devices. Older people regret the lack of "accidental" meeting with friends and neighbors, as the flow of community life bypasses homes.

Shibata Tokue, a city planner, traced the process that made urban life more private over the postwar decades.[33] In the 1950s, there were still small lanes, even dirt roads, in the major cities of Japan. These small lanes did not divide people; in fact, he says, they brought people together, providing points of meeting and communal activity, as members of households brought small hand tasks to perform outside to share neighborhood gossip and information. Children played in these public spaces, less threatened by vehicular traffic than they would be in today's streets.

Family life was more transparent. A house was usually one or two stories and was made of wood, with paper-covered shoji screens and sliding doors to separate spaces. The genkan, or entrance area, was where informal contact occurred without taking off shoes, the marker of more intimacy and access to inside rooms. A fence or hedge, if it existed, was porous and permitted views of the house or even straight through into its interior in good weather, when screens and doors were left open. Surveillance was important for mutual protection in neighborhoods of homes built of such inflammable materials.

The communal, transparent nature of such neighborhoods changed in the 1960s, when more high-rise concrete structures were built, and automobile, bus, and truck traffic increased. Roads were paved, noise and fumes drove people away from their front steps, and accidental socializing became more rare. Homeowners built concrete walls to protect houses, children, and the peace of home from these intrusions and dangers. Both physically and socially, households became limited-access refuges.

These changes in the physical environment coincided with changes in educational and occupational life, as priorities shifted to make institutions outside the home the primary groups with the greatest impact on family and individual life chances. The private household now protected a cluster of individuals centrifugally tied to school and workplace. Meanwhile, its functions dwindled.

We have seen how shifts in consumer culture have accompanied other changes in people's realities, maintaining the expectations of the core family roles but making up for their shortfall. Family functions may have moved into bars, convenience stores, *depaato* food halls, and even vending machines, but the standards have not. Backing and filling around new behavior, the consumer industries have to some degree—but with some limitations—managed the gap. The irony of consumption in Japan today is that while the products and services now available do indeed help people support their households, they subvert the ideological national Family. The very consumption acts that fuel the economy and keep family life going also sanction very different forms of family life than those officials espouse.

Just as filial piety means caring for the elderly at home to obviate the need for state-provided services, domesticity means using goods and services from outside the home to keep it going: official definitions of the Family are more honored in the breach than the observance.

Exceptions Are the Rule

Families as Models of Diversity

To those concerned with the falling birthrate and the care of the elderly, twenty-first-century families may look like patched arrangements among people sharing residence. What is obvious from the cases we have seen, however, is that even without the internal structure and values approved by official ideologies, these families are more than congeries of individuals going it alone together.

The Fujimuras of the 1990s, like the Maruyamas a century earlier, function in spite of rather than because of a heavy-handed family code. In the Maruyamas' multigenerational household, negotiations and strategies of family management refer little to orthodoxy, much more to the practical concerns of business. The Fujimuras' solutions to the problem of multiple and conflicting demands are very much their own, even farther from any code.

Contemporary rural families like the Kandas often have an establishment to pass on to heirs, whether it is a farm or a local business. Though they find a way to transfer the business within the family, it is not to preserve a patriline per se that they adopt a son-in-law.

Postwar families define their households by children and as living units, and the support of both is the job of the parents much as in any nuclear family in most of the world. Sometimes the functions are shared, as in the Takamura and Fujimura families, but often roles are clearly demarcated once children are born. As most mothers today work outside the home at some point while they are raising their children, families adjust domestic tasks according to needs and ability to summon other aids—including those supplied by consumer services and goods at a cost. Very few can manage the division of labor assumed in the postwar household without a stay-at-home mother, and the burden on both parents intensifies in a *tanshin funin* family where the husband lives apart from his wife and children because of a job transfer. Divorced women must raise their children on their own, as *tanshin funin* wives do, but straitened finances often cause them to return to their natal homes. Finally, an ordinary family's impromptu accommodations for care of elderly relatives reveals its basic configuration as a nuclear family with add-ons.

Over a family's life course, now reckoned as the lifetime of the parental couple instead of the centuries of lineage continuity implied in the traditional *ie* model, the household will change several times. At first it is a two-person unit, then it becomes a two-plus-child (or children) unit—both justifying the marriage and existing as add-ons—until once again it shrinks to the couple alone or with a parent or two, again as add-ons, to care for.

That families today "make do" and "get by" should not lead us to think that they believe they fall short of socially approved models. The Fujimuras are pleased with their lives, and others only wish they had the flexibility and resources to deviate more in their own ways. And families always have their own ways, above and beyond grandmother's secret pickle recipe. Within the volatile mix of demographic shift and economic bust, we see a larger picture developing of the relationship between social change, economic environment, and family-making culture in Japan.

The hopeful, energetic postwar families, newly nuclear and practicing gender equality as young couples, coped in their middle years with the demands of their children's schooling and the rigid tracks of employment and roles in family and community. They are now about to hit retirement age with the care of their elders in front of them, and sometimes with children still at home. A little behind their schedules myself, I compared notes with the women of this generation as we raised our children, worrying over them and congratulating each proud parent on their successes. I listened to the men's anecdotes of boredom or anxiety in their work, to their dreams of making a better life for themselves and their families. In their aging parents' stories, I heard echoes of my own parents.

My younger friends, children of these corporate warriors and education mamas, seemed to struggle more with choices than older groups had.

However, choices alone did not offer them freedom or advantage. The most obvious choice was oriented around children—whether or not to have them, how to raise them and finance their education, and how to balance the demands of work and family. As their children grew, they worried in turn over their own parents' care and welfare, even if they knew well that the Confucian golden age of filial reverence never existed.

The family issues of the late twentieth century have become the national concerns of the twenty-first, with political import beyond the private domain of the home. Family itself is a symbol of the nation but families themselves are the butt of criticism, urged by public rhetoric to correct the "distortions." Already beleaguered households act as they must, not as political agenda dictate, to nurture children through the competitive process of reproducing their own social status. They struggle to care for their own elderly relatives and to save for their own future dependency even as they listen to official injunctions on spending to energize the consumer economy in recessionary times. Women must work to afford children and, as mothers, must meet standards for child care that demand a total maternal commitment. Conflicting standards, mixed messages, make the performance intrinsically impossible for many. They defy compliance.

Conservative commentators and politicians in both America and Japan offer moral analyses of how we've gone wrong, and moral programs on how to go right. "Family values" generated by think tanks and conservative publications in America point to the rising rate of divorce, women's abdication from full-time housewifery, and the reluctance of parents to rein in the young as evidence of selfishness and immorality. Families are to blame for delinquency, alienation, depression, drugs, and violent crime. If you substitute "Japan" for "America" in the statements above, some of these would be familiar narratives there too.

Deploring the untidy complexities of families in Japan is a chronic exercise. In 1898, Meiji leaders responded to what they perceived as chaos by creating a Japanese family system. A quarter century later, economic and social changes revealed that this system had not taken hold. In the 1920s the rural exodus to the cities increased the rate of nuclear families, representing to some the decadence of Westernization and to others the essence of modernity. Their descendants, the postwar corporate warrior father and education mama, both in service to economic success, came to epitomize noncompliance with the *ie* model. They were to blame for its apparent attrition and distortion and—the critics went on and on— their children without siblings had indulgence but no proper socialization; in mainstream modern schools with a narrow examination-focused drive for credentials the young had pressure but no discipline.

Laws, schools, workplaces, health and nurturant care facilities, and other entities—institutions and policies aimed at protecting family life—compose strident evocations of the good Family. As demographers, economists, and bureaucrats insist, without strong families the economic future of Japan is in doubt: national security depends on women having children *and* joining the labor force. And as the conservative politicians and commentators remind the nation, filial responsibility prescribes care of the elderly at home.

The institutional narrative of conservative statist economics, institutional entropy, and elite family ideologies traces the decline of families as self-supporting collectivities. For this official chorus, families as they really are do not fill or, more important, "foot" the bill. The families we have seen support their children, their elderly, and the national economy by managing what otherwise the state would have to support. Measured against either the *ie* or the postwar middle-class model of family, they are diverse and irregular. What causes stress in the second postwar generation of families is the official representation of their deviation, along with the policies and practices aimed at restoring them to responsibility, *not* the plurality of their own realities.

Contemporary incursions into the intimate, diverse, and self-generated spheres of family life are as significant as those of wartime mobilization—and resemble them, except for language and enforcement (in fact, the government now offers filial piety as a kind of civil defense program: families caring for the elderly are troops protecting the nation). But this is a very different historical moment: Japan is assiduously democratic, assertively middle class, and actively internationalist. Laws and policies cannot propose that women give birth to support a war effort or demand that children support aged parents. Managers cannot legally dismiss female employees at marriage or at the birth of a child as they once could. The democratic freedoms and models established in the postwar laws are antithetical to the Confucian fundamentalism lurking behind such exhortations.

How then will official Japan cope with deviant families? There is little governmental support for the elderly who increasingly desire independent living arrangements. There are no programs in place to anticipate the shrinking pool of new labor caused by shifts in employment patterns and the lower birthrate. There is no adequate national program of child care to assist working parents (as in France, where families of all classes use public day care, or in Sweden, where some claim that provisions for child care raised the birthrate). Finally, there is little enforcement of equal opportunity for women. The absence of official support amounts to a demand that families become self-sufficient and virtuous: "good families" would not need any such programs.

But would official support foster the *ie* model or the postwar middle-class one? Families with resources or those at the bottom of the economic ladder either do not or cannot choose a traditional family strategy. As Susan Hanley has noted, the middle class takes care of its own but with great sacrifices and without engaging the ideologies of family that care might imply. "The poorest and the richest families are the least likely to have three generations in a household, the poorest for lack of space and the richest because they can afford to live separately. It is the struggling middle class that double up with grandparents."[1]

Diversity often has a commonsense rationale: uniformity may not. American observers have regarded Japanese families in the postwar eras as uniform, middle-class, and homogeneous, imagining them as the opposite of our celebrated diversity. Where other kinds of diversity—race, region, religion, ethnicity—are less obvious in Japan than in America, markers of social class are undeniably present. Thomas Rohlen refers to Japanese class differences as "wafer-thin" distinctions of behavior, the timing of life course events, consumption, and family relations, based in economic resources and power.[2] Homogeneity, as we have seen, is not only relative: it can be an intentional construct, a product of the expectations of public policy, marketing, and law.

In America, families of the working poor have their communities' tolerance if not approval for the strategies they devise to get by.[3] These include cooperation, cohabitation, doubling up housing, and even child labor. In Japan, the equivalent of the American working poor in some respects is the working middle class. The families struggling to stay independent of governmental support for elderly care and child care must find resources within their own walls. These families try to stay in the normative safety zone of the "self-reliant" family if only not to fall into the insubstantial net of governmental social services. They are not attempting to live the ideal for its own sake.

And deviation from the norm too depends on who is doing the talking and what sorts of data are on offer. The dark picture of women's "birth avoidance" uses birthrate data for women of childbearing years, to show 1.30 children per woman ages fifteen to forty-nine. Yet birthrate data for married couples show that on average, the latter have just over two children per family. Similarly, a woman traveling alone to a week-end conference or business meeting abandons her children and husband—even if she has left four days' worth of homemade meals in the freezer—*or* fully engages her professional career, enhancing with her income both her work and family life. And a man avoiding after-hours bar sessions with colleagues either jeopardizes his professional career *or* contributes to domestic role equality if he comes home to cook dinner. Totally new questions arise if there is no child at all: can you call a couple a family? What do you call your spouse if not "Papa" or "Mama"? As the child-less only son of an only son, what do you say to your grandparents who cling to the idea of family name continuity? Who, in a gay or lesbian home, can register as "household head" in the city ward office? Who constitutes the "family" of an unmarried woman in her late thirties and how does she describe her relationship with these people?

These questions, newly framed in public media and forums, heighten the rhetoric and produce backlash. Meanwhile, marketing agencies fur-ther stylize the so-called new kinds of households and families as the audiences for goods and services, new market niches. The dual-income / no-kids types, the bachelor on his own, the elderly couple residing sepa-rately from families, become consumer categories, targets for products to fill the needs these nontraditional units might have.

The answer for non-"normal" but still ordinary families and most oth-ers would not be a restoration of the three-generation household or a re-treat from the workplace to the good wife / wise mother role. It would not be the postwar middle-class "consensual" model of family that would keep them from draining public coffers to supply family needs. Rather, it would be a combination of services offered by public and private sec-tor agencies plus—most important—supports acknowledging diverse conditions in families as they are now.

The practices families create as strategies both of accommodation and resistance show how direct and indirect manipulations (within the fam-ily power structure and from social institutions outside household walls) accumulate and inspire more visible responses and make real change. The women of the first postwar middle-class generation whose emotional in-dependence from their husbands may have presaged the structural inde-pendence of the woman of the 1990s may seem old-fashioned or limited to their daughters.[4] These twenty-something women say, "I don't want to be like my mother." Their brothers resist "being their fathers," whose work took all their time but provided them with little satisfaction. Their parents didn't toe the line completely: they believed in the social changes they saw happening around them and to a great degree valued the difference between their own parents' prewar lives and the promise of a new lifestyle. They hard-wired their children to see different possibilities for themselves and to bring their families along with them.

In fact, Japanese families seem now to have reversed the filiality paradigm. There is no longer an imperial family—the family writ large and embodied in the person of the prewar emperor and his household[5]—to which filial duty is owed, and there are few laws constraining and directing families as wholes. Elderly, at least the oldest elderly, are now more dependent than powerful and need both family-based care and institutional care to serve them and keep them from feeling useless, disengaged, or abandoned. With schedules and commitments beyond the home, women and men alike need workplaces that offer "family-friendly" schedules and recognition of the priorities of families. Children need lives combining support in the efforts to succeed and become self-reliant adults. Further, they need active engagement with their families beyond food, shelter, and clothing. Where can people receive what they need, and how can they feel part of an intimate community if public policy does not validate their actual families?

Everyone living in families individually and collectively participates in activities useful to the state, most as consumers, even if not in the terms and according to the values official Japan recognizes as in the interests of social stability. Families are not the victims of modernization—rent by occupational demands or anomic urbanization—or defined by their adherence to or denial of traditional roles and practices. Families are in fact front-rank agents of change in their strategies to survive, their creative use of resources, and their power to influence the economy. They are coping with the fallout of a future shock we will all experience. A decade ahead of the rest of us, Japan is preparing for the demographic shifts that will be global and for this reason we must examine the ideological crises surrounding the population problem.

In Japan, official rhetoric has at its disposal older story lines of family to employ in crisis management, imaginings of family self-sufficiency with a moral frame. Thus it can use "Japanese family culture" to provide a base rationale for bureaucratic action and political programs. Steven Reed refers to "culture as evolving repertoires," meaning that "standard forms are learned . . . slowly changing and peculiarly adapted to their settings."[6] Culture in this sense is an underlying set of possibilities, not a singular model, and moreover is always adapting and changing.

This has been a protracted essay on family and social change in Japan and on the relationship between state, social policy, and the families on whom the burden rests to enact the models of Family constructed by policymakers. We have seen two significant attempts over the past century to "frame" family in the interests of policy: a new Meiji set of patriarchal norms and practices and a postwar middle-class version of economic reconstruction and global competitiveness. That both patriarchy and democracy as family-constructing forces misrepresent and even distort the experiences of ordinary families over the past century should now be clear.

The representation of family as the source and solution for a national crisis has provided us with an opportunity to look at the interplay between ideologies and actualities of everyday life. Looking to the two moments of family making in the Meiji and postwar periods, we can see parallels in the events and forces driving policymakers to insist on such models. In each case, a geopolitical event occurred to cause officials to see Japan as at risk, and to create programs that would ensure that the bedrock of society, the family, would be a bulwark against changes endangering Japanese social structure and morality. The opening of Japan to modernization in the nineteenth century and the reconstruction of postwar Japan as a democracy under the guidance of an American-led Occupation were moments of family construction somewhat different from today's sense of crisis. However, similar notions of the preservation of the nation and enforcement of civic responsibility lie behind the current construction of family. We also see parallels in ordinary people's responses to the realities behind the current crisis and responses to the attempts and failures of policy to support families. Thus abandoned Grannies and birth strikes are part of wider meaning making, both timely and timeless. So it is with the families we have seen whose sense of being "family" is unwavering even as they are helping create new repertoires of cultures of family.

As we have seen, the protean strategies of men, women, and children in families offer clues to what families in essence have always been, and to what families can do to protect that essence. The very attempt to generate conformity to a model through name-calling and insufficient programs will backfire, forcing the recognition that the Family never existed and that families will function for the state only if it functions for them.

Notes

INTRODUCTION

1. Debra Samuels, personal communication, February 17, 2000.

2. Iwao Sumiko, interview, February 18, 2000; and Iwao Sumiko, editorial, *Japan Echo*, February 2000, 4. Throughout the text, Japanese names are in the conventional Japanese order, with family name preceding given name.

3. "Private Sector Offers Women More," *Asahi Evening News*, February 17, 2000, 4. Whereas once government work such as teaching offered women more flexibility and support to raise children as they continued their jobs, now private sector workplaces may have more flexible schemes to keep long-term workers (and even part-time workers) employed as they tend to family concerns. Recently, IBM Japan announced that it would permit employees caring for family members to work full time from home for up to more than ten years, or until their children graduate from primary school. Other companies offer flextime and child-care leave, beyond the provisions of the Family-Care Leave Act, which allows time off for up to a year without pay for child care—not a viable option for many families who need two incomes and continuous career employment.

4. John Pelzel, "Japanese Kinship: A Comparison," in *Family and Kinship in Chinese Society,* ed. M. Freedman (Stanford: Stanford University Press, 1970), 227–48.

5. Marion Levy, "Contrasting Factors in the Modernization of China and Japan," in *Economic Development and Cultural Change* (Chicago: University of Chicago Press, 1954), 2:161–97.

6. Matthews Hamabata, *The Crested Kimono: Love and Power in the Japanese Family* (Ithaca: Cornell University Press, 1990).

7. Ariga Kizaemon, "The Japanese Family" (manuscript, Tokyo Kyoiku Daigaku, 1953).

8. Ezra Vogel, *Japan's New Middle Class* (Berkeley: University of California Press, 1963).

9. Hamabata, *Crested Kimono.*

10. Ibid., 50.

1. A NATIONAL SECURITY ISSUE

1. Kaji Nobuyuki, "Tsuzoku dotoku e kaere," Chuo Koron, September 9, 1999, 116–25 (translated in *Japan Echo,* June 2000).

2. Since restructuring has cut the numbers of good jobs in the permanent employment sector, young university graduates often choose part-time or freelance work instead and resist frustrating careerism to look for a balance between work, leisure, and other sources of identity ("To Many of Japan's Youths, Work Can Wait," *Boston Globe,* January 5, 2000, A2). "Parasite singles" is a term coined by Yamada Masahiro, a sociologist from Tokyo Gakugei Daigaku.

3. David Plath, ed., *Adult Episodes in Japan* (Leiden: Brill, 1975).

4. Merry White, *The Material Child: Coming of Age in Japan and America* (New York: Free Press, 1993), 55–56.

5. Yukiko Bowman, "Jibun as Number One: Self-Development in Japanese Female Adolescence" (senior honors thesis, Harvard University, 1999).

6. Ezra Vogel, *Japan's New Middle Class* (Berkeley: University of California Press, 1963).

7. There is also a new national program of child-care stipends: for the first two children, $50 per month; for third and more children, $100 per month.

8. Takayama Noriyuki, *Japan Now* (Embassy of Japan, Washington, D.C.), May 1997.

9. Catherine Lewis, *Educating Hearts and Minds* (Cambridge: Cambridge University Press, 1993).

10. Joseph Tobin, Dana Davidson, and David Wu, *Preschool in Three Cultures* (New Haven: Yale University Press, 1992).

11. "The Fertile Takamuras," *Look Japan,* August 1994, 20–21.

12. Broadcasts on NHK Television, from 1992–95.

13. Doug Struck and Katherine Tolbert, "Japan Inc. Workers Get Harsh Dose of Economic Reality," *Washington Post,* January 3, 2000, A14.

14. Stephanie Strom, "In Japan, From a Lifetime Job to No Job at All," *New York Times,* February 3, 1999, 1, A6.

15. Stephanie Strom, "From Japan's Ailing Economy, a Tale of Murder in the Family," *New York Times,* April 15, 1999, 1, 15.

16. Sasaki Yukie, "Happy Holidays?," *Look Japan,* March 1999, 32.

17. Ueno Teruaki, "Dreams Turn to Dust for Japan's Salarymen," Reuters News Service, April 22, 1998.

18. Kevin Sullivan, "Cost of Economic Equality Questioned," *Washington Post,* June 8, 1997; Stephanie Strom, "Tradition of Equality in New Japan," *New York Times,* January 4, 2000, 1, 46.

19. Iwao Suzuki, *Child Welfare Quarterly* 16, no. 4 (March 1996): 2; see appendix A.

20. Ibid., 13.

21. Ibid., 13, 14.

22. Ibid., 11.

23. Uno Mitsuhiro, "Mothers On-Line," *Look Japan,* July 1998, 17.

24. Iizuka Junko, Socioeconomic Research Department, Nomura Institute of Research, April 1996, communication.

25. Sonoi Yuri, "Managing Work and Childcare: Working Women's Lives in Japan" (manuscript, 1996).

26. Daimon Sayori, "'Karōshi' Phenomenon Spreading to Female Workforce," *Japan Times Weekly,* September 30–October 6, 1991.

27. Sasaki, "Happy Holidays?," 40.

28. Yamanaka Keiko, "Return Migration of Japanese-Brazilians to Japan: The *Nikkeijin* as Ethnic Minority and Political Construct,"*Diaspora* 5, no. 1 (spring 1996): 65–97.

29. Kathryn Tolbert, "As Japan Ages, It Plucks Workers from Family Tree Abroad," *International Herald Tribune,* March 8, 2000, 5.

30. Itakura Kimie, "Wifely Concerns," *Look Japan,* November 1988, 40.

31. Yamanaka, "Return Migration."

32. Iwao Sumiko, personal communication, August 1998.

33. Joseph Coleman, "Japan Faces Idea of Childless Future," *Honolulu Star Bulletin,* August 3, 1998, A6.

2. FAMILY UNDER CONSTRUCTION

1. Marilyn Ivy, Discourses of the Vanishing: Modernity, Phantasm, Japan (Chicago: University of Chicago Press, 1995).

2. Kathleen Uno, "The Death of 'Good Wife, Wise Mother,'" in *Postwar Japan as History,* ed. Andrew Gordon (Berkeley: University of California Press, 1993); Ezra Vogel, *Japan's New Middle Class* (Berkeley: University of California Press, 1963).

3. Jill Kleinberg, "When Work and Family Are Almost One," in *Work and Life Course in Japan,* ed. David Plath (Albany: SUNY Press, 1983).

4. Ishihara Kunio, "Trends in Generational Continuity and Succession to Household Directorship," in *Family and Household in Changing Japan,* ed. Koyoma Takashi, Morioka Kiyomi, and Kumagai Fumie (Tokyo: Japan Society for the Promotion of Science, 1980); Hayami Akira, "The Myth of Primogeniture and Impartible Inheritance in Tokugawa Japan," *Journal of Family History* 8, no. 1 (1983): 3–29.

5. Kamiko Takeji, *Nihonjin no kazoku kankei: ibunka to hikakushite "atarashī kateizo" o saguru* (Tokyo: Yuhikaku, 1981). Such a household includes eldest sons of eldest sons, their wives, and unmarried daughters and younger sons.

6. In *The Crested Kimono: Love and Power in the Japanese Family* (Ithaca: Cornell University Press, 1990), Matthews Hamabata describes families engaged in family businesses similar in many ways to the Meiji period Maruyamas; the persistence of some strategies or traits in these families is less about deliberate maintenance of family culture than it is about the corporate and economic strategies they engage to prosper.

7. Kumagai Fumie, "Changing Divorce in Japan," *Journal of American History* 8, no 1 (1983): 87.

8. Shiraishi Saya, personal communication, 2000.

9. Meiji Civil Code of 1898.

10. Muta Kazue, "Images of the Family in Meiji Periodicals: The Paradox Underlying the Emergence of the 'Home,'" *Nichibei Josei Jānaru*, English supplement no. 7 (1994): 53–71; Jordan Sand, "At Home in the Meiji Period: Inventing Japanese Domesticity," in *Mirror of Modernity: Invented Traditions of Modern Japan*, ed. Stephen Vlastos (Berkeley: University of California Press, 1995).

11. Sand, "At Home in the Meiji Period."

12. Tanaka Masako, "Maternal Authority in the Japanese Family," in *Religion and the Family in East Asia*, ed. George deVos and Takao Sofue (Berkeley: University of California Press, 1986); also Kathleen Uno, *Passages to Modernity: Motherhood, Childhood, and Social Reform in Early Twentieth-Century Japan* (Honolulu: University of Hawai'i Press, 1999). Uno refers to the "samuraization" of family life as an aspect of Meiji social mobility but also shows that toward the end of the Meiji era the influence may have gone the other way, the "commonization" of the elite, with this new construction of mother love percolating up to elites, while other aspects of family culture "trickled down" (157).

13. Dorinne Kondo, *Crafting Selves* (Chicago: University of Chicago Press, 1990), 170 ff.

14. I reconstruct the Maruyamas' story from a family tree circulated within the family and from interviews with two of the Maruyama descendants, especially from discussions with the grandson of the youngest son of the 1898 household.

15. Hamabata, *Crested Kimono*.

16. Tetsuo Najita, "Japan's Industrial Revolution in Historical Perspective," in *Japan in the World*, ed. Miyoshi Masao and H. D. Harootunian (Durham, N.C.: Duke University Press, 1993). I am grateful to Jonathan Lipman for suggesting this reference.

17. The concept of samuraization is derived from "sanskritization" discussed by M. Srinivas in *The Changing Position of Indian Women* (Delhi: Oxford University Press, 1978). See note 12 above.

18. Fukuzawa Yukichi, *The Autobiography of Fukuzawa Yukichi* (Tokyo: Hokuseido Press, 1934).

19. Kazuko Smith, trans., *Makiko's Diary: A Merchant Wife in 1910 Kyoto* (Stanford: Stanford University Press, 1995).

20. Herbert Passin, *School and Society in Japan* (New York: Columbia Teachers College Press, 1965).

21. On the constitution, see Beate Sirota Gordon, *The Only Woman in the Room* (Tokyo: Kodansha, 1997).

22. Takie Lebra, "Self and Other in Esteemed Status: The Changing Culture of the Japanese Royalty from Showa to Heisei," *Journal of Japanese Studies* 23 (1997): 257–89. Lebra suggests a comparison between the current image of the imperial family and the British model of a "public" monarchy. The media's new attention to the imperial family's personal lives as well as their roles leaves the

current generation less private space. Empress Michiko, as "Mother," in spite of the problems she is said to have had in her role, is glorified as a self-sacrificing, dignified focus of a child-centered family, a partner in a love marriage that had its origins on a tennis court in Karuizawa. Crown Princess Masako appears caught between generational models of the good woman: a talented career woman, internationalist, and "older" bride, she represents neither the independent feminist nor the three-steps-behind cipher.

3. FAMILIES IN POSTWAR JAPAN

1. Ochiai Emiko, *Nijūsseiki kazoku e: kazoku no sengo taisei no mikata, koekata* (Tokyo: Yuhikaku Shuppansha, 1994).

2. Thomas Rohlen, "Is Japanese Education Becoming Less Egalitarian? Notes on Stratification and Reform," *Journal of Japanese Studies* 3 (winter 1976–77): 37–70.

3. John Dower, *Japan in War and Peace* (New York: New Press, 1993), 317–18.

4. Hironaka Wakako, personal communication. According to Robert Levine ("Why Isn't Japan Happy?" *American Demographics,* 1992), males in the United States who show satisfaction with life are 81 percent, as opposed to 62 percent in Japan; females in the United States are 82 percent, compared to 71 percent in Japan. The quality of life surveys conducted by Gallup polls in the United States and by the Japanese Cabinet Public Information Office in 1989 and 1990 list the rates by percentages:

SATISFACTION WITH LIFE	UNITED STATES	JAPAN
Wages	69	43
Housing	87	65
Jobs	76	66
Leisure	87	47
Overall quality of life	81	67

5. Fujioka Wakao, *Sayonara sengo: atarashī hyogen shakai no tanjo* (1987), cited in Merry White, *The Material Child: Coming of Age in Japan and America* (New York: Free Press, 1993), 111.

6. Andrew Gordon, ed., *Postwar Japan as History* (Berkeley: University of California Press, 1993).

7. John Dower, *Embracing Defeat: Japan in the Wake of World War II* (New York: New Press, 1999); Theodore and Haruko Cook, *Japan at War: An Oral History* (New York: New Press, 1992).

8. David Lodge, *Out of the Shelter* (London: Penguin, 1970).

9. Beate Sirota Gordon, *The Only Woman in the Room* (Tokyo: Kodansha, 1997).

10. Ibid.

11. Samuel Coleman, *Family Planning in Japanese Society: Traditional Birth Control in a Modern Urban Culture* (Princeton: Princeton University Press, 1983).

12. Carmen Johnson, *Wave Rings in Water: My Years with the Women of*

Postwar Japan (Alexandria, Va.: Charles River Press, 1996); Catherine Lewis, "Women in the Consumer Movement," in *Proceedings of the Tokyo Symposium on Women* (Tokyo: International Group for the Study of Women, 1978).

13. John Nathan both directed and produced the documentary film *Farm Song.*

14. Sheldon Garon, *Molding Japanese Minds: The State in Everyday Life* (Princeton: Princeton University Press, 1997).

15. Morioka Kiyomi, "Family and Household in Changing Japan," *Journal of Comparative Family,* no. 3 (1981).

16. Anne Allison, "Japanese Mothers and Obentos:The Lunchbox as Ideological State Apparatus," *Anthropological Quarterly* 64, no. 4 (October 1991): 195–208.

17. Ezra Vogel, *Japan's New Middle Class* (Berkeley: University of California Press, 1963), 107–8.

18. Ronald Dore, *City Life in Japan* (Berkeley: University of California Press, 1963).

19. Vogel, *Japan's New Middle Class.*

20. Ronald Dore, *Diploma Disease* (Berkeley: University of California Press, 1976).

21. Matthews Hamabata, *The Crested Kimono: Love and Power in the Japanese Family* (Ithaca: Cornell University Press, 1990).

22. Suzanne Hall Vogel, "Professional Housewife: The Career of Urban Middle-Class Japanese Women," *The Japan Interpreter* 12, no. 1 (winter 1978).

23. Amy Borovoy, "Domesticity and Strategy: Reading Japanese Self-Sacrifice" (paper presented to American Anthropology Association, Washington, D.C., November 15–19, 1995).

24. Christine Yano, *Shaping Tears of a Nation* (Ann Arbor: University Microfilms, 1995).

25. Laura Shapiro, *Perfection Salad* (New York: Farrar, Straus and Giroux, 1986).

26. Vogel, introduction to *Japan's New Middle Class.*

27. Dower, *Embracing Defeat,* 317–18.

28. Tada Michitaro, "The Glory and Misery of 'My Home,'" in *Authority and the Individual in Japan,* ed. Victor Koschmann (Tokyo: University of Tokyo Press, 1978).

29. Merry White, *The Japanese Educational Challenge* (New York: Free Press, 1986), 145.

30. Kaibara Ekken, cited in Vogel, *Japan's New Middle Class,* 227.

31. Walter Edwards, *Modern Japan through Its Weddings* (Stanford: Stanford University Press, 1989); Joy Hendry, *Marriage in Changing Japan* (New York: St. Martin's Press, 1981).

32. Small living spaces limited full expression and the chance for privacy. Undoubtedly, married couples with small apartments patronized the increasingly popular love hotels, which often have lavishly, whimsically, surreally decorated rooms for sexual encounters—playlands, fantasy palaces, each with a conceptual frame or motif. There are Disney rooms, Las Vegas rooms with roulette

wheels, and many other conceits. These rooms allow for relaxed entertainment and role playing as much as physical pleasure, payable by the hour (see the documentary video, *The Japanese Version* by Andrew Kolker and Louis Alvarez, Center for New American Media [New York, 1991]).

33. Aviad Raz, *Riding the Black Ship: Japan and Tokyo Disneyland* (Cambridge, Mass.: Harvard University Press, 1999).

34. Fujioka Wakao, *Sayonara sengo: atarashī hyogen shakai no tanjo* (Tokyo: PHP Press, 1987).

35. White, *Material Child,* 210.

36. Ministry of Health and Welfare, Statistical Information Department, Minister's Secretariat, "Summary of Vital Statistics" (Tokyo, June 29, 2000).

37. T. K. Ito and Virginia Murray, "Computerized Matchmaking," in *Comparing Cultures,* ed. Merry White and Sylvan Barnet (Boston: Bedford Books, 1996).

38. I thank Christena Turner for her helpful remarks correlating preludes to marriage with new meanings of family.

39. Edwards, *Modern Japan through Its Weddings.*

40. Ono Yumiko, "Here Comes the Bride All Dressed in a Kimono," *Wall Street Journal,* June 9, 1998, A16; Takahashi Kazuko, "Style of Tying the Knot Loosens up a Bit," *Japan Times Weekly,* April 29–May 5, 1991.

41. Kawanishi Yuko, "Breaking Up Still Hard to Do," *Japan Quarterly* (July–September 1998): 84 ff.

42. James Fallows, "A Visit to Sanya," in *Comparing Cultures,* ed. Merry White and Sylvan Barnet (Boston: Bedford Books, 1996).

43. Prime Minister's Office, Survey on Women's Roles, 1995.

44. "Dirty Laundry," *Business Tokyo,* November 1990, 54 (quoted from *Sunday Mainichi*).

45. Miyanagi Kuniko, personal communication, fall 2000; and Mary Brinton, *Women and the Economic Miracle: Gender and Work in Postwar Japan* (Berkeley: University of California Press, 1998).

46. Matsubara Atsuko, *Croissant shokugun* (Tokyo: Bungei Shunsu, 1990).

47. David Plath, *Long Engagements: Maturity in Modern Japan* (Stanford: Stanford University Press, 1980).

4. ELEMENTAL FAMILIES

1. Interview on April 13, 1998, Cambridge, Massachusetts.

2. *Kosodate no shō* (Child-rearing manuals), cited in Merry White, *The Japanese Educational Challenge* (New York: Free Press, 1986), 93.

3. Kathleen Uno, "The Death of 'Good Wife, Wise Mother,'" in *Postwar Japan as History,* ed. Andrew Gordon (Berkeley: University of California Press, 1993).

4. Ezra Vogel, *Japan's New Middle Class* (Berkeley: University of California Press, 1963).

5. Economic Planning Agency, Bureau of Economic Planning, White Paper on Family Life (1986).

6. White, *Japanese Educational Challenge.*

7. Harold Stevenson, "Will the U.S. Be Number 1 by the Year 2000? Comparative Studies of East and West" (lecture at E. O. Reischauer Institute of Japanese Studies, Harvard University, March 5, 1996).

8. Anne Allison, "Japanese Mothers and Obentos: The Lunchbox as Ideological State Apparatus," *Anthropological Quarterly* 64, no. 4 (October 1991): 195–208.

9. Economic Planning Agency of Japan, *Demographic Survey* (Tokyo, 1993).

10. Funabashi Keiko, "Reassessing the Value of Children," *Japan Echo,* February 1999, 32–35 (translated from "Kosodate kara osodachi e," *Ronza,* September 1998, 28–37).

11. Kohno Goro, "Recent Conditions of Child-Raising in Japan," *Child Welfare Quarterly* 17, no. 2 (September 1996): 2–14.

12. Yoshie Nishioka Rice, "The Maternal Role in Japan: Cultural Values and Socio-Economic Conditions" (Ph.D. dissertation, Harvard Graduate School of Education, 1994).

13. Doi Takeo, *The Anatomy of Dependence* (Tokyo: Kodansha, 1973).

14. Vogel, *Japan's New Middle Class,* 243 ff.

15. Suzanne Hall Vogel, personal communication, spring 1999.

16. Tatara Mikihachiro, "Social Change and Its Impact on Family Life in Japan: Some Thoughts on Parent Abuse Syndrome" (manuscript, Austen Riggs Center, May 1981).

17. Wagatsuma Hiroshi, "Some Aspects of the Contemporary Japanese Family: Once Confucian, Now Fatherless?" *Daedalus* (spring 1977): 181–210.

18. Merry White, *The Material Child: Coming of Age in Japan and America* (New York: Free Press, 1993), 59.

19. Esaka Akira, "Job Transfers and the Long Distance Family," *Japan Echo* 25, special issue (1988): 53–59.

20. Tanaka Yuhko, Nakazawa Jun, and Nakazawa Sayuri, "Women's Psychological Stress as Caused by Men's Job Transfers," *Japanese Journal of Educational Psychology* 44 (1996): 156–65; Tanaka Yuhko, "Review of Work-Induced Family Separation Studies," *Japanese Journal of Educational Psychology* 12 (1994): 104–14.

21. Tanaka Yuhko, "The Effects of Relocation-Induced Separation in Families," *Japanese Journal of Educational Psychology* 36 (1988): 229–37.

22. Kashiwagi Keiko and Hisako Nagahisa, "The Change in Value of Children in Japanese Mothers" (paper presented to fifteenth annual ISSBD meetings, Bern, Switzerland, 1998).

23. What is widely called a "Lolita complex" (*Rorita-kon*) among older men refers to a sexual interest in young girls. There are *Rorita* bars where hostesses wear shortened school uniforms, and the young pop idols created for an audience in their early teens include older men among their fans. There are no reliable data on young girls involved in prostitution, though men are said to prefer "virginal" Japanese girls to older or foreign prostitutes because of their fears of contracting the HIV/AIDS virus.

24. *Daily Yomiuri,* August 4, 1997, 14.

25. Anne Allison, *Permitted and Prohibited Desires: Mothers, Comics, and Censorship in Japan* (Berkeley: University of California Press, 2000).

26. Laura Miller, "Beauty Up: Aesthetic Salons in Japan" (paper presented at Association for Asian Studies annual meeting, Boston, 1999).

27. Hara Hiroko and Wagatsuma Hiroshi, *Shitsuke* (Tokyo: Kohbundoh, 1974).

28. William Kelly, "Metropolitan Japan," in *Postwar Japan as History*, ed. Andrew Gordon (Berkeley: University of California Press, 1993).

29. Jeannie Lo, *Office Ladies, Factory Women* (New York: M. E. Sharpe, 1990).

30. Francis Fukuyama, *The End of Order* (Tokyo: Yuzenkaku Shuppansha, 1975), 32.

5. LIFE CHOICES FOR WOMEN AND MEN

1. Kashiwagi Keiko and Hisako Nagahisa, "The Change in Value of Children in Japanese Mothers" (paper presented to fifteenth annual ISSBD meetings, Bern, Switzerland, 1998).

2. "Single Women Mansion Shopping," *Japan Now,* May 1998, 4.

3. Government of Japan, Prime Minister's Office, White Paper on Women in the Workforce (1994).

4. Ginny Parker, "Part-Time Seen as Bane, not Boon for Women," *Japan Times,* October 2, 1998, 8.

5. Yuko Ogasawara, *Office Ladies, Salaried Men* (Berkeley: University of California Press, 1998).

6. Arlie Hochschild, *The Second Shift* (New York: Viking, 1984).

7. Shibata Tokue, interview, July 1986.

8. Brian McVeigh, *Life in a Japanese Women's College: Learning to be Ladylike* (London: Routledge, 1997).

9. Fukuzawa Keiko, "Women's Hiring Woes," *Japan Quarterly* (April–June 1990): 155–61.

10. "Women Allowed Closer to Career Path," *Nihon Keizai Shimbun,* September 12, 1992, 21.

11. Mariko Sugahara Bando, "When Women Change Jobs" *Japan Quarterly* (April–June 1986): 177–82.

12. Ministry of Foreign Affairs, *Foreign Press Bulletin,* May 1, 1992.

13. "Dads Getting More Involved in Childraising," *Asahi Jānaru,* AP wire service release, August 3, 1998.

14. Government of Japan, Prime Minister's Office, Survey on Women's Roles (Tokyo, 1995).

15. *Wall Street Journal,* April 8, 1998; Joseph Coleman, "Japan Faces Idea of Childless Future," *Honolulu Star Bulletin,* August 3, 1998, A6; *Look Japan,* May 1998, 33; Yoshie Nishioka Rice, "The Maternal Role in Japan: Cultural Values and Socio-Economic Conditions" (Ph.D. dissertation, Harvard Graduate School of Education, 1994); Kashiwagi Keiko, "Life-Span Developmental and Socio-Cultural Approach toward Japanese Women/Mothers: Conceptions and Realities of Japanese Women/Mothers," *Annual Report of Educational Psychology in Japan* 37 (1998): 191–200.

16. See chapter 4's section on *ikuji.*

17. Harold Stevenson, "Will the U.S. Be Number 1 by the Year 2000? Comparative Studies of East and West" (lecture at E. O. Reischauer Institute of Japanese Studies, Harvard University, March 5, 1996).

18. Mary Brinton, *Women and the Economic Miracle: Gender and Work in Postwar Japan* (Berkeley: University of California Press, 1993).

19. Shirasuka Mariko, "*Croissant* Syndrome" (manuscript, 1995).

20. Matsubara Atsuko, *Croissant shokugun* (Tokyo: Bungei Shunsu, 1990).

21. Japan Federation of Employers' Associations, survey in *Yomiuri Shimbun*, October 22, 1990.

22. *Mine*, July 1994.

23. Muta Kazue, "Chastity and Romantic Love in Modern Japan" (paper presented at Association for Asian Studies annual meeting, Chicago, Illinois, March 1997).

24. Vogel, *Japan's New Middle Class*, 220–21, 108.

25. Koyama Takashi, cited in Takashi Mochizuki, "Changing Patterns of Mate Selection," in *Family and Household in Changing Japan*, ed. Koyama Takashi, Morioka Kiyomi, and Kumagai Fumie (Tokyo: Japan Society for the Promotion of Sciences, 1980), 79.

26. For a national conference in 1978 I was preparing a paper listed in the program as "The Tonde Iru Onna: Sexual Libertinism and the Japanese Woman." I was unable to attend the meeting and never finished the paper but received mail from Japan and the United States requesting the paper, sometimes even lauding a presentation never made. So compelling was this nonexistent paper's content that I even saw the paper footnoted in a journal article and noted in a published bibliography.

27. Merry White, *The Material Child: Coming of Age in Japan and America* (New York: Free Press, 1993), chs. 7, 2.

28. Sakagami Yuko, *Yukkuri otona ni naranai yoi* (Tokyo: Bunka Shobohakabunsha, 1994).

29. Yukiko Bowman, "Jibun as Number One: Self-Development in Japanese Female Adolescence" (senior honors thesis, Harvard University, 1999).

30. Hirose Yoko, interview, July 1997.

31. Carl Mosk, *Patriarchy and Fertility in Japan and Sweden, 1880–1960* (New York: Academic Press, 1983).

32. Carol Gluck, *Japan's Modern Myths: Ideology in the Late Meiji Period* (Princeton: Princeton University Press, 1985).

33. Miho Ogino, "Abortion and Women's Reproductive Rights: The State of Japanese Women, 1945–1991," in *Women of Japan and Korea: Continuity and Change*, ed. Joyce Gelb and Marian Palley (Philadelphia: Temple University Press, 1994), 70; Samuel Coleman, *Family Planning in Japanese Society: Traditional Birth Control in a Modern Urban Culture* (Princeton: Princeton University Press, 1983).

34. Chupiren disbanded after the failure of its founder's political ambitions. According to news reports, Enoki had struck a bargain with her husband: he would support her campaign for a seat in the Diet, but if she lost, she would repay his efforts with calculated hourly housework at home, retiring from the movement. She lost but, according to some, won the point that women's work is work.

35. Mainichi Shimbun, Population Study Group, *Kiroku nihon no jinkō* (Tokyo, 1992).

36. Jonathan Friedland and Lily Matsubara, "Permission Denied," *Far Eastern Economic Review,* April 14, 1994.

37. Coleman, *Family Planning;* Ono Yumiko, "The Big Yawn, or How the Pill Made Its Way to Japan," *Wall Street Journal,* July 1, 1999, A1.

38. Ogino, "Abortion and Women's Reproductive Rights," 86.

39. Population Action International, *World Access to Contraception* (1992).

40. John Pelzel, personal communication, spring 1976.

41. Elisabeth Bumiller, "Japan's Abortion Agony: In a Country that Prohibits the Pill, Reality Collides with Religion," *Washington Post,* October 25, 1990.

42. Helen Hardacre's work on *mizuko kuyo* in *Marketing the Menacing Fetus* (Berkeley: University of California Press, 1997) demonstrates the economics of abortion in the rise of Buddhist temple rites to appease the spirits of aborted fetuses, a profitable business established to exploit women's unease and guilt over the abortions they have had. These women are often middle-aged, seeking to correct problems they are persuaded relate to abortions they had twenty or more years earlier.

43. Ashino Yuriko, interview, July 1995.

44. Ogino, "Abortion and Women's Reproductive Rights," 89.

45. Ashino interview, July 1995.

46. *Look Japan,* May 1998, 33.

47. Susan Hanley and Kozo Yamamura, *Economic and Demographic Change in Pre-Industrial Japan* (Princeton: Princeton University Press, 1977). Ian Reader supports the view that the primary reason for birth decline is economic, noting that the women who have the most abortions are in their late twenties and thirties, married, and have had one or more children (letters, *Guardian Weekly,* October 22, 1995).

48. Ochiai Emiko, *Nijūsseiki kazoku e: kazoku no sengo taisei no mikata, koekata* (Tokyo: Yuhikaku Shuppansha, 1994), 115.

6. TWENTY-FIRST-CENTURY BLUES

1. David Plath, "Japan: The After Years," in *Aging and Modernization,* ed. Donald O. Cowgill (New York: Meredith, 1972); and Diane Bethel, "Alienation and Reconnection in a Home for the Elderly," in *Comparing Cultures,* ed. Merry White and Sylvan Barnet (Boston: Bedford Books, 1996).

2. "Population Likely to Peak in 2207; Aged Will Exceed Young This Year," *Yomiuri Shimbun,* January 22, 1997, 1, 6.

3. Ministry of Health and Welfare, Statistical Information Department, Ministry's Secretariat, White Paper on Aging (1994).

4. Foundation for Social Development for Senior Citizens, cited in *Look Japan,* January 1999. 5.

5. "Hashimoto Outlines Priorities," *Japan Times,* January 23, 1996, 1.

6. Total social welfare costs could amount to 73 percent of the national income by 2025 creating a huge tax burden on the working population (Sheryl

WuDunn, "The Face of the Future in Japan," *New York Times,* September 2, 1997, D1, D14).

7. Erdman Palmore, "What the U.S.A. Can Learn from Japan about Aging," *Gerontologist* 15, no. 1 (?): 64–67.

8. Edward Norbeck, "Age Grading in Japan," *American Anthropologist* 55 (1953): 373–84.

9. At the age of sixty, referred to as *jitsunen* or age of fruition, many workers can begin to collect pensions, but sixty is also one of the most troublesome *yakudoshi* or "problem years" when ill luck could befall them. Traditionally, people celebrate a second "coming of age" on their sixty-first birthday, after they make it through the difficult year.

10. Ruth Benedict, *Patterns of Culture* (New York: Mentor Books, 1959).

11. Norbeck, "Age Grading in Japan," 381.

12. John Embree, *Suye Mura* (Chicago: University of Chicago Press, 1939); and Robert J. Smith and Ella Wiswell, *The Women of Suye Mura* (Chicago: University of Chicago Press, 1982).

13. Christena Turner, personal communication, July 2000. Marketing and advertising obviously reach across class lines in establishing expectations of a "middle-class" lifestyle. As people can afford to, they may buy into the substance of the middle class, including educational enhancements for children, to create an illusion of upward mobility much like the phenomenon called "samuraization" in the Tokugawa period, when merchant families began to emulate the lifestyles of elites.

14. Gordon Mathews, *What Makes Life Worth Living? How Japanese and Americans Make Sense of Their Worlds* (Berkeley: Univ. of California Press, 1996).

15. Nakamura Noriko, personal communication, May 1999.

16. Takeda Akio and Sumiko, interviews, May 1999.

17. Nakamura refers to this as "new 'aged' tourism" (personal communication).

18. Kuraoka Masataka, personal communication, May 2000.

19. Maruki Iri, personal communication, 1989.

20. Merry White, *The Material Child: Coming of Age in Japan and America* (New York: Free Press, 1993), ch. 5.

21. Ibid., 105–6.

22. Howard French, "New Pressures Alter Japanese Family's Geometry," *New York Times,* July 27, 2000, 4.

23. Ministry of Health and Welfare, *Statistical Handbook of Japan* (Tokyo, 2001); "Solving Social Security's Problems," *Japan Now,* May 1997, 3.

24. *Japan Times Weekly,* March 7, 1993.

25. John Creighton Campbell, personal communication, 1999. Exchange with Sheldon Garon, September 1997, Social Science Japan Forum, Institute of Social Science, University of Tokyo, website, http://www/iss.u-tokyo.ac.jp/.

26. *When Traditional Mechanisms Fail: Aging in Japan* (Tokyo: NHK, 1990), documentary film.

27. Hisashi Hirayama, "Public Policies and Services for the Aged in Japan," in *Ethnicity and Gerontological Social Work* (New York: Haworth Press, 1987,) 47.

28. James Schulz and Allan Borowski, *Economics of Population Aging* (New York: Auburn House, 1991).

29. Akiko Hashimoto, *The Gift of Generations Japanese and American Perspectives on Aging and the Social Contract* (New York: Cambridge University Press, 1996), 13.

30. Nashima Mitsuko, "Retirement Homes Prove Popular with Elderly," *Japan Times Weekly,* March 4–10, 1991.

31. Ono Yumiko, "An Army of 'Home Helpers' Is Ready to Descend on Japan's Seniors," *Wall Street Journal,* October 7, 1999, B1, B4.

32. Ibid.

33. Katsumata Yukiko, "Financing Japan's Social Security System," *Social Science Japan,* no. 5 (November 1995).

34. Nigel Holloway, "Taxing Times," *Far Eastern Economic Review,* September 7, 1989; and WuDunn, "Face of the Future in Japan."

35. Christena Turner, personal communication, July 2000.

7. MARKETING THE BITE-SIZE FAMILY

1. Stephanie Coontz, *The Way We Never Were* (New York: Basic Books, 1992).

2. Sheldon Garon, *Molding Japanese Minds: The State in Everyday Life* (Princeton: Princeton University Press, 1997).

3. Tamara K. Hareven, "The Life Course and Aging in Historical Perspective," in *Aging and Life Course Transitions: An Interdisciplinary Perspective,* ed. Tamara K. Hareven (New York: Guilford Press, 1982).

4. John Demos, *Past, Present and Personal* (Oxford: Oxford University Press, 1986).

5. Robert Bellah et al., *Habits of the Heart: Individualism and Commitment in American Life* (Berkeley: University of California Press, 1985).

6. Kumakura Isao, "Seikatsu to geijutsu nihon seikatsu bunkashi" (Chiba: Hoso Shuppan Kyokai, 1990).

7. Sakai Toshihiko, cited in Jordan Sand, "At Home in the Meiji Period: Inventing Japanese Domesticity," in *Mirror of Modernity: Invented Traditions of Modern Japan,* ed. Stephen Vlastos (Berkeley: University of California Press, 1998), 199.

8. Except as opportunities to buy flowers, cards, or fancy foods, Mother's Day and Father's Day are not celebrated in Japan, in spite of the advent of Hallmark Cards and other novelty companies ready to take advantage of lucrative holidays. In a recent survey, 45 percent of families say they celebrate both Mother's and Father's Days, 22 percent celebrate only Mother's Day, and 2 percent only Father's Day. The rest celebrate neither (Miyashita Hiroshi, "Retirees to Get Their Just Deserts?," *Look Japan,* September 1997, 13).

9. Takemura Tamio, "The Embryonic Formation of a Mass Consumption Society and Innovation in Japan in the 1920s," *Japan Review* 10 (1998): 173–97.

10. The incident reported in chapter 5, in which my presentation of attitudes about the relationship between mother's work and children's school failure was represented as a warning to Japanese mothers not to work, is evidence of the persistence of this responsibility and attitude.

11. *The Colonel Comes to Japan,* documentary film, directed and produced by John Nathan, for WGBH-TV "Enterprise" series, 1981.

12. Andrew Painter, "Japanese Daytime Television, Popular Cultures, and Ideology," *Journal of Japanese Studies* 19 (1993): 295–325.

13. "TV Series Popular," *Japan Now,* summer 1998, 4.

14. The Ministry of Education enacted a new policy making first one, then two Saturdays per month nonschool days, in an effort to encourage more freedom for children (William Kelly, Oxford University, personal communication, 1999).

15. In Merry White, *The Material Child: Coming of Age in Japan and America* (New York: Free Press, 1993), 111.

16. Millie Creighton, "Marriage, Motherhood, and Career Management in a Japanese 'Counter Culture,'" in *Re-Imaging Japanese Women,* ed. Anne Imamura (Berkeley: University of California Press, 1996).

17. Victor Turner, *The Ritual Process: Structure and Anti-Structure* (Chicago: University of Chicago Press, 1969).

18. Merry White, *The Material Child: Coming of Age in Japan and America* (New York: Free Press, 1993).

19. Stephanie Strom, "Shopping for a Recovery," *New York Times,* May 29, 1998, 2.

20. "Signs of Change in Japan's Economy," *Japan Now,* March 1999, 2.

21. White, *Material Child.*

22. Washida Kiyokazu, "Kombini," *Look Japan,* June 1997, 11.

23. Creighton, "Marriage, Motherhood, and Career Management."

24. Umesao Tadao, "Terminal Culture."

25. Ministry of Foreign Affairs, *Foreign Press Bulletin,* May 1, 1992.

26. Nostalgic songs make older people weep as they invoke "the taste of my mother's miso soup" (Christine Yano, *Shaping Tears of a Nation* [Ann Arbor: University Microfilms, 1995]). On a television game show, five kindergarten boys were asked to identify their own mother's miso soup from a collection of all the mothers' soups. All did.

27. Anne Allison, "Japanese Women and Obentos: The Lunchbox as Ideological State Apparatus," *Anthropological Quarterly* 64, no. 4 (October 1991): 195–208.

28. Emiko Ohnuki-Tierney, *Rice as Self: Japanese Identities Through Time* (Princeton: Princeton University Press, 1993).

29. Fast foods do not enhance or complement domestic foods in the same ways as do prepared foods, even from *konbini.* As Emiko Ohnuki-Tierney notes (James Watson, ed., *Golden Arches in East Asia* [Stanford: Stanford University Press, 1997]), especially for the older generations, fast food such as a hamburger or fried chicken would not be seen as a replacement for a meal but act only as a "snack." Nor would lingering at a fast-food emporium represent the same niche for respite as would a bar or coffee shop, except for young people. In other East Asian societies, however, a fast-food store might encourage people to stay and might become a meeting place or place to read or work.

30. Anne Allison, *Nightwork* (Chicago: University of Chicago Press, 1994).

31. Ibid., ch. 9.

32. Anne Allison, *Permitted and Prohibited Desires: Mothers, Comics, and Censorship in Japan* (Berkeley: University of California Press, 2000).

33. Shibata Tokue, personal communication, 1985.

CONCLUSION

1. Susan Hanley, "Traditional Housing and Unique Lifestyles" (1992), quoted in Steven Reed, *Making Commonsense of Japan* (Pittsburgh: University of Pittsburgh Press, 1993), 29.

2. Thomas Rohlen, "Is Japanese Education Becoming Less Egalitarian? Notes on Stratification and Reform," *Journal of Japanese Studies* 3 (winter 1976–77): 37–70.

3. Louis Uchitelle, "Working-Class Families Strain to Live Middle-Class Life," *New York Times,* September 10, 2000, 1, 28.

4. Suzanne Hall Vogel, "Professional Housewife: The Career of Urban Middle-Class Japanese Women," *The Japan Interpreter* 12, no. 1 (winter 1978).

5. Takie Lebra, "Self and Other in Esteemed Status: The Changing Culture of the Japanese Royalty from Showa to Heisei," *Journal of Japanese Studies* 23 (1997): 257–89.

6. Reed, *Making Commonsense,* 53.

Bibliography

Allison, Anne. "Japanese Mothers and Obentos: The Lunchbox as Ideological State Apparatus." *Anthropology Quarterly* 64, no. 4 (October 1991): 195–208.

———. *Nightwork*. Chicago: University of Chicago Press, 1994.

———. *Permitted and Prohibited Desires: Mothers, Comics, and Censorship in Japan*. Berkeley: University of California Press, 2000.

Amemiya, Kozy. "Balancing Women's Autonomy and the Good of the Community: Pro-Choice Women in Japan." Paper presented to Association for Asian Studies, Boston, March 1994.

Amino Takehiro. "Current Environment for Child Rearing in Japan—Child Rearing by Working Mothers." *Child Welfare Quarterly* 16, no.3 (December 1995): 2–11.

Anderson, Joseph, and Donald Richie. *The Japanese Film: Art and Industry*. Princeton: Princeton University Press, 1982.

Ariga Kizaemon. "The Japanese Family." Manuscript, Tokyo Kyoiku Daigaku, 1953.

Ariyoshi Sawako. *Twilight Years*. New York: Harper and Row, 1984. First published as *Kōkotsu no hito* (Tokyo: Shinchōsa, 1972).

Atoh, Makoto. *Attitude Toward Marriage Among Youth*. Tokyo: Institute of Population Problems, 1993.

Bando, Mariko Sugahara. "When Women Change Jobs." *Japan Quarterly* (April–June 1986): 177–82.

———. "The Change of Status of Women in Japan: Can We Change the *Kaisha* Society?" Paper presented to Japan Society, New York, May 30, 1990.

Befu Harumi. "Corporate Emphasis and Patterns of Descent in the Japanese Family." In *Japanese Culture: Its Development and Characteristics,* ed. Robert J. Smith and Richard Beardsley. Viking Fund Publications in Anthropology, no. 34. New York: Viking Fund Publications, 1962.

Bellah, Robert, et al. *Habits of the Heart: Individualism and Commitment in American Life.* Berkeley: University of California Press, 1985.

Benedict, Ruth. *Patterns of Culture.* New York: Mentor Books, 1959.

———. *The Chrysanthemum and the Sword.* Boston: Houghton Mifflin, 1989.

Bernstein, Gail, ed. *Recreating Japanese Women: 1600–1945.* Berkeley: University of California Press, 1991.

Bethel, Diane. "Alienation and Reconnection in a Home for the Elderly." In *Comparing Cultures,* ed. Merry White and Sylvan Barnet. Boston: Bedford Books, 1996.

Borovoy, Amy. "Domesticity and Strategy: Reading Japanese Self-Sacrifice." Paper presented to American Anthropology Association, Washington, D.C., November 15–19, 1995.

Bosanquet, Nick. "New Remedy for Old." *Far Eastern Economic Review,* May 10, 1990.

Bowman, Yukiko. "Jibun as Number One: Self-Development in Japanese Female Adolescence." Senior honors thesis, Harvard University, 1999.

Brinton, Mary. "Christmas Cakes and Wedding Cakes: The Social Organization of Japanese Women's Life Course." In *Japanese Social Organization,* ed. Takie Lebra. Honolulu: University of Hawai'i Press, 1992.

———. *Women and the Economic Miracle: Gender and Work in Postwar Japan.* Berkeley: University of California Press, 1993.

———. "Harvesting the Green Shoot: Japanese Employers' Recruitment of New Graduates." Paper presented at Harvard University, November 7, 1995.

Bumiller, Elisabeth. "Japan's Abortion Agony: In a Country that Prohibits the Pill, Reality Collides with Religion." *Washington Post,* October 25, 1990.

Butler, Robert N., and Kenzo Kiikuni, eds. *Who Is Responsible for My Old Age?* New York: Springer Publishing, 1995.

Caudill, William. "Interrelations of Psychiatry, Culture, and Emotion in Japan." In *Medicine and Anthropology.* New York: Wenner Gren, 1962.

Chira, Susan. "Many Working Women in Japan Remain Invisible." *New York Times,* December 4, 1988.

Chudacoff, Howard P. *How Old Are You? Age Consciousness in American Culture.* Princeton: Princeton University Press, 1989.

Chudacoff, Howard P., and Tamara K. Hareven. "Family Transitions into Old Age." In *Transitions,* ed. Tamara K. Hareven. New York: Academic Press, 1978.

Coleman, James. "Hit Japanese Software Lets Male Players Raise 'Daughter.'" Associated Press wire release, April 5, 1997.

Coleman, Joseph. "Japan Faces Idea of Childless Future." *Honolulu Star Bulletin,* August 3, 1998, A6.

Coleman, Samuel. *Family Planning in Japanese Society: Traditional Birth Control in a Modern Urban Culture.* Princeton: Princeton University Press, 1983.

———. "The Tempo of Family Formation." In *Work and Life Course in Japan,* ed. David Plath. Albany: SUNY Press, 1983.

Cook, Theodore, and Haruko Cook. *Japan at War: An Oral History.* New York: New Press, 1992.

Coontz, Stephanie. *The Way We Never Were.* New York: Basic Books, 1992.

Cornell, Laurel. "Retirement, Inheritance, and Intergenerational Conflict in Pre-Industrial Japan." *Journal of Family History* 8, no. 1 (1983): 55–69.

———. "Gender Differences in Remarriage after Divorce in Japan and the United States." *Journal of Marriage and the Family* 51, no. 2 (1989): 457–63.

Creighton, Millie R. "Marriage, Motherhood, and Career Management in a Japanese 'Counter Culture.'" In *Re-Imaging Japanese Women,* ed. Anne Imamura. Berkeley: University of California Press, 1996.

Daimon Sayuri. "'Karōshi' Phenomenon Spreading to Female Workforce." *Japan Times Weekly,* September 30–October 6, 1991, 7.

Demos, John. *Past, Present and Personal.* Oxford: Oxford University Press, 1986.

deVos, George, and Takao Sofue. *Religion and the Family in East Asia.* Berkeley: University of California Press, 1986.

Dickensheets, Tony. "The Role of the Education Mama." *Japan Quarterly* (July–September 1996): 73–78.

"Dirty Laundry." *Business Tokyo,* November 1990, 54.

Doi Takeo. *The Anatomy of Dependence.* Tokyo: Kodansha, 1973.

Dore, Ronald. *City Life in Japan.* Berkeley: University of California Press, 1958.

———. *Diploma Disease.* Berkeley: University of California Press, 1976.

Dower, John. *Japan in War and Peace.* New York: New Press, 1993.

———. *Embracing Defeat: Japan in the Wake of World War II.* New York: New Press, 1999.

Economic Planning Agency of Japan. *Demographic Survey.* Tokyo, 1993.

Edwards, Linda. "Equal Employment Opportunity in Japan: A View from the West." *Industrial and Labor Relations Review* 41, no. 2 (January 1988): 240–50.

Edwards, Walter. *Modern Japan through Its Weddings.* Stanford: Stanford University Press, 1989.

"Elderly Outnumber Children in Rapidly Ageing Japan." Reuters News Service, June 26, 1997.

11th International Congress of Gerontology. *Aging in Japan.* 1978.

Embree, John. *Suye Mura.* Chicago: University of Chicago Press, 1939.

Esaka Akira. "Job Transfers and the Long-Distance Family." *Japan Echo* 25, special issue (1988).

Eto Jun. "A Nation in Search of Reality." *Japan Echo* 22 (1995).

Fallows, James. "A Visit to Sanya." In *Comparing Cultures,* ed. Merry White and Sylvan Barnet. Boston: Bedford Books, 1996.

Foreign Press Center. *Japan's Population.* Tokyo, 1992.

Formanek, Susanne, and Sepp Linhart. *Japanese Biographies: Life Histories, Life Cycles, Life Stages.* Vienna: Verlag der Osterreichschen Akademie der Wissenschaften, 1992.

French, Howard. "New Pressures Alter Japanese Family's Geography." *New York Times,* July 27, 2000.

Friedland, Jonathan, and Lily Matsubara. "Permission Denied." *Far Eastern Economic Review,* April 14, 1994.

Fujioka Wakao. *Sayonara sengo: atarashī hyogen shakai no tanjo.* Tokyo: PHP, 1987.

Fukuyama, Francis. *The End of Order.* Tokyo: Yuzenkaku Shuppansha, 1975.

Fukuzawa Keiko. "Women's Hiring Woes." *Japan Quarterly* (April–June 1995): 155–61.

Fukuzawa Yukichi. *The Autobiography of Fukuzawa Yukichi.* Tokyo: Hokuseido Press, 1934.

Funabashi Keiko. "Reassessing the Value of Children." *Japan Echo,* February 1999.

Fuse Akiko. "Role Structure of Dual Career Families." In *Family and Household in Changing Japan,* ed. Koyama Takashi, Morioka Kiyomi, and Kumagai Fumie. Tokyo: Japan Society for the Promotion of Sciences, 1980.

Gamber-Eck, Stephanie. "A Woman's Place." *Look Japan,* December 1992, 14.

Garon, Sheldon. *Molding Japanese Minds: The State in Everyday Life.* Princeton: Princeton University Press, 1997.

Gelb, Joyce, and Marian Lief Palley, eds. *Women of Japan and Korea: Continuity and Change.* Philadelphia: Temple University Press, 1994.

Gluck, Carol. *Japan's Modern Myths: Ideology in the Late Meiji Period.* Princeton: Princeton University Press, 1985.

Goode, William. "The Resistance of Family Forces to Industrialization." Presented to Korean National Academy of Sciences, 7th International Symposium, Seoul, 1979.

Gordon, Andrew, ed. *Postwar Japan as History.* Berkeley: University of California Press, 1993.

Gordon, Beate Sirota. *The Only Woman in the Room.* Tokyo: Kodansha 1997.

Government of Japan. Prime Minister's Office. *Statistical Analysis of Elderly Population in Japan.* Tokyo: Foreign Press Center, 1983.

———. White Paper on Women in the Workforce. 1994.

———. Survey on Women's Roles. 1995.

Graven, Kathryn. "Japan Women Begin to Address Problem of Sexual Harassment in the Workplace." *Asian Wall Street Journal Weekly,* December 25, 1989.

Greenfeld, Karl Taro. "Marriage? Girls Just Wanna Have Fun." *Japan Times,* international edition, July 13–19, 1992.

Hakuhodo, Seikatsu Sogo Kenkyujo. *Japanese Seniors, Pioneers in the Era of Aging Populations.* Tokyo, 1987.

Hamabata, Matthews. "Love and Work in Japanese Society: The Role of Women in Large-Scale Family Enterprise." Paper presented to Association for Asian Studies, San Francisco, March 27, 1983.

———. *The Crested Kimono: Love and Power in the Japanese Family.* Ithaca: Cornell University Press, 1990.

Hamaguchi Keiichiro. "New Patterns of Work in Japan." *News and Views from Japan* (Japanese Mission to the European Union), December 1996, 3.

Hanley, Susan. "Traditional Housing and Unique Lifestyles: The Unintended Outcomes of Japan's Land Policy." In *Land Issues in Japan: A Policy Failure,* ed. John. O. Haley and Kozo Yamamura. Seattle: Society for Japanese Studies, 1992.

————, ed. *Family and Population in East Asian History.* Stanford: Stanford University Press, 1985.

Hanley, Susan, and Kozo Yamamura. *Economic and Demographic Change in Pre-Industrial Japan.* Princeton: Princeton University Press, 1977.

Hara Hiroko, and Mieko Minagawa. "From Productive Dependents to Precious Guests: Historical Changes in Japanese Children." In *Japanese Childrearing: Two Generations of Scholarship,* ed. David and Barbara Shwalb. New York: Guilford Press, 1996.

Hara Hiroko and Wagatsuma Hiroshi. *Shitsuke.* Tokyo: Kohbundoh, 1974.

Harada Hisashi. *Kazoku keitai no hendo to rojin fukushi.* Tokyo: Toshi Mondai Kenkyū, 1994.

Hardacre, Helen. *Marketing the Menacing Fetus.* Berkeley: University of California Press, 1997.

Hareven, Tamara K. *Themes in the History of the Family.* Worcester: American Antiquarian Society, 1978.

————. "The Life Course and Aging in Historical Perspective." In *Aging and Life Course Transitions: An Interdisciplinary Perspective,* ed. Tamara K. Hareven. New York: Guilford Press, 1982.

Hashimoto, Akiko. *The Gift of Generations: Japanese and American Perspectives on Aging and the Social Contract.* New York: Cambridge University Press, 1996.

Hashimoto Meiko. "Becoming Aware of Child Abuse." *Japan Quarterly* (April–June 1996): 145–52.

Hayami, Akira. "The Myth of Primogeniture and Impartible Inheritance in Tokugawa Japan." *Journal of Family History* 8, no. 1 (1983): 3–29.

————. "Population Changes." In *Japan in Transition from Tokugawa to Meiji,* ed. Marius Jansen and Gilbert Rozman. Princeton: Princeton University Press, 1986.

Hendry, Joy. *Marriage in Changing Japan.* New York: St. Martin's Press, 1981.

Hill, M. Anne. "Female Labor Supply in Japan." *Journal of Human Resources* 24, no. 1 (1988): 143–61.

Hirayama, Hisashi. "Public Policies and Services for the Aged in Japan." In *Ethnicity and Gerontological Social Work.* New York: Haworth Press, 1987.

Hirayama, T. *Life-Style and Mortality: A Large-Scale Census-Based Cohort Study in Japan.* Basel: Karger, 1990.

Hochschild, Arlie. *The Second Shift.* New York: Viking, 1984.

Hodge, Robert W., and Naohiro Ogawa. *Fertility Change in Contemporary Japan.* Chicago: University of Chicago Press, 1991.

Holloway, Nigel. "Taxing Times." *Far Eastern Economic Review,* September 7, 1989.

Holloway, Susan. "Images of Close Relationships in Japanese Preschools." Manuscript, April 1997.

Houseman, Susan, and Katharine Abraham. "Female Workers as a Buffer in the Japanese Economy." *American Economic Review* 83, no. 2 (May 1993): 45–51.

Iizuka Junko. "Discount Coupons for Home Baby-Sitting Services—A Child Care Assistance Program for Employees." Nomura Institute of Research, April 1996.

Imamura, Anne. *Urban Japanese Housewives: At Home and in Community.* Honolulu: University of Hawai'i Press, 1987.

———, ed. *Re-Imaging Japanese Women.* Berkeley: University of California Press, 1996.

Ishihara Kunio. "Trends in Generational Continuity and Succession to House-hold Directorship." In *Family and Household in Changing Japan,* ed. Koyama Takashi, Morioka Kiyomi, and Kumagai Fumie. Tokyo: Japan Society for the Promotion of Sciences, 1980.

Ishizuka Yukio. "Japan's Feminists Take Their Message to Screen, Stage." *Mainichi Shimbun,* January 10, 1991.

Itakura Kimie. "Wifely Concerns." *Look Japan,* November 1988, 40.

Itasaka Kikuko. "Bursting the Bubbles: Japan's New Soap Operas." *Japan Society Newsletter* 35, no. 7 (March 1988): 2–5.

Ito, T. K., and Virginia Murray. "Computerized Matchmaking." In *Comparing Cultures,* ed. Merry White and Sylvan Barnet. Boston: Bedford Books, 1996.

Ivy, Marilyn. *Discourses of the Vanishing: Modernity, Phantasm, Japan.* Chicago: University of Chicago Press, 1995.

Iwai Tomoaki. "The Madonna Boom: Women in the Japanese Diet." *Journal of Japanese Studies* 19 (1983): 103–20.

Iwao Sumiko. "How About a Little Smile, Honey?" *Nihon Keizai Shimbun,* March 16, 1992.

———. Editorial. *Japan Echo,* February 2000.

Iwao Suzuki. "Government Administrative Actions Concerning Day-Care and Issues." *Child Welfare Quarterly* 16, no. 4 (March 1996): 2.

Japanese Organization for International Cooperation in Family Planning. *Bird's Eye View of Population and Family Planning in Japan.* Tokyo, 1987.

Johnson, Carmen. *Wave Rings in Water: My Years with the Women of Postwar Japan.* Alexandria, Va.: Charles River Press, 1996.

Jordan, Mary. "Tired of Subway Molesters, Japanese Women Say They Favor Separate Cars." *Washington Post,* October 4, 1997.

Kageyama, Yuri. "TV Soap Opera of Suffering Woman Strikes Chord in Japanese Society." Associated Press wire release, July 10, 1992.

Kaji Nobuyuki. "Tsuzoku dotoku e kaere." *Chuo Koron,* September 9, 1999.

Kamerman, Sheila B., and Alfred J. Kahn, eds. *Family Policy.* New York: Columbia University Press, 1978.

Kamiko Takeji. *Nihonjin no kazoku kankei: ibunka to hikakushite "atarashī kateizo" o saguru.* Tokyo: Yuhikaku, 1981.

Kanabayashi Masayoshi. "More Women in Japan Get Jobs, Shaking Up Traditional Marriages." *Wall Street Journal,* May 14, 1985.

Kashima Takashi. "More Workers Quit to Care for Elderly." *The Nikkei Weekly,* January 25, 1993.

Kashiwagi Keiko. "Life-Span Developmental and Socio-Cultural Approach toward Japanese Women / Mothers: Conceptions and Realities of Japanese Women / Mothers." *Annual Report of Educational Psychology in Japan* 37 (1998): 191–200.

Kashiwagi Keiko and Hisako Nagahisa. "The Change in Value of Children in

Japanese Mothers." Paper presented to fifteenth annual International Society for the Study of Behavioral Development meetings, Bern, Switzerland, 1998.

Katayama Osamu. "Life Support." *Look Japan,* October 1998, 26.

Katsumata Yukiko. "Financing Japan's Social Security System." *Social Science Japan,* no. 5 (November 1995).

Kawamata Takeo. "A New Look at a Society with Fewer Children: White Paper [no. 30] on Health and Welfare." Japanese Mission to the European Union, Brussels, September 1998.

Kawanishi Yuko. "Breaking Up Still Hard to Do." *Japan Quarterly* (July–September 1998): 84 ff.

Kelly, William. "Metropolitan Japan." In *Postwar Japan as History,* ed. Andrew Gordon. Berkeley: University of California Press, 1993.

Kinoshita Yasuhiro and Christie W. Kiefer. *Refuge of the Honored: Social Organization in a Japanese Retirement Community.* Berkeley: University of California Press, 1993.

Kitano Seiichi. "Dōzoku and Ie in Japan: The Meaning of Family Genealogical Relationships." In *Japanese Culture: Its Development and Characteristics,* ed. Robert J. Smith and Richard Beardsley. Viking Fund Publications in Anthropology, no. 34. New York: Viking Fund Publications, 1962.

Kitaoji Hironobu. "The Structure of the Japanese Family." *American Anthropologist* 73 (1971): 1036–57.

Kleinberg, Jill. "When Work and Family Are Almost One." In *Work and Life Course in Japan,* ed. David Plath. Albany: SUNY Press, 1983.

Kohno Goro. "Recent Conditions of Child Raising in Japan." *Child Welfare Quarterly* 17, no. 2 (September 1996): 2–14.

Kondo, Dorinne. *Crafting Selves.* Chicago: University of Chicago Press, 1990.
———. *About Face.* New York: Routledge, 1997.

Kono, Shigemi, and Mitsuru Shio. *Interprefectural Migration in Japan, 1956, 1961.* New York: Asia Publishing House, 1965.

Kou Sueoka. "Reproductive Medicine in Japan: Progress and Paradox." *Japan Echo,* February 1999, 40–44.

Koyama Shizuko. "The 'Good Wife and Wise Mother' Ideology in Post–World War I Japan." *Nihon Josei Jānaru,* no. 7 (1994): 31–52.

Koyama Takashi, Morioka Kiyomi, and Kumagai Kumie, eds. *Family and Household in Changing Japan.* Tokyo: Japan Society for the Promotion of Sciences, 1980.

Koyano, Wataru. "Japanese Attitudes Towards the Elderly: A Review of Research Findings." *Journal of Cross-Cultural Gerontology* 4 (1989): 335–45.

Krauss, Ellis, et al., eds. *Conflict in Japan.* Honolulu: University of Hawai'i Press, 1988.

Kristof, Nicholas. "Japan Is a Woman's World Once the Front Door Is Shut." *New York Times,* June 19, 1996.

Kumagai Fumie. "Changing Divorce in Japan." *Journal of Family History* 8, no.1 (1983): 85–108.
———. "The Life Cycle of the Japanese Family." *Journal of Marriage and the Family* 46, no. 1 (1984): 191–204.

————. "Modernization and the Family in Japan." *Journal of Family History* 11, no. 4 (1986): 371–82.

————. "Satisfaction among Rural and Urban Japanese Elderly in Three-Generation Families." *Journal of Cross-Cultural Gerontology* 2 (1987): 225–39.

Kumakura Isao. "Seikatsu to geijutsu nihon seikatsu bunkashi." Hoso Daigaku Kyoiku Shinkokai. Chiba: Hoso Shuppan Kyokai, 1990.

Kyodo News Service. "Ministers Agree to Promote 'Angel Plan' Nursery Project." *Japan Economic Newswire,* December 16, 1994.

LaFleur, William. *Liquid Life.* Princeton: Princeton University Press, 1992.

Lebra, Takie. "Self and Other in Esteemed Status: The Changing Culture of the Japanese Royalty from Showa to Heisei." *Journal of Japanese Studies* 23 (1997): 257–89.

Lebra, Takie, and William Lebra. *Japanese Culture and Behavior.* Honolulu: University of Hawai'i Press, 1974.

Levine, Robert. "Why Isn't Japan Happy?" *American Demographics,* 1992.

Levy, Marion. "Contrasting Factors in the Modernization of China and Japan." In *Economic Development and Cultural Change.* Chicago: University of Chicago Press, 1954.

Lewis, Catherine. "Women in the Consumer Movement." In *Proceedings of the Tokyo Symposium on Women.* Tokyo: International Group for the Study of Women, 1978.

————. *Educating Hearts and Minds.* Cambridge: Cambridge University Press, 1993.

Lo, Jeannie. *Office Ladies, Factory Women.* New York: M. E. Sharpe, 1990.

Lock, Margaret. "Protests of a Good Wife and Wise Mother: The Medicalization of Distress in Japan." In *Health, Illness, and Medical Care in Japan,* ed. Edward Norbeck and Margaret Lock. Honolulu: University of Hawai'i Press, 1987.

Lodge, David. *Out of the Shelter.* London: Penguin, 1990.

Long, Susan Orpett. "Nurturing and Femininity: The Ideal of Caregiving in Postwar Japan." In *Re-Imaging Japanese Women,* ed. Anne Imamura. Berkeley: University of California Press, 1996.

McVeigh, Brian. *Life in a Japanese Women's College: Learning to be Ladylike.* London: Routledge, 1997.

Mainichi Shimbun. Population Study Group. *Summary of Twentieth National Survey on Family Planning.* Tokyo, 1990.

————. *Kiroku nihon no jinkō.* Tokyo, 1992.

————. *The Population and Society of Postwar Japan.* Tokyo, 1994.

Makihara, Kumiko. "Who Needs Equality?" *Time,* December 3, 1990.

Marsh, William. "Japan's Generation X." *Mangajin,* n.d.

Martin, Linda. *The Graying of Japan.* Washington, D.C.: Population Reference Bureau, July 1989.

Masson, Paul R. "Long-Term Macroeconomic Effects of Aging Populations." *Finance and Development* 27, no. 2 (June 1990): 6–9.

Matsubara Atsuko. *Croissant shokugun.* Tokyo: Bungei Shunsu, 1990.

Matsumoto, Yoshiharu Scott. *Demographic Research in Japan, 1955–1970.* Honolulu: East-West Center, 1974.

Mathews, Gordon. *What Makes Life Worth Living? How Japanese and Americans Make Sense of Their Worlds.* Berkeley: University of California Press, 1996.

Minami Ryozaburo. *An Outlook of Studies of the Population Problems in Japan.* Tokyo: Japanese National Commission for UNESCO, 1956.

Mine (Tokyo), July 1994.

Ministry of Foreign Affairs. *Foreign Press Bulletin,* May 1, 1992.

Ministry of Health and Welfare. "Opinions on the Formulation of a Comprehensive Policy for the Protection of Mother and Child Health." Tokyo, 1968.

———. Statistical Information Department, Ministry's Secretariat. White Paper on Aging. 1994.

———. Summary of Vital Statistics, June 29, 2000.

———. *Statistical Handbook of Japan.* Tokyo, 2000–2001.

Minoguchi Tokijiro. *An Outlook of Studies on Population Problems in Japan.* Tokyo: Japanese National Commission for UNESCO, 1956.

Miyashita Hiroshi. "Retirees to Get Their Just Deserts?" *Look Japan,* September 1997, 13.

Mochizuki Takashi. "Changing Patterns of Mate Selection." In *Family and Household in Changing Japan,* ed. Koyama Takashi, Morioka Kiyomi, and Kumagai Fumie. Tokyo: Japan Society for the Promotion of Sciences, 1980.

Morioka Kiyomi. "Family and Household in Changing Japan." *Journal of Comparative Family,* no. 3 (1981): 365–96.

———. *Gendai kazoku hendō ron.* Tokyo: Minerva, 1993.

Mosk, Carl. "Nuptuality in Meiji Japan." *Journal of Social History* 13, no. 3 (spring 1980): 474–89.

———. *Patriarchy and Fertility in Japan and Sweden, 1880–1960.* New York: Academic Press, 1983.

Muta Kazue. "Chastity and Romantic Love in Modern Japan." Paper presented at Association for Asian Studies annual meeting, Chicago, Illinois, March 1997.

———. "Images of the Family in Meiji Periodicals: The Paradox Underlying the Emergence of the 'Home.'" *Nichibei Josei Jānaru,* English supplement no. 7 (1994): 53–71.

Najita, Tetsuo. "Japan's Industrial Revolution in Historical Perspective." In *Japan in the World,* ed. Miyoshi Masao and H. D. Harootunian. Durham, N.C.: Duke University Press, 1993.

Nakanishi Tamako. "Women and Leadership in Japan Today." Lecture at Harvard University, October 26, 1995.

Nambu Yasuyuki. "Temps Are Here to Stay." *Look Japan,* January 1996, 16.

Nashima Mitsuko. "Retirement Homes Prove Popular with Elderly." *Japan Times Weekly,* March 4–10, 1991.

National Institute for Research Advancement. *An International Comparison of Aid to Working Women: A Study of Conditions in the Low-Birthrate Countries of Japan, Germany, and Italy.* Tokyo, 1994.

Nishimura Kunio. "Life Begins at Sixty." *Look Japan,* October 1997, 36 ff.

Noguchi, Yukio, and David A. Wise. *Aging in the United States and Japan.* Chicago: University of Chicago Press, 1994.

Norbeck, Edward. "Age Grading in Japan." *American Anthropologist* 55 (1953): 373–84.

Ochiai Emiko. *Nijusseiki kazoku e: kazoku no sengo taisei no mikata, koekata.* Tokyo: Yuhikaku Shuppansha, 1994.

Ogasawara, Yuko. *Office Ladies, Salaried Men.* Berkeley: University of California Press, 1998.

Ogino, Miho. "Abortion and Women's Reproductive Rights: The State of Japanese Women, 1945–1991." In *Women of Japan and Korea: Continuity and Change,* ed. Joyce Gelb and Marian Palley. Philadelphia: Temple University Press, 1994.

Ohnuki-Tierney, Emiko. *Rice as Self: Japanese Identities Through Time.* Princeton: Princeton University Press, 1993.

Omori Maki. "Gender and the Labor Market." *Journal of Japanese Studies* 19 (1993): 79–102.

Ono Yumiko. "Here Comes the Bride All Dressed in a Kimono." *Wall Street Journal,* June 9, 1998.

———. "The Big Yawn, or How the Pill Made Its Way to Japan." *Wall Street Journal,* July 1, 1999.

———. "An Army of 'Home Helpers' Is Ready to Descend on Japan's Seniors." *Wall Street Journal,* October 7, 1999.

Osako Masako Murakami. "Dilemmas of Japanese Professional Women." *Social Problems* 26 (1978): 15–25.

Painter, Andrew. "Japanese Daytime Television, Popular Cultures, and Ideology." *Journal of Japanese Studies* 19 (1993): 295–325.

Palmore, Erdman. "What the U.S.A. Can Learn from Japan about Aging." *Gerontologist* 15, no. 1 (1975): 64–67.

Parker, Ginny. "Part-Time Seen as Bane, not Boon for Women."*Japan Times,* October 2, 1998.

Passin, Herbert. *Society and Education in Japan.* New York: Columbia Teachers College Press, 1965.

Pelzel, John. "Japanese Kinship: A Comparison." In *Family and Kinship in Chinese Society,* ed. M. Freedman. Stanford: Stanford University Press, 1970.

Pharr, Susan. "The Revolt of the Tea Pourers." In *Conflict in Japan,* ed. Ellis Krauss et al. Honolulu: University of Hawai'i Press, 1988.

Plath, David. "When the Family of God Is the Family: The Role of the Dead in Japanese Households." *American Anthropologist* 66 (1964): 300–317.

———. "Japan: The After Years." In *Aging and Modernization,* ed. Donald O. Cowgill. New York: Meredith Press, 1972.

———. *Long Engagements: Maturity in Modern Japan.* Stanford: Stanford University Press, 1980.

———. "Resistance at Forty-Eight: Old-Age Brinksmanship and Japanese Life Course Pathways." In *Aging and Life Course Transitions: An Interdisciplinary Perspective,* ed. Tamara K. Hareven. New York: Guilford Press, 1982.

Population Action International. *World Access to Contraception.* Washington, D.C., 1992.

"Population Likely to Peak in 2007." *Yomiuri Shimbun,* January 22, 1997.

"Private Sector Offers Women More." *Asahi Evening News,* February 17, 2000.

"Proposals Target Women's Status." *Japan Times Weekly,* April 22–28, 1991.

Raz, Aviad. *Riding the Black Ship: Japan and Tokyo Disneyland.* Cambridge, Mass.: Harvard University Press, 1999.

Reader, Ian. "Cost of Living Explains Japan's Low Birth Rate." *Guardian Weekly,* October 22, 1995.

Reed, Steven. *Making Commonsense of Japan.* Pittsburgh: University of Pittsburgh Press, 1993.

Rice, Yoshie Nishioka. "The Maternal Role in Japan: Cultural Values and Socio-Economic Conditions." Ph.D. dissertation, Harvard Graduate School of Education, 1994.

Richie, Donald. "Caging the Japanese Woman." *Japan Times,* June 23, 1990.

Rohlen, Thomas. "Is Japanese Education Becoming Less Egalitarian? Notes on Stratification and Reform." *Journal of Japanese Studies* 3 (winter 1976–77): 37–70.

Rosenberger, Nancy. *The Japanese Sense of Self.* New York: Cambridge University Press, 1992.

Rudolph, Ellen. "Women's Talk." *New York Times Sunday Magazine,* September 1, 1996.

Sadowsky, Richard. "The Quest for 'My Home.'" *Mangajin* 3 (1996): 12–15.

Sakagami Yuko. *Yukkuri otona ni naranai yoi.* Tokyo: Bunka Shobohakabunsha, 1994.

Sakamoto Kazue. "Analyzing the Relationship Between the Elderly and Their Children in Japan." *Sociology of Aging* (1997): 444–52.

Sand, Jordan. "At Home in the Meiji Period: Inventing Japanese Domesticity." In *Mirror of Modernity: Invented Traditions of Modern Japan,* ed. Stephen Vlastos. Berkeley: University of California Press, 1998.

Sasaki Yukie. "Happy Holidays?" *Look Japan,* March 1999, 40.

Sato Kunio. "Wives for Farmers: A Critical Import." *Japan Quarterly* (January–March 1988): 253–59.

Schlesinger, Jacob. "Japanese Women Break Taboo, Using Maiden Names on the Job." *Wall Street Journal,* July 2, 1992.

Schooler, Carmi, and Karen C. Smith. "'. . . and a Japanese wife': Social Structural Antecedents of Women's Role Values in Japan." *Sex Roles* 4, no. 1 (1978): 23–41.

Schulz, James, and Allan Borowski. *Economics of Population Aging.* New York: Auburn House, 1991.

Shapiro, Laura. *Perfection Salad.* New York: Farrar, Straus and Giroux, 1986.

Shimada Haruo. "The Labor Shortage and Workers From Abroad." *Japan Echo* 17, no. 1 (spring 1990).

Shirasuka Mariko. "*Croissant* Syndrome." Manuscript, Boston University, 1995.

"Shopping Again." *Economisto,* June 8, 1996.

Shwalb, David, and Barbara Shwalb. *Japanese Childrearing: Two Generations of Scholarship.* New York: Guilford Press, 1996.

"Signs of Change in Japan's Economy." *Japan Now* (Embassy of Japan, Washington, D.C.), March 1999, 2.

"Single Women Mansion Shopping." *Japan Now,* May 1998, 4.

Skov, Lise, and Brian Moeran. *Women and the Media and Consumption in Japan.* London: Curzon Press, 1995.

Smith, Kazuko, trans. *Makiko's Diary: A Merchant Wife in 1910 Kyoto.* Stanford: Stanford University Press, 1995.

Smith, Robert J. "Stability in Japanese Kinship Terminology: The Historical Evidence." In *Japanese Culture: Its Development and Characteristics,* ed. Robert J. Smith and Richard Beardsley. Viking Fund Publications in Anthropology, no. 34. New York: Viking Fund Publications, 1962.

———. "Small Families, Small Households and Residential Instability: Town and City in 'Pre-Modern' Japan." In *Household and Family in Past Time,* ed. Peter Laslett. Cambridge: Cambridge University Press, 1972.

———. "Making Village Women into 'Good Wives and Wise Mothers' in Prewar Japan." *Journal of Family History* 8, no. 1 (1983): 70–84.

Smith, Robert J., and Ella Wiswell. *The Women of Suye Mura.* Chicago: University of Chicago Press, 1982.

Sodei Takako. "The Fatherless Family." *Japan Quarterly* (January–March 1982): 77–82.

"Solving Social Security's Problems." *Japan Now,* May 1997, 3.

Sonoi Yuri. "Managing Work and Childcare: Working Women's Lives in Japan." Manuscript, 1996.

Srinivas, M. *The Changing Position of Indian Women.* Delhi: Oxford University Press, 1978.

Stevenson, Harold. "Will the U.S. Be Number 1 by the Year 2000? Comparative Studies of East and West." Lecture at E. O. Reischauer Institute of Japanese Studies, Harvard University, March 5, 1996.

Stone, Deborah. "Work and the Moral Woman." *The American Prospect,* November–December 1997.

Strom, Stephanie. "Shopping for a Recovery." *New York Times,* May 29, 1998.

———. "In Japan, From a Lifetime Job to No Job at All." *New York Times,* February 3, 1999.

———. "From Japan's Ailing Economy, a Tale of Murder in the Family." *New York Times,* April 15, 1999.

Struck, Doug, and Katherine Tolbert. "Japan Inc. Workers Get Harsh Dose of Economic Reality." *Washington Post,* January 3, 2000.

Sugiyama Mieko. "Josei 'Womankind.'" *Asahi Gendai,* 1992.

Sullivan, Kevin. "Cost of Economic Equality Questioned." *Washington Post,* June 8, 1997.

Suzuki Kazue. "Equal Job Opportunity for Whom." *Japan Quarterly* (July–September 1996): 54–60.

Tada Michitaro. "The Glory and Misery of 'My Home.'" In *Authority and the Individual in Japan,* ed. Victor Koschmann. Tokyo: University of Tokyo Press, 1978.

Takada Masatoshi. "Woman and Man in Modern Japan." *Japan Echo* 16, no. 2 (summer 1989): 39–44.

Takahashi Kazuko. "Style of Tying the Knot Loosens up a Bit." *Japan Times Weekly International,* April 29–May 5, 1991.

Takahashi, Keiko. "Are the Japanese More Interdependent?: A Cross-Cultural Perspective on Social Relationships." Manuscript, April 1997.

Takayama Hideko. "The Main Track at Last." *Newsweek,* January 22, 1990.

Takemura Tamio. "The Embryonic Formation of a Mass Consumption Society and Innovation in Japan in the 1920s." *Japan Review* 10 (1998): 173–97.

Takeuchi Hiroshi. "Working Women in Business Corporations." *Japan Quarterly* (July–September 1982): 319–23.

Tanabe Seiko. "Prodigal Children, Impoverished Parents." *Japan Echo* 17, special issue (1990).

Tanaka Masako. "Maternal Authority in the Japanese Family." In *Religion and the Family in East Asia,* ed. George deVos and Takao Sofue. Berkeley: University of California Press, 1986.

Tanaka Yasumasa. "Women's Growing Role in Contemporary Japan."*International Journal of Psychology* 25 (1990): 751–65.

Tanaka Yuhko, Nakazawa Jun, and Nakazawa Sayuri. "The Effects of Relocation-Induced Separation in Families." *Japanese Journal of Educational Psychology* 36 (1988): 229–37.

———. "Review of Work-Induced Family Separation Studies." *Japanese Journal of Educational Psychology* 42 (1994): 104–14.

———. "Women's Psychological Stress as Caused by Men's Job Transfers." *Japanese Journal of Educational Psychology* 44 (1996): 156–65.

Tatara Mikihachiro. "Some Thoughts on Life Cycle and Generational Cycle in Japan." Manuscript, Austen Riggs Center, 1980.

———. "Identity and Social Change in Japan." Manuscript, Austen Riggs Center, 1981.

———. "Social Change and Its Impact on Family Life in Japan: Some Thoughts on Parent Abuse Syndrome." Manuscript, Austen Riggs Center, 1981.

Tezuka Kazuaki. *Gaikokujin Rodosha.* Tokyo: Nihon Keizai Shimbunsha, 1989.

"To Many of Japan's Youths, Work Can Wait." *Boston Globe,* January 5, 2000.

Tobin, Joseph, Dana Davidson, and David Wu. *Preschool in Three Cultures.* New Haven: Yale University Press, 1992.

Tokyo, City of. *Tōkyō josei hakusho.* 1998.

Tsuya Noriko and Linda Martin. "Living Arrangements of Elderly Japanese and Attitudes Towards Inheritance." *Journal of Gerontology* 47, nos. 45–54 (1992).

Turner, Victor. *The Ritual Process: Structure and Anti-Structure.* Chicago: University of Chicago Press, 1969.

"2007 Called Critical Time in Society's Rapid Aging." *Japan Times Weekly,* March 1–7, 1993.

Uchihashi Katsuto. "Downsizing, Japanese Style." *Japan Echo* 21, special issue (1994).

Uchitelle, Louis. "Working-Class Families Strain to Live Middle-Class Life." *New York Times,* September 10, 2000.

Ueno, Chizuko. "The Position of Japanese Women Reconsidered." *Current Anthropology* 28, no.4 (August–October 1987): 75–84.

Ueno Teruaki. "Dreams Turn to Dust for Japan's Salarymen." Reuters News Service, April 22, 1998.

Ujihara Shojiro. "The Job Market for the Middle-Aged." *Japan Quarterly* 33 (April–June 1986): 172–75.

Uno, Kathleen. "The Death of 'Good Wife, Wise Mother.'" In *Postwar Japan as History,* ed. Andrew Gordon. Berkeley: University of California Press, 1993.

———. *Passages to Modernity: Motherhood, Childhood, and Social Reform in Early Twentieth-Century Japan.* Honolulu: University of Hawai'i Press, 1999.

Uno Mitsuhiro. "Mothers On-Line." *Look Japan,* July 1998, 17.

Vlastos, Stephen. *Mirrors of Modernity.* Berkeley: University of California Press, 1998.

Vogel, Ezra. *Japan's New Middle Class.* Berkeley: University of California Press, 1963.

Vogel, Suzanne Hall. "Professional Housewife: The Career of Urban Middle-Class Japanese Women." *The Japan Interpreter* 12, no. 1 (winter 1978).

———. "Urban Middle-Class Japanese Family Life, 1958–1996: A Personal and Evolving Perspective." In *Japanese Childrearing: Two Generations of Scholarship,* ed. David and Barbara Shwalb. New York: Guilford Press, 1997.

Wagatsuma Hiroshi. "Some Aspects of the Contemporary Japanese Family: Once Confucian, Now Fatherless?" *Daedalus* (spring 1977): 181–210.

Washida Kiyokazu. "Kombini." *Look Japan,* June 1997, 11.

Watanabe, Teresa. "In Japan You Spell Birth Control: C-O-N-D-O-M." *Number One Shimbun,* September 15, 1994.

Watson, James, ed. *Golden Arches in East Asia.* Stanford: Stanford University Press, 1997.

White, James. *Migration in Metropolitan Japan: Social Change and Political Behavior.* Berkeley: Institute of East Asian Studies, 1982.

White, Merry. *The Japanese Educational Challenge.* New York: Free Press, 1986.

———. "The Virtue of Japanese Mothers: Cultural Definitions of Women's Lives." *Daedalus* (summer 1987): 149–63.

———. *Challenging Tradition: Women in Japan,* New York: Japan Society, 1991.

———. "Home Truths: Women and Social Change in Japan." *Daedalus* (fall 1992): 61–82.

———. *The Material Child: Coming of Age in Japan and America.* New York: Free Press, 1993.

———. "Renewing the New Middle Class: Japan's Next Families." In *Japanese Childrearing: Two Generations of Scholarship,* ed. David and Barbara Shwalb. New York: Guilford Press, 1997.

White, Merry, and Sylvan Barnet, eds. *Comparing Cultures.* Boston: Bedford Books, 1996.

WuDunn, Sheryl. "Japan May Approve the Pill, But Women May Not." *New York Times,* November 27, 1996.

———. "The Face of the Future in Japan." *New York Times,* September 2, 1997.

Yagi Hidetsugu. "The Folly of Imploring Women to Have Babies." *Japan Echo,* February 1999.

Yamada Waka. "The Social Status of Japanese Women." Tokyo: Bunka Shinko-kai, 1935.

Yamanaka Akiko. "Changing Japanese Women." Manuscript, n.d.

Yamanaka Keiko. "Factory Workers and Convalescent Attendants: Japanese-Brazilian Migrant Women and Their Families in Japan." In *International Female Migration and Japan: Networking, Settlement, and Human Rights.* Tokyo: Meiji Gakuin University, 1996.

———. "I Will Go Home But When? Labor Migration and Circular Diaspora Formation by Japanese Brazilians in Japan." Paper presented to Pacific Sociological Association, Seattle, March 21–24, 1996.

———. "Return Migration of Japanese-Brazilians to Japan: The *Nikkeijin* as Ethnic Minority and Political Construct." *Diaspora* 5, no. 1 (spring 1996): 65–97.

Yanagisako, Sylvia Junko. "Family and Household: The Analysis of Dominant Groups." *Annual Review of Anthropology* (1979): 161–205.

Yanagishita, Machiko. "Japan's Declining Fertility: '1.53 shock.'" *Population Today,* April 1992.

———. "Slow Growth Will Turn to Decline of the Japanese Population." *Population Today,* May 1993.

Yano, Christine. *Shaping Tears of a Nation.* Ann Arbor: University Microfilms, 1995.

Yashiro Naohiro. *Japan's Rapidly Aging Population.* Tokyo: Foreign Press Center, 1982.

Index

Illustrations:	Bill Nelson
Index:	Susan Stone
Compositor:	Integrated Composition Systems
Text:	10/13 Sabon
Display:	Sabon
Printer and binder:	Sheridan Books, Inc.